DEPICTING THE DIVINE
MIKHAIL BULGAKOV AND THOMAS MANN

LEGENDA

LEGENDA is the Modern Humanities Research Association's book imprint for new research in the Humanities. Founded in 1995 by Malcolm Bowie and others within the University of Oxford, Legenda has always been a collaborative publishing enterprise, directly governed by scholars. The Modern Humanities Research Association (MHRA) joined this collaboration in 1998, became half-owner in 2004, in partnership with Maney Publishing and then Routledge, and has since 2016 been sole owner. Titles range from medieval texts to contemporary cinema and form a widely comparative view of the modern humanities, including works on Arabic, Catalan, English, French, German, Greek, Italian, Portuguese, Russian, Spanish, and Yiddish literature. Editorial boards and committees of more than 60 leading academic specialists work in collaboration with bodies such as the Society for French Studies, the British Comparative Literature Association and the Association of Hispanists of Great Britain & Ireland.

The MHRA encourages and promotes advanced study and research in the field of the modern humanities, especially modern European languages and literature, including English, and also cinema. It aims to break down the barriers between scholars working in different disciplines and to maintain the unity of humanistic scholarship. The Association fulfils this purpose through the publication of journals, bibliographies, monographs, critical editions, and the MHRA Style Guide, and by making grants in support of research. Membership is open to all who work in the Humanities, whether independent or in a University post, and the participation of younger colleagues entering the field is especially welcomed.

ALSO PUBLISHED BY THE ASSOCIATION

Critical Texts
Tudor and Stuart Translations • *New Translations* • *European Translations*
MHRA Library of Medieval Welsh Literature

MHRA Bibliographies
Publications of the Modern Humanities Research Association

The Annual Bibliography of English Language & Literature
Austrian Studies
Modern Language Review
Portuguese Studies
The Slavonic and East European Review
Working Papers in the Humanities
The Yearbook of English Studies

www.mhra.org.uk
www.legendabooks.com

STUDIES IN COMPARATIVE LITERATURE

Studies in Comparative Literature are produced in close collaboration with the British Comparative Literature Association, and range widely across comparative and theoretical topics in literary and translation studies, accommodating research at the interface between different artistic media and between the humanities and the sciences.

ALSO PUBLISHED IN THIS SERIES

Depicting the Divine

Mikhail Bulgakov and Thomas Mann

❖

Olga G. Voronina

l

LEGENDA

Studies in Comparative Literature 47
Modern Humanities Research Association
2019

Published by Legenda
an imprint of the Modern Humanities Research Association
Salisbury House, Station Road, Cambridge CB1 2LA

ISBN 978-1-78188-545-1 (HB)
ISBN 978-1-78188-546-8 (PB)

First published 2019
Paperback edition 2021

Copy-Editor: Dr Birgit Mikus

CONTENTS

❖

For my parents
Irina and Georgii

ACKNOWLEDGEMENTS

❖

This study looks at how stories change as they are told and retold, written down and edited, each reader taking them in a different and often unexpected direction. The same is true of the readers of this monograph. I would like to express my deep gratitude to my supervisors, Professor Stephanie Bird and Professor Pamela Davidson, for their patient guidance, inspirational mentoring, and for their complete selflessness with their time. This study benefited from the generous advice given by my examiners Professor J. A. E. Curtis and Professor Martin Swales, as well as the anonymous reviewer of the book proposal at Legenda. I would also like to thank Dr Sarah Young for her comments on the early drafts of the Bulgakov chapters. I am profoundly grateful to the Legenda readers, Professor Edythe C. Haber and Dr Ernest Schonfield, whose expert advice and attention to detail saved this monograph from *non sequiturs*. Any mistakes left in this study are mine.

It is thanks to Dr Jon Hesk's encouragement that I embarked on this project during my time in Scotland. At Legenda I am thankful to Dr Graham Nelson and Dr Dorota Goluch, for their valuable advice and support, to Dr Birgit Mikus for her help with copy-editing the manuscript, and to Dr Emily Finer for her help and Professor Wen-chin Ouyang, for allowing me to take the time that I needed.

For reading endless drafts of the monograph, I wish to thank my dear friend Nabeelah Shabbir. This is a conclusion (but not the end) of our discussions of *The Master and Margarita*, which started when we were both students. For giving me a home while I was writing, as well as for unexpected food deliveries at crucial moments, I thank Olga Nuryaeva. I am grateful to none more for their support than my family. I would like to remember my aunt, Galina Voronina, whose erudition and keen interest in the divine helped me take my first steps on this journey. To my parents, Irina and Georgii, you are a constant source of inspiration for me and this monograph is dedicated to you with deepest love. And, of course, Lui, without you I would never have emerged from this biblical maze unscathed.

o.v., February 2018

TRANSLITERATION AND TRANSLATIONS

❖

The Library of Congress system of Cyrillic transliteration is used throughout, even when the resulting spelling of writers' names is different from their usual English forms, e.g. 'Merezhkovskii' rather than 'Merezhkovsky'. Diacritics are omitted in Russian names with the exception of 'Savel'eva' and 'El'baum'.

Translations in the text are my own unless otherwise stated. When this is the case, quotation marks are omitted. The translations from *Мастер и Маргарита* are taken from Diana Burgin and Katherine Tiernan O'Connor's version: Mikhail Bulgakov, *The Master and Margarita*, trans. by Diana Burgin and Katherine Tiernan O'Connor (London: Picador, 1997). The translations from *Joseph und seine Brüder* are taken from the version by John E. Woods: Thomas Mann, *Joseph and His Brothers. The stories of Jacob, Young Joseph, Joseph in Egypt, Joseph the Provider*, trans. by John E. Woods (New York, NY: Knopf, 2005). In the few instances where the translation does not render the original Russian and German precisely (or at all), the translations are mine, and are not enclosed in quotation marks.

PREFACE

❖

For a study that is, in many ways, concerned with reliability of records, it is perhaps fitting that no authoritative final text of Mikhail Bulgakov's *The Master and Margarita* exists. Illness prevented the writer from finishing editorial work on the novel past chapter nineteen.[1] Following Bulgakov's death, his widow Elena Sergeevna Bulgakova relied on the notebooks and the typescript of the novel to prepare a text which was used 'as a basis for the abridged' version of *The Master and Margarita* published in *Moskva* in 1966 and 1967.[2] Since then there have been several determined attempts to reconstruct the final text of Bulgakov's last novel. In 1973 Anna Saakiants compiled the so-called Soviet *Romany* redaction making use of the writer's notebooks and typescripts as well as the materials in the Bulgakov archive, housed in the Lenin Library, to revise Bulgakova's text.[3] Another version of *The Master and Margarita* was published in 1989 and then again in 1990 by the textologist Lidiia Ianovskaiia, who had a good working knowledge of Bulgakov's drafts of the novel and knew Elena Sergeevna personally.[4] This study primarily refers to the most recent 2014 version of *The Master and Margarita*, which is based on Elena Kolysheva's meticulous archival research of all the surviving redactions of the novel. A decision has been made not to use Viktor Losev's 2006 version of Bulgakov's text criticized by Kolysheva for a very significant number of mistakes and omissions.[5]

Burgin and Tiernan O'Connor's translation of Bulgakov's novel is based on a text prepared by Ellendea Proffer which draws on both Ianovskaia and Saakiants's redactions. Significant discrepancies between the different redactions relevant to this study are acknowledged and discussed.

Notes to the Preface

1. Lidiia Ianovskaia, *Treugol'nik Volanda. K istorii romana 'Master i Margarita'* (Kiev: Libid', 1992), p. 56. See also Mikhail A. Bulgakov, *'Master i Margarita': Polnoe sobranie chernovikov romana. Osnovnoi tekst. V dvukh tomakh*, ed. by Elena Iu. Kolysheva, 2 vols (Moscow: Pashkov dom, 2014), II, p. 24. Henceforth Bulgakov, *'Master i Margarita'*.
2. Donald M. Fiene, 'A Comparison of the Soviet and Possev Editions of *The Master and Margarita*, with a Note on Interpretation of the Novel', *Canadian-American Slavic Studies*, 15 (1981), 330–54 (p. 332).
3. Ibid, p. 332. See Mikhail A. Bulgakov, *Belaia gvardiia. Teatral'nyi roman. Master i Margarita*, ed. by V. Volina, Anna Saakiants and A. Vinogradov (Moscow: Khudozhestvennaia literatura, 1973). Henceforth Bulgakov, *Belaia gvardiia*.
4. Mikhail A. Bulgakov, *Sobranie sochinenii v piati tomakh*, ed by Gennadii S. Gots and others, 5 vols (Moscow: Khudozhestvennaia literatura, 1989–1990), V: *'Master i Margarita'. Pis'ma*, ed. by Lidiia Ianovskaia, Violetta Gudkova and Elena Zemskaia (1990). Henceforth Bulgakov, *Sobranie sochinenii v piati tomakh*. This text was first published in 1989 in Kiev by Dnipro and then again in 1990 in Moscow by Khudozhestvennaia literatura.

5. Bulgakov, *'Master i Margarita'*, I, 23. Incidentally, Losev's version of Bulgakov's novel was also left unfinished at the time of his death. See Mikhail A. Bulgakov, *"Moi bednyi, bednyi master..."* *Polnoe sobranie redaktsii i variantov romana 'Master i Margarita,'* ed. by Viktor I. Losev (Moscow: Vagrius, 2006), p. 22. Henceforth Bulgakov, *"Moi bednyi"*.

INTRODUCTION

❖

Mikhail Bulgakov's *The Master and Margarita* and Thomas Mann's *Joseph and His Brothers* share a number of remarkable and hitherto virtually unexplored similarities in their approach to the biblical text.[1] Bulgakov's novel, written between 1928 and 1940 and published in 1966 and 1967, reimagines the New Testament Passion narrative, portraying the Christian messiah Jesus Christ as a mortal Yeshua Ha-Notsri. Mann's tetralogy, started in 1926 and published between 1933 and 1943, narrates the emergence of monotheism against the background of the Genesis story of Joseph and his brothers. Both texts polemicize against the scripture, offering their versions of biblical events as the truth in relation to what they represent as the incomplete and inaccurate canonical text; polemic itself becomes a subject of critical reflection.[2] The readers bear witness to the biblical events as they unfold in the narrative, which results in an 'амбивалентный эффект: миф превращается в реальность, но и реальность тем самым превращается в миф' [ambivalent effect: myth turns into reality but the reality thereby turns to myth].[3]

Neither writer was religious. Mann came from a culturally Protestant family but declared himself to be agnostic, citing profound scepticism both 'auf sogenannten Glauben und sogenannten Unglauben' [towards so-called belief and so-called unbelief].[4] He secularized the concept of religion and the 'religious' by defining the latter idiosyncratically, in abstract terms, as the thought of death, and the former:[5]

> als Gegenteil der Nachlässigkeit und Vernachlässigung, als Acht geben, beachten, bedenken, Gewissenhaftigkeit, als ein *behutsames* Verhalten, ja als metus und schließlich als sorgend achtsame Empfindlichkeit gegenüber den Regungen des Weltgeistes.[6]

> [as the opposite of negligence and disregard, as taking care, respecting, considering, conscience, as a *vigilant* attitude, indeed as dread, and finally as a concerned, attentive receptivity to the movements of the universal spirit.][7]

Mann ascribed his growing attention to myth and religious history over the years to a change in taste, a shift 'vom Bürgerlich-Individuellen [...] zum Typischen, Generellen und Menschheitlichen' ['away from the bourgeois-individualistic toward the typical, the general, the universally human'].[8] Indeed, the orientation of his theology is essentially anthropological. The religious in his writing is always linked to the human:

> Die Stellung des Menschen im Kosmos, sein Anfang, seine Herkunft, sein Ziel, das ist das große Geheimnis, und das religiöse Problem ist das humane Problem, die Frage des Menschen nach sich selbst.[9]

[The position of man in cosmos, his beginnings, his origin, his destination
— that is the great mystery. The religious problem is the human problem,
mankind's quest for itself.]

Mann posited religious questions in relation to his work, not the other way around.
In *Joseph* the divine and the human often reflect and find realization in each other,
their relationship mediated hermetically by art. Quite apart from Mann's general
scepticism towards religion and religious belief, his rejection of an idea of God the
creator, who is due adoration and prostration, is to be understood in these terms:

Ein 'Werk', eine 'Welt', einen äußerst komplizierten und in sich ruhenden
Mechanismus mit irrationalen Einschlägen herstellen kann ich auch; das ist
keine Kunst, vielmehr: es ist nichts weiter als Kunst und kein Grund, mit dem
Stirn den Boden zu schlagen.[10]

[I, too, can create a work, a world, an extremely complicated self-contained
mechanism with irrational features. There's no art to it or, on the contrary,
it is nothing but art and artifice and no reason to strike the floor with the
forehead.]

The writer's letters and essays present a nexus of ideas that underpin *Joseph*'s
humanist poetics: the interconnection of the human and the divine, and the notion
of an artist whose creativity is divinely productive.

Bulgakov's writing is marked by anticlericalism despite his family's ecclesiastical
roots; both of his grandfathers, Mikhail Vasilievich Pokrovskii and Ivan Avraamovich
Bulgakov, were priests, and his father, Afanasii Ivanovich Bulgakov, was a professor
of Comparative Religion at the Kiev Ecclesiastical Academy, specializing in the
History and Analysis of Western Creeds.[11] Bulgakov's deep scepticism towards
organized religion was influenced in no small part by the ambiguous political
role played by the church after the Bolshevik revolution in 1917.[12] He paid close
attention to Soviet religious politics, noting Patriarch Tikhon's declaration of
neutrality towards the regime in a diary entry in 1923, as well as the '[н]евероятная
склока' [unbelievable squabble] between the Russian Orthodox Church and the
Living Church, a schismatic movement supported by the Bolsheviks.[13] Turning to
this subject in a sketch 'Киев-город' ('The City of Kiev') published in the same
year, he predicted that the mutual hatred and the divisions between the old, the
Living and the Ukrainian Autocephalous Churches, would lead to a mass rise in
atheism amongst their congregations.[14] Notably, in Bulgakov's novel *Белая гвардия*
(*The White Guard*), which depicts Kiev during the Civil War, God is above politics.
He does not take sides. There is a space reserved not just for the Whites but also
for the atheist Bolsheviks in heaven.[15] Moreover, according to a humorous report
by Zhilin in Alexei Turbin's dream in the novel, God is frustrated and embarrassed
by the behaviour of the priests.[16] In another memorable scene in *The White Guard*
Bulgakov touches on the precarious relationship between the religious and the
political once more when he describes a service to celebrate the arrival of Simon
Petliura, the most recent victor in the bloody conflict, held amidst the sound of a
terrible, satanic cacophony of 'barking' church bells at the St. Sophia Cathedral.[17]
From the comical and pathetic to cruel and opportunistic, representatives of

organized religion do not fare well in Bulgakov's work. His negative attitude towards organized religion did not, however, necessarily reflect his feelings towards faith.[18] Indeed, he turned to the thought of God as a source of strength on several occasions, writing in his diary in 1923:

> Может быть, сильным и смелым он не нужен, но таким, как я, жить с мыслью о нем легче. Нездоровье мое осложненное, затяжное. Весь я разбит. Оно может помешать мне работать, вот почему я боюсь его, вот почему я надеюсь на Бога.[19]

> [Maybe He's not needed by the bold and the brave, but for such as myself it is easier to live with the thought of Him. My illness is a complex and lingering one, and I am completely run down. It could hinder me from working, which is why I fear it; and that's why I place my hopes in God.][20]

In the 1920s, when these lines were written, Bulgakov was a published author and a dramatist who enjoyed popular recognition. His phenomenally successful play *Дни Турбиных* (*The Days of the Turbins*), which depicted the White movement sympathetically, was running on the stage of the Moscow Arts Theatre and was seen by Stalin several times. His writing, however, was notably out of kilter with the spirit of the time, which favoured simple linear narratives with positive protagonists and a Socialist message. Over the next couple of years Bulgakov's refusal to adapt to the artistic and ideological demands of the time led to a widespread ban on his works. In 1930 Bulgakov referred to the fate of his works in a passionate letter addressed to the Soviet government, documented the relentless press campaign against him and pleaded to be allowed to leave the Soviet Union, a request that was never granted.[21] Although the writer did secure a position at the Moscow Arts Theatre following Stalin's intervention in response to the letter, there was now no longer any realistic prospect of publication for his work. In 1931 Bulgakov would write 'Помоги, Господи, кончить роман' [Lord, help me finish writing the novel] on a draft page of *The Master and Margarita*, a novel which would place the gospel story at the heart of a biting satire of Soviet Russia.[22]

No one writing about biblical figures in the first half of the twentieth century, as Mann and Bulgakov did, could fail to notice a broad change in cultural attitudes towards the scripture, from devotional to critical. This originated in a fundamental paradigm shift in Bible studies, briefly surveyed below. Prior to the eighteenth century, Western Christian readings of the Bible assumed that the biblical corpus formed a consequential narrative to be taken literally, as a realistic portrayal of historical reality with profound theological significance.[23] As these certitudes gradually eroded, the emphasis of biblical criticism shifted to scrutiny of the scripture's historical reliability, and its interpretation as allegory and myth.[24]

New methods of biblical exegesis, historical criticism and comparative mythology, entered the cultural mainstream in the nineteenth century. Two seminal works in this context were David Friedrich Strauss's *Das Leben Jesu, kritisch bearbeitet* (*The Life of Jesus Critically Examined*), published in 1835, and Ernest Renan's *La Vie de Jésus* (*The Life of Jesus*), published in 1863; both were used by Bulgakov to flesh out his poetic version of the biblical story.[25] Renan treated the gospels as idealized legendary narratives and dismissed miracles, arguing that they are only possible in times when they are believed. He offered a naturalistic, if sentimental biography of the historical Christ, a figure he greatly admired.[26] Renan was by no means the first writer to devote himself to the search for the gospels' historical origins, but his work had wide international resonance and contributed to the popularity of the so-called quest for the historical Jesus literature.[27]

Strauss pointed out the crucial importance of time and culture-specific mythical group consciousness 'not yet capable of rising to abstract conceptualization' that had shaped the gospels.[28] His work paved the way for mythological readings of the scripture which focused on the affinities between the Bible and myths of the Ancient Near East. The discovery mentioned in *Joseph*, of cuneiform tablets inscribed with Babylonian myths in the mid-nineteenth century, which bore a striking resemblance to Old Testament stories, also furthered the research of the mythological school of biblical criticism and gave rise to Pan-Babylonianism, a dedicated movement within Assyriology.[29] Its main proponents, such as Alfred Jeremias, explored these parallels in order to enhance the understanding of biblical texts.[30] Jeremias's work *Das Alte Testament im Lichte des Alten Orients* (*The Old Testament in the Light of Ancient Orient*) is a key source for *Joseph*.[31] Other prominent German Assyriologists focused their attention on the New Testament, seeking to demonstrate that the story of Christ was Babylonian in origin, with roots in myths such as the Gilgamesh epic.[32] Scholars like Jeremias aimed only to contextualize the Old Testament. However, the shift in biblical hermeneutics ultimately led to an interrogation of the status and dogmatic authority of the scripture as a unique text, grounded in divine revelation. This raised a number of urgent questions: could biblical narratives be treated as reliable historical sources? Were parts of the Old Testament inspired by ancient Near Eastern myths? Was Jesus of Nazareth a messiah, a historical figure or just a compelling but unoriginal myth?

These debates saw a radical politicization of biblical criticism in Russia and Germany in the early twentieth century, exacerbated in the 1920s and 1930s under the Soviet and Nazi regimes. In Germany the debate about the origins and the authenticity of the Old Testament led to a re-evaluation of its relevance for contemporary Christianity, providing anti-Semitism with an academic basis.[33] In the so-called Bible-Babel debate at the beginning of the 1900s, Friedrich Delitzsch, a respected German Assyriologist and one of the more radical figures to emerge from the Pan-Babylonian movement, asserted that Israelite culture and religion were assimilated by the Jews from Babylon and that it was, as such, inferior to Babylonian culture and religion.[34] Delitzsch's project attempted to divorce Western Christianity from Judaism, and relied on highly questionable assertions that Jesus may have been a descendant of non-Semitic Sumerians or Yaturean nomads who were converted to Judaism.[35]

Delitzsch's pseudo-academic work fuelled the anti-Semitic mood and was symptomatic of the tendentious direction taken by biblical criticism in Germany. The attempt to redefine Christianity as an Aryan, Germanic religion by the German Christian movement, a pro-Nazi group within the German Protestant Church, was another example of this trend.[36] Key to this effort was the opening in 1939 of the Institute for the Study and Eradication of Jewish Influence on German Church Life (*Institut zur Erforschung und Beseitigung des jüdischen Einflusses auf das deutsche kirchliche Leben*).[37] The tasks of the Institute included the dejudaization of biblical texts and liturgical materials and a search for 'the historically genuine' Christ, which, in practice, entailed his racialization as a Galilean Gentile of Aryan origin, whose teachings, moreover, had opposed Judaism.[38] The Institute was not officially supported by the Nazi Party, which regarded the church as competition; however its publications, that developed 'biblical exegesis and religious history using racial methods', aided and legitimated the anti-Semitic Nazi discourse both before and during the Holocaust.[39]

Mann became a *persona non grata* in Hitler's Germany long before assuming the role of a vocal critic of the Nazi regime and before the philosemitic angle of the tetralogy rendered it unpublishable in his native country.[40] Mann's conception of *Joseph and His Brothers* predated Hitler's rise to power by roughly a decade and was, in fact, inspired by Goethe's remark that Joseph's story in the Old Testament is too short.[41] Mann stated that his choice of the Old Testament, a Jewish subject, stood '[g]anz gewiß [...] in geheimem, trotzig-polemischem Zusammenhang mit Zeit-Tendenzen' [certainly in a secret defiantly polemical relation to the tendencies of the time], in particular, to its 'Rassenwahn' [racist madness]; that it was 'zeitgemäß, gerade weil es unzeitgemäß schien' [of the time precisely because it did not seem to be of the time].[42] However, 'das Jüdische' [Jewish], as he put it, was only 'ein Stilelement' [one stylistic element] of the novel's language.[43] His primary interest in Joseph's story was artistic, closely linked to the definition and the uses of myth. He described the subject matter of the tetralogy as the 'Fleischwerdung des Mythos' [incarnation of myth].[44] One of its tasks, in this context, was to prove 'daß man auf humoristische Weise mythisch sein kann' [that it was possible to be mythical in a humorous way].[45]

With the emergence of National Socialism in Germany as a dominant political force, and the Nazis' redefinition of myth as irrational and nationalist, Mann's long-standing interest in religious history and mythology acquired new meaning.[46] Recovery of myth from misuse at the hands of Nazi ideologues is a crucial part of *Joseph*'s humanistic program.[47] Mann saw psychology as a means 'den Mythos den faschistischen Dunkelmännern aus den Händen zu nehmen und ihn ins Humane "umfunktionieren"' ['whereby myth may be wrested from the hands of the Fascist obscurantists to be "transmuted" for humane ends'].[48] He created an ironic distance to myth in *Joseph* through a combination of humour and psychology.[49] In the tetralogy myth is conceived as future- rather than past-oriented, a means for mankind's conscious spiritual emancipation. Its protagonist Joseph, moreover, is blessed both by spirit and nature, embodying their perfect synthesis, and is, as such, a figure symbolically antithetical to primacy of nature in Nazi ideology.[50] Mann's writing as a whole stood in polemical relation to the tendencies of the time, of which he was acutely aware.

To a certain extent the same is true for Bulgakov's *The Master and Margarita*.

Woland is astonished to learn the subject of the Master's novel — Pontius Pilate, who is, of course, also one of Bulgakov's subjects: 'Вот теперь? (737) ['In these times?' (245)]. Bulgakov's Satan has good cause to be surprised. The Bolshevik revolution of 1917 was followed by a radical overhaul in religious politics. The Bolshevik regime saw organized religion, especially the powerful Russian Orthodox Church, as a political threat and regarded religious belief as a sign of backwardness, incompatible with new Soviet values of materialism and rationalism.[51] The legal separation of church and state in 1918 was followed by an offensive against Orthodoxy and sectarianism as the new regime sought to modernize and secularize Soviet society.[52] Its optimism that religious belief would disappear naturally, once the right conditions were created, however, was disappointed.[53] Instead, religious belief would have to be demystified and eliminated through a series of state-sponsored interventions. Consequently, an Antireligious Commission was established in 1922, a State Publishing House for Antireligious Literature, responsible (amongst other things) for translation of foreign works two years later, and an All Union League of the Militant Godless, an association promoting scientific materialism through atheist propaganda, in 1925.[54]

The Soviet antireligious campaign combined cultural education through atheist propaganda with aggressive intervention, which included exerting legal and economic pressure on the church, clergy and congregation, as well as subjecting them to violence and terror.[55] Culturalists, headed by Emelian Iaroslavskii, editor of the League's antireligious weekly *Bezbozhnik* (*The Godless*), made extensive use of biblical criticism; they even came under attack for publishing complex criticism of religion based on a comparison of myths and 'third-rate German translations'.[56] One of Iaroslavskii's many publications, *Как родятся, живут и умирают боги* (*The birth, life and death of gods*), which was first published in 1923 and reprinted in 1925, is a case in point.[57] Here, his language brings to mind Mikhail Berlioz, also editor of a journal, which is nameless in the final redaction of *The Master and Margarita*, but is suggestively titled *Bogoborets* [*The Godfighter*] in the early drafts of the novel (1928–1930).[58] Like Berlioz, Iaroslavskii claims that Christ never existed, referring to stories about him as later fraudulent interpolations and fairy tales.[59] Indeed, Bulgakov's research for the novel comprised a number of works which belonged to both the historical and mythological schools of biblical criticism. Apart from Renan and Strauss, some of the other sources used to deck his poetic vision of ancient Jerusalem with historical detail included Frederic William Farrar's *The Life of Christ*, Arthur Drews's *Die Chrystusmythe* (*The Christ Myth*) and Henri Barbusse's *Jésus*.[60] Bulgakov also took a keen interest in *Bezbozhnik*, visiting its Moscow office to collect eleven back issues of the newspaper from the previous year. He recorded his impressions from this expedition in a diary entry on 5 January 1925:

> Когда я бегло проглядел у себя дома вечером номера «Безбожника», был потрясен. Соль не в кощунстве, хотя оно, конечно, безмерно, если говорить о внешней стороне. Соль в идее, ее можно доказать документально: Иисуса Христа изображают в виде негодяя и мошенника, именно его. [...] Этому преступлению нет цены.[61]

[I was astounded once I had looked through the issues of *Bezbozhnik* at home in the evening. The point is not the blasphemy, although it is, of course, without measure, if one speaks about the superficial side of things. The point is in the idea, which can be reliably proven: none other than Jesus Christ is depicted as a scoundrel and a conman [...] This is an unprecedented crime.]

The Master and Margarita, begun three years later, would feature references to the Soviet antireligious project and a discussion about the different ways in which Jesus Christ may be interpreted and represented.

Bulgakov and Mann's poetic engagement with the Bible in the 1920s and 30s is significant, coming as it did against the background of changing cultural attitudes and the instrumentalization of biblical criticism for political purposes. In part, the remarkable similarities in their treatment of biblical texts can be traced to their reading of literature on Bible study, both scholarly and pseudo-academic. However, both writers use biblical criticism only to refine their poetic vision, not to define or delimit it.[62] Similarities in Mann and Bulgakov's approach to biblical stories in this context raise a number of questions. In what ways do they take inspiration from the Bible, a subject that, to borrow Mann's words, did not seem to be of the time? How do they retell ancient biblical narratives with divine protagonists in a secular modern age? What does their biblical fiction tell us about the time when it was written, when religious sentiment became radically politicized?

This book is the first comparative study of *Joseph and His Brothers* and *The Master and Margarita* to address the implications of Bulgakov and Mann's engagement with religious themes against the background of politicization of religious discourse in Germany and Soviet Russia. Its focal point is the narrative strategies used to represent the Jewish God Yahweh and the Christ figure Yeshua Ha-Notsri, the divine protagonists of biblical stories reimagined in *Joseph and His Brothers* and *The Master and Margarita*. Narrative strategies are considered here as a specifically poetic mode of engagement with the scripture and an important contribution to understanding Mann and Bulgakov's literary interaction with their contemporary political and cultural landscape.

Mann's Yahweh and Bulgakov's Yeshua lend themselves to many disparate interpretations. Past scholarship treats *Joseph* as a novel 'with a modern anthropological approach to religion.'[63] Abraham's discovery of a transcendent God, in this context, has been read as an emancipation of an individual consciousness, a recognition of the self as being separate from the world.[64] Abraham's God is a reflection of man as he can and ought to be, the aim of his path towards self-fulfilment.[65] This 'highest condition of humanity' in *Joseph* is also an enlightened 'narrative' condition, in which a morally responsible adult consciously "narrates" the epic of his own life.'[66] *Joseph* combines this narrative anthropology with a narrative theology,[67] a poetics 'einer erzählenden und erzählten Theologie' [of a narrating and narrated theology].[68] Mann's Yahweh, seen from this perspective, appears as 'a figurative expression for the author' or the Schopenhauerian 'will behind the story'.[69]

The relationship of Yeshua Ha-Notsri to the gospel Jesus Christ and the question of his divinity are amongst the most contested in Bulgakov scholarship. Yeshua has been variously interpreted as a fundamentally human figure, uncommonly kind, honest and disinterested,[70] a demythologized[71] or an apocryphal Jesus,[72] an embodiment of the highest philosophical religious truth, who appears in his earthly hypostasis only as its preacher,[73] a Gnostic saviour figure, a Son of God whose 'divinity' is manifested through his 'superior humanity',[74] a Bogomil and a Manichean character.[75]

This study takes as its point of departure the fact that Mann and Bulgakov's divine protagonists Yahweh and Yeshua appear primarily as objects of fascination and contemplation for the other characters in *The Master and Margarita* and *Joseph*. Their representation is addressed here through a close textual analysis of the narratives about them authored by the characters of the two novels, with close attention paid to the discontinuities and the contradictions which emerge as a result.[76]

Chapter One focuses on the production and transmission of oral and written narratives about Jesus Christ and Yeshua Ha-Notsri in Soviet atheist Moscow and in the ancient city of Yershalaim, Bulgakov's Jerusalem, in *The Master and Margarita*. It considers how these narratives are authored, recorded and edited by Bulgakov's characters, addressing various narrative formats, ranging from the protocol of Yeshua's interrogation by Pilate to an antireligious poem about Christ, commissioned to a young conformist Soviet poet. Central to this chapter is the journey undertaken by the readers of the novel as they witness Yeshua's story unfold through the eyes of Pontius Pilate. It explores the factors that influence the integrity of narrative production, such as institutional pressures and censorship but also subjectivity, as manifested through prejudices and personal beliefs.

Chapter Two explores the ways in which the portrayal of Yeshua Ha-Notsri changes if the four chapters set in ancient Yershalaim, which reinterpret the Passion narrative, are read as the text of the Master's novel about the moral dilemma of Pontius Pilate, where the Christ figure is used as a measure of the procurator's humanity. The chapter addresses the implications of interpreting Yeshua as the Master's character, inspired by the gospels, intuited and imagined by him as a vulnerable and, crucially, a mortal man rather than a divine messiah.

Bulgakov's novel ostensibly demythologizes the figure of the Son of God as a man, Yeshua Ha-Notsri. Nevertheless, a certain degree of ambivalence about Yeshua's immortality and divinity remains unresolved in the narrative. Chapter Three assesses the significance of ambiguity about Yeshua's figure, generated by the instances in the text, which imply, if not his divinity, then a certain degree of transcendence. The chapter also considers Yeshua's narrative as it is related in his own words. The element of doubt resulting from the many ambiguities inherent to the way Yeshua's story is told and retold in *The Master and Margarita* is addressed in this chapter as a dimension of faith.

In the different versions of his story in *Joseph*, biblical Abraham either invents God out of existential doubt or is miraculously chosen by him. Chapter Four examines the demystification of God in *Joseph* as Abraham's construct, where Yahweh is conceptualized by the patriarch as the highest state of spiritual emancipation achievable by man. It juxtaposes the notion of Yahweh as a transcendent spiritual deity that emerges from this intellectual process, to his other portrayals in *Joseph* as a comical protagonist of rabbinic folklore and the God of the Old Testament.

The focal point of this chapter is the relationship between these contrasting representations, which emerge from the different ways of telling Yahweh's story in the tetralogy. The chapter pays particular attention to the narrator's commentary on the rehearsal, embellishment and politicization of Abraham's narrative by his descendants in faith.

Chapter Five explores the ways in which Yahweh in *Joseph* is constituted hermeneutically, through contemplation and imaginative interpretation of the world in which the patriarchs live. It argues that the patriarchs Jacob and Joseph, the heirs of Abraham's story, mythologize their lives, imagining them to be divinely intended, and, to that end, see God as a silence that can be interpreted and endowed with meaning. In this context it considers the patriarchs' visions of Yahweh as emotionally motivated wish projections and focuses on the protagonist of the tetralogy, Joseph, who sets up narrative creativity as a mode of worship. The chapter addresses his understanding of man as God's co-creator, whose intellect enables him to organize chaotic reality into a meaningful narrative and whose language constructs what it describes.

Chapter Six assesses how ambiguous fragments of the text in *Joseph* that suggest the existence of the transcendent may be reconciled with the consistent demystification of Yahweh as a human projection in the rest of the tetralogy. In this context it pays particular attention to Mann's reinterpretation of sources such as Gnostic narratives and medieval Jewish folklore, incorporated into the tetralogy as stories about God. The chapter argues that the coexistence of two logically irreconcilable realities in *Joseph*, where man thinks God into being and God creates man, results in an Aporia, which constitutes an integral part of Mann's poetic design.

Notes to the Introduction

1. Boris M. Gasparov, 'Iz nabliudenii nad motivnoi strukturoi romana M. A. Bulgakova *Master i Margarita*', *Daugava*, 10 (1988), 96–106 (p. 96). Gasparov is the only critic to date to have addressed the parallels between the two texts in this context in any detail. For a different comparative reading of the two novels see Mihai I. Spariosu, *Modernism and Exile. Play, Liminality, and the Exilic-Utopian Imagination* (Basingstoke: Palgrave Macmillan, 2015), pp. 151–79. Szilárd notes the baffling similarity of Mann and Bulgakov's late works (p. 348). Léna Szilárd, 'Der Mythos im Roman und der Wechsel der literarisch-stilistischen Formationen: Von Joyce und A. Belyj zum späten Th. Mann und zu M. Bulgakov,' in *Evolution of the Novel. L'Evolution du Roman. Die Entwicklung des Romans. Proceedings of the IXth congress of the International Comparative Literature Association*, ed. by Zoran Konstantinovič, Eva Kuschner and Béla Köpeczi, Innsbrucker Beiträge zur Kulturwissenschaft, 53 (Innsbruck: Institut für Sprachwissenschaft der Universität Innsbruck, 1982), pp. 347–52. For examples of comparative readings of Bulgakov and Mann's other works see Ekaterina Rogachevskaya, 'Thomas Mann's *Mario und der Zauberer* and Bulgakov's *The Master and Margarita* as Political Commentaries on the Events of the 1930s', *Australian Slavonic & East European Studies*, 9 (1995), 119–28 and Claudia Natterer, *Faust als Künstler. Michail Bulgakovs 'Master i Margarita' und Thomas Manns 'Doktor Faustus'*, Beiträge zur Slavischen Philologie, 9 (Heidelberg: Winter, 2002).
2. Gasparov, 'Iz nabliudenii', 10, 96–97.
3. Gasparov, 'Iz nabliudenii', 10, 97.
4. Thomas Mann, *Gesammelte Werke in dreizehn Bänden*, 13 vols (Frankfurt a.M.: Fischer: 1960), XI, 424. Henceforth *GW*.

5. *GW*, XI, 423. Beck writes that for Mann religion is equivalent to rules for human behaviour. Mann secularizes the religious concept with the help of irony and extends it into 'Ethisch-Humane' [the ethical-human] (p. 24). Helmut Beck, 'Thomas Manns Josephstetralogie und das Gestaltungsprinzip der epischen Ironie', in *Betrachtungen und Überblicke zum Werk Thomas Manns*, ed. by Georg Wenzel (Berlin: Aufbau, 1966), pp. 11–106. Hartwich states in this context that in *Joseph* Mann sets up 'the sacred as ethically normative and, at the same time, as aesthetically autonomous' (p. 153). (Wolf-Daniel Hartwich, 'Religion and Culture: *Joseph and his Brothers*', trans. by Ritchie Robertson, in *The Cambridge Companion to Thomas Mann*, ed. by Ritchie Robertson (Cambridge: Cambridge University Press, 2006), pp. 151–67.

6. Karl Kerényi, ed, *Thomas Mann — Karl Kerényi. Gespräch in Briefen* (Zurich: Rhein, 1960), p. 75 (7 October 1936). Henceforth *Gespräch in Briefen*.

7. Thomas Mann and Karl Kerényi, *Mythology and Humanism. The Correspondence of Thomas Mann and Karl Kerényi*, trans. by Alexander Gelley (Ithaca, NY: Cornell University Press, 1975), pp. 73–74 (7 October 1936). Henceforth *Mythology*.

8. Kerényi, *Gespräch in Briefen*, p. 41. *Mythology*, p. 37 (20 February 1934).

9. *GW*, XI, 424.

10. *GW*, XI, 424.

11. Marietta Chudakova, *Zhizneopisanie Mikhaila Bulgakova*, 2nd edn (Moscow: Kniga, 1988), p. 12. In 1910, Bulgakov's sister Nadezhda noted her thoughts about his temporary turn towards atheism in her diary (Chudakova, *Zhizneopisanie*, p. 43). Edythe C. Haber, 'The Lamp with the Green Shade: Mikhail Bulgakov and His Father', *Russian Review*, 44 (1985), 333–50 (p. 333). See also Vladimir Golstein, 'What Does a Saint Do amidst MASSOLIT Revelers? Mikhail Bulgakov, Father John of Kronstadt, and Julien Benda's *La Trahison des clercs*', *Russian Review*, 63 (2004), 673–87.

12. Ellendea Proffer, *Bulgakov. Life and Work* (Ann Arbor, MI: Ardis, 1984), p. 579 and p. 541.

13. Viktor I. Losev, ed, *Mikhail i Elena Bulgakovy. Dnevnik Mastera i Margarity* (Moscow: Vagrius, 2004), p. 26. Henceforth Losev, *Dnevnik*.

14. Mikhail A. Bulgakov, *Sobraniie sochinenii v vos'mi tomakh*, ed. by Losev, Viktor I., 8 vols (St. Petersburg: Azbuka-klassika, 2002–2004), I: *Zapiski pokoinika: Avtobiograficheskaia proza* (2002), p. 304. Henceforth Bulgakov, *Sobraniie sochinenii v vos'mi tomakh*.

15. Bulgakov, *Sobraniie sochinenii v vos'mi tomakh*, II: *Belaia gvardiia: Grazhdanskaia voina v Rossii* (2002), p. 149.

16. Ibid, p. 150.

17. Ibid, p. 322.

18. Proffer writes: 'On the whole, Bulgakov seems to have respected the miracle and mystery of religion [...] but he had no use for the authority which resides in the priesthood of any religion' (Proffer, *Bulgakov*, p. 579). Curtis asserts that: 'For Bulgakov as a writer, religion would come to figure not so much as a matter of dogma, but rather as a central dimension of a common European heritage, the defining feature of European civilization' (p. 14). Julie A. E. Curtis, *Mikhail Bulgakov*, Critical Lives (London: Reaktion Books, 2017).

19. Losev, *Dnevnik*, p. 34.

20. Julie A. E. Curtis, *Manuscripts Don't Burn. Mikhail Bulgakov: A Life in Letters and Diaries*, trans. by Julie A. E. Curtis (London: Bloomsbury, 2012), p. 54.

21. In the letter dated 28 March 1930 Bulgakov refers to three hundred and one reviews of his work collected over ten years. Of these two hundred and ninety-eight are 'враждебно-ругательны[е]' [hostile and abusive] and only three are 'похвальны[е]' [positive] (p. 280). He concludes that the Soviet press and censorship bodies clearly prove that his works 'в СССР не могут существовать' [cannot exist in the USSR] (p. 281). Bulgakov, *Sobraniie sochinenii v vos'mi tomakh*, VIII: *Zhizneopisanie v dokumentakh* (2004).

22. Bulgakov, '*Master i Margarita*', I, 127.

23. Hans W. Frei, *The Eclipse of Biblical Narrative: A Study in Eighteenth and Nineteenth Century Hermeneutics* (New Haven, CT: Yale University Press, 1974), pp. 1–3.

24. Frei, *The Eclipse of Biblical Narrative*, pp. 4–6.

25. Lidiia Ianovskaia, *Tvorcheskii put' Mikhaila Bulgakova* (Moscow: Sovetskii Pisatel', 1983), p. 249, p. 252. Henceforth Ianovskaia, *Tvorcheskii Put'*.

26. Ernest Renan, *The Life of Jesus*, [n. trans], Thinker's Library, 53 (London: Watts, 1935).

27. On the Quest see James Carleton Paget, 'Quest for the historical Jesus', in *The Cambridge Companion to Jesus*, ed. by Markus Bockmuehl (Cambridge: Cambridge University Press, 2001), pp. 138–55.

28. Frei, *The Eclipse of Biblical Narrative*, pp. 236–38 (p. 238). See David Friedrich Strauss, *The Life of Jesus Critically Examined*, trans. by George Eliot (London: SCM, 1973).

29. Yaacov Shavit and Mordechai Eran, *The Hebrew Bible Reborn: From Holy Scripture to the Book of Books. A History of Biblical Culture and the Battles over the Bible in Modern Judaism*, trans. by Chaya Naor, Studia Judaica 38 (Berlin: De Gruyter, 2007), pp. 214–15.

30. Alfred Jeremias, *Das Alte Testament im Lichte des Alten Orients. Handbuch zur biblisch-orientalischen Altertumskunde* (Leipzig: Hinrichs, 1904), p. vii.

31. See Herbert Lehnert, 'Thomas Manns Vorstudien zur Josephstetralogie', *Jahrbuch der Deutschen Schillergesellschaft*, 7 (1963), 458–520 (pp. 467–71).

32. Susannah Heschel, *The Aryan Jesus. Christian Theologians and the Bible in Nazi Germany* (Princeton, NJ: Princeton University Press, 2008), pp. 56–58. Discovery of parallels between Christ and the dying and resurrecting fertility deities of antiquity did not, however, always result in the same conclusions. Russian religious philosopher Dmitrii Merezhkovskii had argued in 1925 in his *Taina trekh. Egipet i Vavilon (The Mystery of the Three: Egypt and Babylon)* that such parallels need not necessarily lead to Christ's mythologization, suggesting instead that his death and resurrection were mystically foreshadowed by Adonis and Tammuz. See Dmitrii Merezhkovskii, *Taina trekh. Egipet i Vavilon*, ed. by Aleksandr N. Nikoliukin, Sobranie sochinenii D. S. Merezhkovskogo, 3 (Moscow: Respublika, 1999), p. 131. Mann was indebted to Georg Brandes and Merezhkovskii for the motif of Joseph's identification with a series of dying and resurrecting fertility deities (Tammuz-Adonis-Osiris) and, through them, a parallel to Jesus Christ. See Georg Brandes, *Jesus: A Myth*, trans. by Edwin Björkman (London: Brentano, 1927), p. 73. For Mann's reading of Brandes and Merezhkovskii see Lehnert, 'Thomas Manns Vorstudien zur Josephstetralogie', pp. 499–502, p. 503.

33. See Friedrich Delitzsch, *Die grosse Täuschung. Kritische Betrachtungen zu den alttestamentlichen Berichten über Israels Eindringen in Kanaan, die Gottesoffenbarung vom Sinai und die Wirksamkeit der Propheten*, 2 vols (Stuttgart: Deutsche Verlags-Anstalt, 1920), I, 93–96.

34. Shavit and Eran, *The Hebrew Bible Reborn*, pp. 200–01, p. 212, p. 230. See Friedrich Delitzsch, *Zweiter Vortrag über Babel und Bibel. 26. bis 30. Tausend. Mit 20 Abbildungen und einem Wort 'Zur Klärung'* (Stuttgart: Deutsche Verlags-Anstalt, 1903). For example, Delitzsch suggested that the origin of the Mosaic laws lies in human invention (and in Babylon) rather than in a divine revelation (pp. 21–27).

35. Shavit and Eran, *The Hebrew Bible Reborn*, p. 234, p. 240, p. 299. Heschel, *The Aryan Jesus*, p. 27.

36. Heschel, *The Aryan Jesus*, p. 1, p. 3.

37. Heschel, *The Aryan Jesus*, p. 1.

38. Heschel, *The Aryan Jesus*, pp. 1–2, pp. 32–37 (p. 2).

39. Heschel, *The Aryan Jesus*, p. 1, p. 9 (p. 13).

40. The third volume of the tetralogy was published in Vienna and the fourth in Stockholm.

41. *GW*, XI, p. 654.

42. *GW*, XI, p. 663.

43. *GW*, XI, p. 663.

44. *GW*, XI, p. 625.

45. *GW*, XI, p. 625.

46. Swales writes that *Joseph* juxtaposes myth as married 'to sophistication, urbanity, self-consciousness' that makes possible 'a universal, tolerant, syncretic consciousness and intelligence' to its regressive definition in 1930s Nazi Germany as 'synonymous with primitivism', 'nationalist, exclusive, suffused with cultic irrationalism' (p. 76). See Martin Swales, *Thomas Mann: A Study* (London: Heinemann, 1980).

47. Beck sees Mann's engagement with Nazi ideology through an exploration of a modern understanding of myth as the writer's central artistic task (Beck, 'Thomas Manns Josephstetralogie', pp. 74–75). Lörke reads Mann's conception of myth in *Joseph* as juxtaposed to its politicization by

the Nazis. See Tim Lörke, 'Politische Religion und aufgeklärter Mythos: der Nationalsozialismus und das Gegenprogramm Hermann Brochs und Thomas Manns', in *Totalitarismus und Literatur. Deutsche Literatur im 20 Jahrhundert — Literarische Öffentlichkeit im Spannungsfeld totalitärer Meinungsbildung*, ed. by Hans Jörg Schmidt and Petra Tallafuss, Schriften des Hannah-Arendt-Instituts für Totalitarismusforschung, 33 (Göttingen: Vandenhoeck & Ruprecht, 2007), pp. 119–34. Schwöbel points out that humanization of myth required its subversion in order to make it a medium for the development of the vision and realization of a humane future rather than reaction (p. 206). See Christoph Schwöbel, *Die Religion des Zauberers: Theologisches in den großen Romanen Thomas Manns* (Tübingen: Mohr Siebeck, 2008). On Mann's well-documented rejection of Oswald Spengler's fatalism and polyhistoric mysticism and Alfred Baeumler's tendentious interpretation of Johann Jakob Bachofen as a mythologist of Romanticism see Willy R. Berger, *Die mythologischen Motive in Thomas Manns Roman 'Joseph und seine Brüder'*, Literatur und Leben. Neue Folge, 14 (Cologne: Böhlau, 1971), pp. 21–27.

48. Kerényi, *Gespräch in Briefen*, p. 98. *Mythology*, p. 100 (18 February 1941). Gerth points out the tetralogy's juxtaposition of the psychology of enlightened spirit to regressive irrationality in German politics (p. 165). Klaus Gerth, *"Das Problem des Menschen". Zu Leben und Werk Thomas Manns* (Seelze: Friedrich, 2004).

49. Beck, 'Thomas Manns Josephstetralogie', p. 62, p. 95.

50. Swales writes that 'Thomas Mann's involvement [...] with the dialectic of "Geist" and "Leben" has profoundly to do with an urgent cultural debate which is inseparable from the history of his times' (p. 11). For Mann's understanding of the conflict between nature and spirit [Geist] as inherent to fascist ideology see Lothar Pikulik, *Thomas Mann und der Faschismus: Wahrnehmung, Erkenntnisinteresse, Widerstand*, Germanistische Texte und Studien, 90 (Hildesheim: Olms, 2013) and Dierk Wolters, *Zwischen Metaphysik und Politik. Thomas Manns Roman 'Joseph und seine Brüder' in seiner Zeit*, Studien zur deutschen Literatur, 147 (Tübingen: Niemeyer, 1998), pp. 11–12. On Mann's belief in the necessity of politicization of 'Geist' [intellect] in this context see Børge Kristiansen, 'Ägypten als symbolischer Raum der geistigen Problematik Thomas Manns. Überlegungen zur Dimension der Selbstkritik in *Joseph und seine Brüder*', *Thomas-Mann-Jahrbuch*, 6 (1993), 9–36 (p. 29).

51. Daniel Peris, *Storming the Heavens. The Soviet League of the Militant Godless* (Ithaca, NY: Cornell University Press, 1998), p. 22.

52. Peris, *Storming the Heavens*, p. 6.

53. David E. Powell, *Antireligious Propaganda in the Soviet Union: A Study of Mass Persuasion* (Cambridge, Massachusetts: the MIT Press, 1975), p. 23.

54. Powell, *Antireligious Propaganda in the Soviet Union*, p. 35. Peris, *Storming the Heavens*, pp. 42–44. See also Arto Luukkanen, *The Religious Policy of the Stalinist State. A Case Study: The Central Standing Commission on Religious Questions, 1929–1938*, Studia Historica, 57 (Helsinki: SHS, 1997).

55. See Dimitry V. Pospielovsky, *A History of Soviet Atheism in Theory and Practice, and the Believer. Soviet Antireligious Campaigns and Persecutions*, 3 vols (London: Macmillan, 1988), II. Powell, p. 3, p. 23, p. 25.

56. Peris, *Storming the Heavens*, pp. 50–53 (p. 52). For example, a series of articles in the 1926 November issue of *Bezbozhnik* explored the influence of 'pagan' myths on Christianity, drawing parallels between Jesus Christ, Babylonian Marduk, Persian Mithras, Zarathustra, Egyptian Osiris, Tammuz, Greek Adonis and Roman Apollo. See G. Daian, 'K istorii religii', *Bezbozhnik*, November 1926, pp. 11–14.

57. Emelian Iaroslavskii, *Kak rodiatsia, zhivut i umiraiut bogi* (Moscow: Gosudarstvennoe Antireligioznoe Izdatel'stvo, 1938). I use the 1938 extended edition of Iaroslavskii's book here.

58. Bulgakov, *'Master i Margarita'*, I, 76.

59. Iaroslavskii, *Kak rodiatsia*, p. 225, p. 65, p. 167. Iaroslavskii, like Berlioz, also draws on Josephus Flavius (p. 63), pointing out similarities between virgin birth myths of Attis, Adonis, Osiris, Mithras and Uitzilopochtli (p. 41, p. 44), concluding that Christians had invented nothing new (p. 65). Curtis writes that 'Berlioz's arguments identify him as a representative of the 'mythological' school of thought represented in Bulgakov's sources by the writings of A. Drews' (p. 161). See Julie A. E. Curtis, *Bulgakov's Last Decade: The Writer as Hero* (Cambridge: Cambridge University

Press, 1987). On Drews's understanding of Jesus Christ as a mythical figure see Arthur Drews, *The Christ Myth*, 3rd edn, trans. and rev. by Cecil Delisle Burns (London: Fisher Unwin, 1910), p. 235. Haber notes that during the 1920s the notions expounded in *The Christ Myth* were 'a central part of the Christological "party line", with an untold number of popular mass-produced works enlisting Drews's Christ myth to the cause of atheism' (pp. 347–48). Edythe C. Haber, 'The Mythic Bulgakov: *The Master and Margarita* and Arthur Drews's *The Christ Myth*', *Slavic and East European Journal*, 43 (1999), 347–60.

60. On Bulgakov's research for the Yershalaim chapters see Ianovskaia, *Tvorcheskii Put'*, pp. 249–60. Ianovskaia demonstrates that Bulgakov was primarily concerned with factual details, especially those which confirmed his poetic vision, not the essence of the different schools of Bible criticism (Ianovskaia, *Tvorcheskii Put'*, p. 253). On this subject also see Ianovskaia, *Treugol'nik*, p. 57 and p. 146 and Lidiia Ianovskaia, 'Pontii Pilat i Yeshua Ga-Notsri. V zerkalakh bulgakovedeniia', *Voprosy Literatury*, 3 (2010), 5–72, pp. 31–55. (Henceforth Ianovskaia, 'Pontii'.)

61. Losev, *Dnevnik*, p. 55. Bulgakov followed the writing of Demian Bednyi, a popular antireligious writer (Chudakova, *Zhizneopisanie*, p. 296). The newspaper *Gudok (The Hooter)*, where Bulgakov worked in the 1920s, ran a column entitled 'Гибель богов!' [The death of gods!]. See Natalia Kuziakina, 'Mikhail Bulgakov i Demian Bednyi', in *M. A. Bulgakov — dramaturg i khudozhestvennaia kul'tura ego vremeni*, ed. by Aleksandr A. Ninov and Violetta V. Gudkova (Moscow: Soiuz teatral'nykh deiatelei RSFSR, 1988), pp. 392–410 (p. 398).

62. Lidiia Ianovskaia, *Zapiski o Mikhaile Bulgakove* (Moscow: Tekst, 2007), p. 87.

63. Vladimir Tumanov, 'Jacob as Job in Thomas Mann's *Joseph und seine Brüder*', *Neophilologus*, 86 (2002), 287–302 (p. 298).

64. Käte Hamburger, *Thomas Manns biblisches Werk: Der Joseph-Roman, Die Moses-Erzählung, "Das Gesetz"*, Fischer Taschenbücher, 1230 (Frankfurt a.M.: Fischer, 1984), p. 108. Murdaugh explores this in psychoanalytical terms, as 'the emergence of the ego out of the unconscious' (p. 30). Elaine Murdaugh, *Salvation in the Secular: The Moral Law in Thomas Mann's 'Joseph und seine Brüder'*, Stanford German Studies, 10 (Bern: Lang, 1976). Abraham's covenant with God is seen by Nolte as being 'parallel to the union between ego and the Self, in which neither loses its intrinsic qualities' (p. 125). Charlotte Nolte, *Being and Meaning in Thomas Mann's 'Joseph' Novels*, MHRA texts and dissertations, 44, Bithell series of dissertations, 22 (Leeds: Maney for the Modern Humanities Research Association and the Institute of Germanic Studies, University of London, 1996).

65. Hamburger, *Thomas Manns biblisches Werk*, p. 100.

66. Murdaugh, *Salvation in the Secular*, p. 14.

67. Schwöbel, *Die Religion des Zauberers*, p. 38.

68. Christoph Jäger, *Humanisierung des Mythos — Vergegenwärtigung der Tradition. Theologisch-hermeneutische Aspekte in den Josephsromanen von Thomas Mann* (Stuttgart: M&P, 1992), p. 284. This narrative theology is underpinned in the novel by the dichotomy between the level of 'Wirklichkeit' [reality], where Mann follows the letter of the biblical story and the level of 'Wahrheit' [truth], where its meaning is expounded (Jäger, *Humanisierung des Mythos*, p. 127). The contradiction between Mann's choice of the flexible form of the modern novel and myth and the inflexible subject of absolutist monotheist God, whose origin lies in the unique historical event of revelation, fixed in a canonical text as inviolable law and historical truth, is reconciled through art, the medium of fine discourse and the festive reinstallation of the biblical text (Seibt, p. 88, p. 93). Gustav Seibt, 'Jaakobs Gott'. in *Das Buch der Bücher — gelesen: Lesearten der Bibel in den Wissenschaften und Künsten*, ed. by Steffen Martus and Andrea Polaschegg, Publikationen zur Zeitschrift für Germanistik, 13 (Bern: Lang, 2006), pp. 85–100.

69. Alan J. Swensen, *Gods, Angels and Narrators. A Metaphysics of Narrative in Thomas Mann's 'Joseph und seine Brüder'*, Studies in Modern German literature, 57 (New York: Lang, 1994), p. 10, p. 120. Assmann notes the analogy between the 'invention' of God and the 'invention' of literary fiction in the tetralogy (p. 36). See Jan Assmann, *Thomas Mann und Ägypten. Mythos und Monotheismus in den Josephsromanen* (Munich: Beck, 2006).

70. Olga Kushlina and Iurii Smirnov, 'Magiia slova (zametki na poliakh romana M. Bulgakova Master i Margarita', *Pamir*, 5 (1986), 152–67 (p. 164). For Haber Christ in Bulgakov's novel 'takes

the form of a ragged vagabond' (Haber, 'The Mythic Bulgakov', p. 395). Ianovskaia speculates that Yeshua may be deprived of the knowledge of his divinity while he is incarnated on earth as a human (Ianovskaia , 'Pontii', p. 59).

71. Igor F. Belza, 'Genealogiia *Mastera i Margarity*', *Kontekst*, 78 (1978), 156–248 (p. 158). Savel'eva treats Yeshua as a desacralized Christ-like character (p. 177). See Olga Savel'eva, 'Russkii apokrificheskii Khristos: K postanovke problemy', *Slavia Orientalis*, 52 (2003), 159–78.

72. Edward E. Ericson, 'The Satanic Incarnation: Parody in Bulgakov's *The Master and Margarita*', *Russian Review*, 33 (1974), 20–36 (p. 25). Zerkalov sees Yeshua as a pseudo-Jesus (p. 48). Aleksandr Zerkalov, 'Iisus iz Nazareta i Yeshua Ga-Notsri', *Nauka i Religiia*, 9 (1986), 47–52.

73. Georgii A. Lesskis, '*Master i Margarita* Bulgakova (manera povestvovaniia, zhanr, makrokompozitsiia)', *Izvestiia Akademii Nauk SSSR, Seriia literatury i iazyka*, 38 (1979), 52–59 (pp. 56–57).

74. George Krugovoy, 'The Jesus of the Church and the Yeshua of Mikhail Bulgakov', *Transactions of the Association of Russian-American Scholars in the USA*, 18 (1985), pp. 201–22 (p. 206, p. 208, p. 213). See also Anthony Colin Wright, *Mikhail Bulgakov. Life and Interpretations* (Toronto: University of Toronto Press, 1978). Wright avers that in spite of Yeshua's considerable differences from the gospel Christ 'we have little difficulty in recognizing him as divine' (pp. 262–63). Davies writes about 'the Divine Humanity of Jesus' but sees Yeshua as 'a human being exemplary in his compassion and honesty rather than [...] a new metaphysical Messiah' (p. 128, p. 134). J. M. Q Davies, 'Bulgakov: Atheist or "Militant Old Believer"? *The Master and Margarita* Reconsidered', *ASEES*, 6 (1992), 125–33.

75. Williams sees an echo of the Bogomil teaching of 'passive disobedience [...] to the authorities' in Yeshua's words (p. 247). The Bogomil doctrine 'became the state religion of Bosnia' in the twelfth century and 'was frequently called Manichaeism in Western Europe' (p. 249). See Gareth Williams, 'Some Difficulties in the Interpretation of Bulgakov's *Master and Margarita* and the advantages of a Manichean Approach, with Some Notes on Tolstoi's Influence on the Novel', *Slavonic and East European Review*, 68 (1990), 234–56 (pp. 244–48). The question of Yeshua's identity in this context has been linked with attempts to understand the cosmology of *The Master and Margarita* in terms of either Orthodox monistic or Manichean and Gnostic dualist organization. Critical attention has focused on Yeshua and Woland's correspondence to Christ and to Satan, and on the balance of power between them. Ericson offers a monistic reading when he interprets Bulgakov's Satan as an 'imitation' of God who has 'no existence independent of him' (p. 23) and who is an agent of 'impartial justice' (p. 25). Amert sees God and the Devil in *The Master and Margarita* as 'by no means separate or equal' and asserts that in Bulgakov's metaphysics 'the Devil takes orders from God' (p. 612). Susan Amert, 'The Dialectics of Closure in Bulgakov's *Master and Margarita*', *Russian Review*, 61 (2002), 599–617. Baker argues that Woland 'has been coopted to the divine' (p. 16). Harold D. Baker, 'Voland's Seventh Proof: The Event in Bulgakov's *Master i Margarita*', *Russian, Croatian and Serbian, Czech and Slovak, Polish Literature*, 49 (2001), 1–23. Kreps states that there are two equal and cooperating departments, one headed by Yeshua and the other by Woland, and that both of them are under the jurisdiction of God (p. 88). Mikhail Kreps, *Bulgakov i Pasternak kak romanisty. Analiz romanov 'Master i Margarita' i 'Doktor Zhivago'* (Ann Arbor, MI: Ermitazh, 1984). Longinović compares the relationship between Jesus and Woland to 'the relationship between the Gnostic transcendental god' and 'the demiurge, the creator of the material world' and sees Woland as 'the agent of the invisible god' (pp. 57–58). Tomislav Longinović, *Borderline Culture: The Politics of Identity in Four Twentieth-Century Slavic Novels* (Fayetteville, AK: University of Arkansas Press, 1993). Another monistic reading is provided by Weeks who interprets Woland as an agent of 'divine justice', a representation of Old Testament Law (p. 225). Weeks believes Woland to be subservient to Yeshua, proposing that the 'binary good-evil system' (p. 225) of the novel can be resolved in unity. Laura D. Weeks, 'Hebraic Antecedents in *The Master and Margarita*: Woland and Company Revisited', *Slavic Review*, 42 (1984), 224–41.

76. God in *Joseph* has been described by Murdaugh as 'a number of images', the transcendent 'God-of-the-Fairy-tales' and the 'immanent' God who appears as 'a non-miraculous psychological and philosophical phenomenon' (p. 55). She believes that this representation may be the result of

God's becoming 'historicized', whereby he moves from the 'position of narrator to the place of the narrated', but does not pursue this reading further (Murdaugh, *Salvation in the Secular*, p. 55).

CHAPTER 1

❖

Fairy Tales About God

The Master and Margarita famously opens with a discussion about how the narrative of Jesus Christ, represented in the Bible as a messiah and God made man, might be articulated in atheist Soviet Russia. The first two chapters offer three alternatives to the gospel story: Ivan's satirical antireligious poem, Berlioz's mythical narrative and Woland's account, where Christ appears as Yeshua Ha-Notsri, a likeable man of uncertain parentage.

Bulgakov deliberately uses two variants of the name 'Jesus' in the novel: 'Иисус Христос' (Jesus Christ) and the less familiar 'Иешуа Га-Ноцри' (Yeshua Ha-Notsri). The second variant is a russified Hebrew version of 'Jesus from Nazareth', conventionally rendered from the Greek as 'Иисус' (Iisus) in the Russian translation of the Bible.[1] 'Christ' means 'the anointed one' and has messianic connotations, whereas 'Nazareth' denotes geographical origin. Choosing either reference to Christ provides a small but significant shift in emphasis on the different aspects of his identity. With just two exceptions, the four Yershalaim chapters refer to Yeshua, and the Moscow chapters — to Jesus Christ.[2]

Another specificity of Bulgakov's portrayal of Christ in *The Master and Margarita*, which is still awaiting a detailed analysis, is that he, like Woland, 'appears as the object of another's perceptions'.[3] This chapter, therefore, considers how the depiction of the biblical messiah is problematized in the context of the production, transmission and reception of narratives about Christ and Yeshua, understood broadly as third-person accounts, both written and oral, composed by the Moscow and the Yershalaim characters. Taking twentieth-century Soviet Moscow as its point of departure, the chapter addresses a conflict between aesthetically and ideologically determined narrative production in *The Master and Margarita*. The second part of the chapter takes a close look at the three Yershalaim fragments. Here, at the historical genesis point for the gospel narrative, particular attention is paid to how Yeshua is perceived by his contemporaries. The way in which subjective perceptions of individual characters, their prejudices, knowledge horizons and personal beliefs motivate and shape the narrative construction of Christ and Yeshua in the novel, is considered to be of central importance.[4]

Mikhail Berlioz and Ivan Bezdomny

The first chapter of *The Master and Margarita* introduces the readers to two authors of narratives about Christ: a young Soviet poet called Ivan Bezdomny and his mentor, editor of a 'thick' journal, Mikhail Berlioz. Berlioz, a chairman of MASSOLIT, the Moscow writers' association, and thus a prominent member of the Soviet literary establishment, commissions an antireligious poem about Christ from Bezdomny.[5] Ivan is a safe choice. His poetry is conformist and, as such, so aesthetically uninventive that the Master is able to confidently dismiss it when he meets him: 'Никаких я ваших стихов не читал [...] как будто я других не читал? (632–33) ['I haven't read any of your poetry [...] Well [...] it's not as if I haven't read other things like it, now is it?' (111)]. Ivan writes a satirical poem that inadvertently paints Christ as a vital albeit a negative historical personage. The poem fails to meet the editor's exacting standards for antireligious propaganda precisely because of its success as a work of art, which is all the more surprising because of Ivan's 'полное незнакомство' (547) ['complete ignorance' (5)] of his subject. Ivan shares his unexpected artistic success with Bulgakov's Satan, another unlikely narrator of a realistic and believable take on the Passion of Christ, the first Yershalaim chapter, which magically transports the readers to the past.

Berlioz, Ivan's censor and editor, treats stories about Christ as 'простые выдумки, самый обыкновенный миф' (547) ['mere fabrications, myths of the most standard kind' (5)]. He suggests that Ivan re-write his poem in that vein, depicting the birth of Christ and the coming of the Magi as: 'нелепые слухи' (549) ['nonsense' (6), 'rumours' in the original].[6] Berlioz's language reflects his understanding of the gospels as mythical narratives, rooted in a horizon of perception as a rationalist and an atheist. He sees this as a fact, an objective truth, confirmed by the absence of references to Jesus in the records by prominent ancient historians Philo of Alexandria and Josephus Flavius, as well as by the typological similarities between Christ and a number of dying and resurrecting deities:

> Нет ни одной восточной религии, — говорил Берлиоз, — в которой, как правило, непорочная дева не произвела бы на свет бога. И христиане, не выдумав ничего нового, точно так же создали своего Иисуса, которого на самом деле никогда не было в живых [...] соль-то в том, что до Иисуса родился целый ряд сынов божиих, как, скажем, финикийский Адонис, фригийский Аттис, персидский Митра. (548)

> ['There is not a single Eastern religion,' Berlioz was saying, 'where an immaculate virgin does not, as a matter of course, bring forth a god into the world. And the Christians, displaying no originality whatsoever, followed the same pattern when they created their Jesus, who, in fact, never existed at all. [...] the fact is that a whole host of sons of God were born even before Jesus, like, say, the Phoenician Adonis, the Phrygian Attis, the Persian Mithras.' (5–6)]

Berlioz's extensive academic knowledge is evident from his casual mention of the controversy surrounding the authenticity of the reference to Christ in Tacitus's *Annals*, which he treats as 'позднейшая поддельная вставка' (547) ['a later, fraudulent interpolation' (5)]. The reliability of written records (religious or not), their vulnerability to questionable editing practices and the problematic status of truths they purport to contain are a major concern in both Mann and Bulgakov's novels.

This brief episode in the beginning of the novel provides interesting insights into the mechanisms behind the production of narratives about Christ in *The Master and Margarita*. Berlioz's disagreement with Ivan generates two competing narratives, both of which subjectivize the biblical original. Although Ivan's negative portrayal of Christ springs from his attempts to fulfil the criteria of the commission, his artistic decisions, such as the use of satire, are his own. Similarly, Berlioz's proposed mythologization of the birth of Jesus represents a distortive rewriting of the gospels, which treat Christ as a real historical figure. Berlioz controls the process of narrative production and is directly responsible both for Ivan's negative portrayal of Christ and for the alternative mythical depiction, a vehicle for programmatic rhetoric which embodies the intellectual values of the atheist Soviet establishment. His censorial intervention normalizes a mythologization of the gospel narrative about Christ in public discourse.

However, in spite of the editor's aplomb and formidable knowledge, his intellectual authority and objectivity are implicitly critiqued on the level of his language usage. One need only consider one of Berlioz's axiomatic statements to see the fallibility of his rhetoric: 'большинство нашего населения сознательно и давно перестало верить сказкам о Боге' (549) ['The majority of our population made a conscious decision long ago not to believe the fairy tales about God' (7)]. The truthfulness of this confident assertion and, in particular, Berlioz's use of the word 'conscious', is inadvertently undermined by Ivan, whom the editor explicitly includes in this atheist majority when he declares to Woland: 'Да, мы не верим в Бога' (549) ['That's right, we don't believe in God' (7)].[7] Ivan, of course, also claims to be in agreement with Berlioz when Woland queries him about the editor's claim that Jesus never existed: 'А вы соглашались с вашим собеседником? [...] На все сто!' (549) ['And do you agree with your friend? [...] A hundred percent!' (7)]. However, his point of view about the existence of Christ develops uncritically under the influence of Berlioz who educates him about the mythological roots and historical contexts of the gospel narrative: 'Поэт, для которого все, сообщаемое редактором, являлось новостью, внимательно слушал Михаила Александровича' (547) ['The poet, for whom everything the editor said was a novelty ... listened to him attentively' (5)]. There is a marked difference between his passive acceptance of Berlioz's words from a position of complete ignorance and the editor's assertion that the majority of the population had consciously embraced atheism.[8] Ivan's atheism is received, a result of conformist uncritical thinking. The factuality of Berlioz's rhetoric, at least in this case, turns out to be a wishful projection.

Berlioz's intellectual authority is further compromised when he shares his atheist rationalist beliefs with Woland. The reality of Woland's appearance in Moscow is central to the poetic design of Bulgakov's novel. It enables Bulgakov to reclaim the notion of objective fact from rationalists like Berlioz, who seek to monopolize it, and to re-signify it in *The Master and Margarita* as the expression of irrational truth and poetic justice. The facticity of Berlioz's assertions about the existence of Christ is juxtaposed to fact as it is defined by Woland: 'Голова отрезана женщиной, заседание не состоялось, и живу я теперь в вашей квартире. Это факт' (727) ['Your head was cut off by a woman, the meeting never took place, and I'm living in your apartment. That is a fact' (233)]. Woland casts the improbable and the irrational, such as the circumstances of Berlioz's impending death and his own clairvoyance, which the editor treats with understandable scepticism, as irrefutable facts. Woland's prediction of Berlioz's death functions as 'the seventh proof', a guarantee of the existence of the Devil, which, by implication also establishes the existence of God in the novel.[9] It effectively and cruelly refutes Berlioz's rejection of the supernatural, and highlights the fact that the narrative of *The Master and Margarita* is underpinned by a poetic rather than a rationalist logic. Berlioz's factual knowledge about Christ is later also implicitly pitted against Woland's vivid version of the gospel narrative: the first Yershalaim chapter.

In this context, it is interesting that Berlioz chooses the format of an artistic narrative — a poem rather than an educational pamphlet or an essay — as a vehicle for antireligious propaganda. Although the editor lectures Ivan on comparative mythology and ancient history, he wants him to translate this academic knowledge into a poetic form.[10] As a form of mass propaganda, a poem has clear mnemonic advantages. The commission, however, also suggests that Berlioz recognizes the significance of the gospels not as rational and believable texts, but as narratives which create a compelling image. Berlioz seeks to displace this image with another one, a poetic counter-narrative. This process of displacement, a template for which is set up in the first chapter of *The Master and Margarita*, will be repeated several times in the Yershalaim chapters where, time and again, fictional narratives about Yeshua Ha-Notsri will displace those, which are rooted in fact.[11]

The editor and the poet reject Christ's existence, the one consciously, the other uncritically. Their narratives ultimately serve as vehicles for antireligious propaganda and represent an intentional and ideologically motivated distortion and subjectivization of the original gospel text, sanctioned by a Soviet functionary and implicitly legitimated in the public discourse through its institutional origin. In a certain limited sense, Berlioz's censorial intervention into Ivan's writing dramatizes the collision between the literary establishment and the poetic visionary. This narrative situation is mirrored in the novel in the Master's conflict with a MASSOLIT editor where a narrative about Jesus Christ is once again at the heart of contention.

The Master

Yeshua and Pilate's stories are as inextricably linked in *The Master and Margarita* as they are in the Bible. Indeed, in the novel Yeshua tells the procurator in a dream: 'Помянут меня — сейчас же помянут и тебя!' (760) ['When people remember me, they will immediately remember you too!' (272)].[12] The Judean procurator inevitably recalls his most famous arrestee. The Master's novel about Pontius Pilate can, therefore, also be read as a narrative about Christ. Its transmission and critical reception are considered below.

Unlike Ivan, the Master does not come from a literary background. Nor is he a member of MASSOLIT, Moscow's main professional literary body. Instead, he emphatically distances himself from the writing it represents:

— Вы — писатель? — с интересом спросил поэт.
Гость потемнел лицом и погрозил Ивану кулаком, потом сказал:
— Я — мастер. (635)

['You're a writer?' asked the poet with interest.
The guest's face darkened, and he shook his fist at Ivan and then said, 'I am the Master.' (114)]

The Master's title, given to him by Margarita, reflects her recognition of his craftsmanship and her delight in his poetic achievement. A former museum worker and translator, his first encounter with the professional literary world takes place when he makes an attempt to publish his manuscript. The attempt is doomed to failure. His novel is too out of kilter with the dominant atheist discourse, reproduced by MASSOLIT writers and editors such as Ivan and Berlioz. Biblical subjects are acceptable to the Soviet literary establishment only when framed in rationalist secular rhetoric. The Master, however, is driven by his poetic vision and is either blind or indifferent to expectations of ideological literacy. Unsurprisingly, he sees the editor's questions about his novel as 'сумасшедши[е]' ['insane'] and 'совсем идиотски[е]' (639) ['totally idiotic' (119)]. The editor, for his part, looks at the Master as if he has 'an abscess' (119) ['флюс[]' (639)] and refers to his subject as strange.[13] The imagery of abnormality and mental illness reflects the fact that the interlocutors do not share a common understanding of what constitutes a 'normative' artistic practice under the Soviet regime, or, rather that the Master is completely unaware of it. The Master's ignorance of MASSOLIT politics leads him to inadvertently challenge its narrative monopoly and he is subsequently subjected to a critical campaign in the press. One of its most striking features is the aggressive use of language, which deserves our attention here as it, too, constructs and projects a particular image of Christ.

The Master's brief incursion into the Soviet literary world is treated with indignation by critics Ariman and Latunsky and the writer Lavrovich who see it as a dangerous encroachment, a contamination of public discourse which has to be stamped out and eradicated.[14] Ariman's review of the Master's novel — 'Вылазка врага' [The enemy's sortie] — identifies him as a hidden enemy who has made an attempt to 'протащить в печать апологию Иисуса Христа' (640) ['sneak into print an apologia for Jesus Christ' (120)].[15] Ariman's literary vigilantism testifies to establishment paranoia and casts positive depictions of Christ as a threat to its values, whilst also implying that there are legitimate and illegitimate modes of representation. Lavrovich's violent self-righteous article proposes 'ударить, и крепко ударить, по пилатчине и тому богомазу, который вздумал ее протащить [...] в печать' (640) ['striking a blow, and a strong one at that, against Pilatism and against that religious freak who had tried to sneak [...] it into print'

(120)]. The language used by the critics is an example of a particular kind of Soviet speak, ideologically tinted, unliterary and low in register. Derogatory coinage such as 'Pilatism' and 'religious freak', as well as terms like 'старообрядец' (640) ['Old Believer' (120)] and 'apologia', form a prescriptive lexicon which affirms the dominant cultural practice.[16] The word 'богомаз' ['religious freak'] operates on a number of levels. It implies the Master's artistic inferiority but also indicates that the critics see his Christ as a divine figure and that they react aggressively to this aspect of his work.[17] Their comparison of the Master to an Old Believer references the schism in the Russian Orthodox Church over the disagreements in liturgical reforms in the 1600s, exemplifying defiance and alterity, which is problematic in the value system of conformist Soviet Moscow. It also suggests the incongruity and the irrelevance of a novel about Pilate and Christ to the Soviet modernity.

The integrity of the critics' language is important as they have exclusive access to the press, controlling both the mechanisms of narrative production and the official channels of communication with the reading public.[18] Neither Ivan nor the Master are able to publish their work without the prior approval of MASSOLIT editors. Latunsky's reference to the Master as a 'militant Old Believer' attributes an aggressive and confrontational identity to him on the basis of his nonconformist narrative about Pilate and Christ. This label is ill fitting for the man who cannot stand 'шума, возни, насилий' (632) ['noise, rows, violence' (110)]. The critics also misinterpret and distort the original poetic design of the Master's novel by deliberately politicizing its agenda.[19] Finally, their allegation that the Master had tried to sneak the novel into print is simply false, as he makes no secret of the attempt to publish his work.

It is interesting that the Master draws on the Christian vocabulary of salvation and damnation when he refers to the words to 'sneak in' as 'это проклятое слово' (640) ['that damned word' (120)]. Given that Berlioz, another MASSOLIT editor who rejects Christ, is temporarily resurrected by Woland at his ball, where he is surrounded by the damned — and so quite literally in hell — the Master's subconscious response is symbolic. His sensitivity to the literal meaning of language contrasts with its casual misuse by the critics. He also suggests that the critics are constrained by the internalized interpretative norms they are reinforcing, and that the anger, that is ostensibly directed at him, is actually displaced: 'Мне все казалось, [...] что авторы этих статей говорят не то, что они хотят сказать, и что их ярость вызывается именно этим' (640) ['I kept thinking [...] that the authors of these articles weren't saying what they wanted to say, and that that was why they were so furious' (121)]. In *The Master and Margarita*, the literary establishment assumes the role of the custodian of truth, where truth is defined as objective, factual and rational by characters such as Berlioz. Yet Ariman and Lavrovich's language is arbitrary, subjective and underpinned by ideological conformism rather than integrity or real critical insight. None of the so-called 'critics' offer a valid literary criticism of the Master's novel, instead interpreting it narrowly in formulaic ideological terms. Professional literary bodies such as MASSOLIT in *The Master and Margarita* have become an obliging appendage to the state and a mouthpiece for its ideology.

After the Master's failed publication attempt, the manuscript is returned to him 'порядочно засаленный и растрепанный' (639) ['really tattered and soiled' (119)], which may be read as a physical manifestation of the novel's transmission, the critics' reading in preparation for their denunciatory articles, a calculated and underhand action.[20] The Master's failure to publish the novel means that the critics attack an unpublished text by an unknown author.[21] Their campaign proves to be highly effective. Ivan recalls the negative reviews of the novel when he meets the Master. More importantly, Azazello reveals that the Master is arrested after a complaint made by a certain Aloysius Mogarych: 'вы, прочитав статью Латунского о романе этого человека, написали на него жалобу с сообщением о том, что он хранит у себя нелегальную литературу?' (738) ['you [are] the one who read Latunsky's article on this man's novel and then filed a complaint against him, saying that he had illegal literature in his possession?' (246)]. The denunciation actualizes Lavrovich's suggestion of striking a blow against Pilatism, albeit motivated by private gain rather than ideology: Mogarych moves into the Master's flat after his arrest. It is often the willing complicity or moral indifference rather than true conviction of *Homo Sovieticus* that underpins the success of establishment politics in *The Master and Margarita*, here exploited by Mogarych for the improvement of his personal circumstances. Although the Master burns the manuscript and its only surviving fragment is taken by Margarita for safekeeping, he is arrested as the author of an 'illegal' narrative about Christ.

The literary establishment, represented by MASSOLIT in *The Master and Margarita*, enforces its monopoly on narrative production by containing what it considers to be nonconformist or ideologically fallible texts. The Master's novel is never published and its author is placed under arrest. The resulting psychological trauma is expressed in self-effacement; the Master characterizes himself as 'никто' (736) ['no one' (244)] when he meets Woland. The long-term consequences of the Master's incarceration and of the psychological pressure of the campaign against him result in the erosion of his sense of identity as a writer and the internalization of his novel. When Ivan, a sympathetic listener, implores the Master to tell him what has happened next to Yeshua and Pilate the writer refuses: 'Ах нет, нет, — болезненно дернувшись, ответил гость, — я вспомнить не могу без дрожи мой роман' (644) ['"Oh, no, no," the guest answered, twitching painfully, "I can't think of my novel without a shudder"' (125)]. Words in *The Master and Margarita* have a magical generative power. The language of illness used in the Master's first conversation with a MASSOLIT editor is eventually actualized in his condition. The Master also claims to have lost both his inspiration and 'способность описывать что-нибудь' (643) ['the facility [...] for describing things' (124)]. His powerful poetic evocation of love as 'убийца в переулке' (637) ['a murderer [...] in an alley' (116)] who strikes like lightning or like a Finnish knife belies his loss of eloquence as a loss of confidence, reclaimed only through Woland's magical intervention. Without Woland, the agent of poetic justice in the novel, and Margarita, who is moved by her love for the Master (a different kind of magic that overcomes all obstacles), the novel and its author would disappear.

The Secretary

Moscow narratives about Christ in *The Master and Margarita* are all subjective interpretations or imaginative reconstructions of the gospel events, produced as they are almost two thousand years after the canonical gospels were written. In contrast, Yershalaim is a site where narratives about Yeshua are recorded by the characters who witness them unfold first-hand. The immediacy of their experience holds a promise that their accounts will constitute accurate representations of Yeshua. This assumption is tested in the following analysis of third-person narratives about him in the four Yershalaim chapters, with special attention paid to the dynamics of their production and transmission.

When an arrestee called Yeshua Ha-Notsri is brought before the Judean procurator Pontius Pilate, charged with disturbance of peace in Yershalaim, a character anachronistically referred to as his secretary compiles a protocol of his interrogation. This bureaucratic document represents an official eyewitness record of the proceedings and, in this limited sense, a narrative about Yeshua. What starts as a routine interrogation unexpectedly turns into a philosophical conversation about human nature and other subjects, which have little to do with the criminal proceedings. The secretary's surprise at this turn of events disrupts his writing and results in omissions in the protocol.[22] At first, he simply lifts up his head from the parchment in reaction to Yeshua's denial of the allegations that he incited people to destroy the temple:

> Удивление выразилось на лице секретаря, сгорбившегося над низеньким столом и записывавшего показания. Он поднял голову, но тотчас же опять склонил ее к пергаменту [...] Секретарь перестал записывать и исподтишка бросил удивленный взгляд, но не на арестованного, а на прокуратора. (557)

> [A look of surprise crossed the face of the secretary, who was bent over a low table, writing down the testimony. He raised his head, but then immediately lowered it to the parchment [...] The secretary stopped writing and cast a furtive, surprised glance not at the prisoner but at the procurator. (16)]

However, when the arrestee states, apparently without rhyme or reason, that the procurator is suffering from a headache, the secretary drops the parchment and stops writing altogether:

> Секретарь вытаращил глаза на арестанта и не дописал слова [...] секретарь ничего более не записывал, а только, вытянув шею, как гусь, старался не проронить ни одного слова. (558)

> Секретарь смертельно побледнел и уронил свиток на пол [...] Секретарь поднял свиток, решил пока что ничего не записывать и ничему не удивляться. (559)

> [The secretary looked goggle-eyed at the prisoner and stopped writing in the middle of a word [...] the secretary no longer wrote any of it [the prisoner's speech] down, he just craned his neck like a goose, not wanting to miss a single word [...] The secretary turned deathly pale and dropped the scroll on the floor [...] The secretary picked up the scroll, decided not to write anything down for the time being and not to be surprised at anything. (18)]

Pilate eventually orders the secretary to stop writing, a superfluous request since the secretary has already made that decision himself. It is only after Yeshua starts recounting his beliefs about the power of the Caesars that put him in breach of the law pertaining to insults to the sovereign that the secretary starts writing again, this time 'стараясь не проронить ни слова' (562) ['[t]rying not to miss a word' (22)]. By taking the decision to stop writing before he is ordered to do so, the secretary subjectively filters the information preserved in the protocol and omits what he deems to be irrelevant to the proceedings in an act of 'editorial displacement'.[23] He leaves out all that is potentially miraculous in Yeshua's behaviour. The record excludes all references to Yeshua's inexplicable telepathic insight into the procurator's predicament, his longing for death and for his dog. The secretary fails to document that Yeshua cures Pilate's headache and omits his denial of entering Yershalaim on an ass greeted by the crowds as a prophet. Admittedly, all of the above (perhaps with the exception of the last allegation) has little to do with the subject of the interrogation, Yeshua's alleged call for the destruction of the temple. In this sense, the secretary's decision is entirely justified.

Crucially, the reason that motivates the secretary's selective recording, his decision to stop writing, is his astonishment at Yeshua's 'неслыханна[я] дерзость[]' (559) ['unprecedented insolence' (18)] and Pilate's willingness to engage in a dialogue with the arrestee, in other words, his lack of belief in what he sees. Unlike Pilate, the secretary does not experience Yeshua's healing, nor does he realize the true extent of his insight into the procurator's thoughts. As a result, Yeshua's words carry a different weight and meaning for the secretary, who perceives them only as peculiar. In this context, his response to one of Yeshua's more outlandish assertions about the procurator's loss of faith in people is highly symbolic: 'Секретарь думал теперь только об одном, верить ли ему ушам своим или не верить. Приходилось верить' (559) ['The secretary now had only one thought: whether or not to believe his own ears. There was no other choice but to believe' (18)]. The verb to 'believe', used three times in two short sentences in the Russian original, emphasizes the secretary's incredulity and symbolically underscores the importance of belief, as a facet of subjectivity, for narrative production. The emphasis on belief, created through the repeated use of this word, sets up another important parallel to the Moscow characters whose depictions of Christ are determined by their individual horizons of perception.

The importance of the protocol of the interrogation, as a narrative about Yeshua, lies in its format as a legal document, essentially a record of a sequence of questions and answers that should leave little room for subjectivization. It is worth noting here that the procurator also edits Yeshua's words recorded in the protocol by imposing convenient and subjective labels on the arrestee. When Yeshua says: 'У меня нет постоянного жилища [...] я путешествую из города в город' (556) ['I have none [permanent residence] [...] I travel from town to town' (15)], his movement, 'traveling,' has a purpose and a direction (from town to town). Pilate rephrases his words: 'одним словом — бродяга' (556) ['in one word — vagrant' (15)]. The omissions and editorial interventions in the protocol highlight the centrality of subjectivity to narrative production even in this uncreative bureaucratic format. The editorial activity of the procurator and his secretary, both of whom are functionaries and representatives of the Roman establishment, forges a disturbing parallel to the revision of the gospel narrative about Christ by the Moscow *literati*. Ironically, the protocol also clearly demonstrates the gap between the secretary's experience of the interrogation and its written account. It is, to a certain extent, a selective and subjective record of the proceedings, which ultimately reflects only the establishment beliefs and represents Yeshua as an ordinary criminal, guilty of breaching 'Закон об оскорблении величества' (561) ['The law pertaining to insults to the sovereign' (21)].

Pontius Pilate and Afranius

The next set of narratives about Yeshua is composed by two senior members of the Roman administration of Judea: the procurator Pontius Pilate and his chief of secret police Afranius. Plagued by a splitting headache and drawn into Sanhedrin affairs much against his will, the procurator initially has little time for Yeshua, who he calls, in turn, a vagrant, a common criminal and a liar and whom he irritably orders to stop pretending to be insane. All this changes when Yeshua inexplicably cures his headache. This captures the procurator's attention, who now sees Yeshua as 'великий врач' (559) ['a great physician' (18)]), another label rejected by the arrestee. Lending him a more favourable ear, Pilate becomes intrigued by Yeshua's unconventional beliefs in the kingdom of truth, the inherent goodness of people and his rejection of every kind of power as a form of violence. Yeshua's utopian ideas ultimately lead the procurator, who holds a very different view of the world, to perceive him as a philosopher and a 'юродив[ый]' (566) ['holy fool' (27)]. Creating convenient labels for Yeshua and consistently revising his words enables Pilate to rationalize and normalize his experience by subjectively framing it in familiar terms. Put simply, Pilate sees what he wants to see.

Although the procurator comes to believe that there is little substance in the allegations against Yeshua he decides to incarcerate him close to his residence. He intends to appease Kaifa but also to keep the extraordinary healer and fascinating interlocutor close to himself. In order to justify Yeshua's imprisonment Pilate creates a legend for the protocol: 'Бродячий философ оказался душевнобольным' (561) ['The vagrant philosopher turned out to be mentally ill' (20–21)], which belies his beliefs as 'безумные утопические речи' (561) ['insane, utopian speeches' (21)]. He later exploits the rhetoric of this fictional depiction of Yeshua as 'явно сумасшедший человек, [который] повинен в произнесении нелепых речей' (565) ['clearly a deranged individual [...] guilty of making absurd speeches' (26)] in a conversation with Kaifa in the hope of saving him. Although the procurator does not, in actual fact, believe Yeshua to be insane, his story capitalizes on the arrestee's unorthodox idealistic views, his naiveté and honesty, reframing alterity as mental illness in a parallel to the Moscow editor's treatment of the Master. However, Pilate's fiction ultimately falls on deaf ears as the High Priest Kaifa, the main addressee and the only recipient of his narrative about Yeshua's insanity, is unwilling to change his view of Ha-Notsri as a dangerous rabble-rouser.

Afranius's conversations with Pilate form one of the centrepieces of the Yershalaim narrative. His account of Yeshua's execution is suggestive both because of what it includes and because of what it leaves out. In the gospels, after Christ's sentencing the governor's soldiers offer him vinegar mixed with gall, which he refuses to drink. Then, just before his death, he is given vinegar.[24] In *The Master and Margarita*, when Pilate asks his chief of secret police if the condemned had accepted a drink before the hanging on the posts, Afranius, inscrutable and, for some reason, closing his eyes as he speaks, replies that Yeshua had refused it. At the same time, he chooses not to tell the procurator that Yeshua had, in fact, gladly accepted water just before his death.[25] Afranius also reports to Pilate (again closing his eyes) that Yeshua made the two following statements: '[он] не винит за то, что у него отняли жизнь' (750) ['he [...] cast no blame for the taking of his life' (260)] and 'в числе человеческих пороков одним из самых главных он считает трусость' (750) ['he considered cowardice one of the worst of all human vices' (260)]. The format and purpose of Afranius's report are similar to that of the protocol compiled by Pilate's secretary. He provides information about the execution only in response to the procurator's questions. Perhaps it is because of this that the picture of the execution which emerges from his report about Yeshua does not overlap with what the readers have borne witness to. They see the moments just before Yeshua's death, when he is so weakened by his ordeal that he can hardly muster the strength to say a few simple words. He manages to ask the executioner: 'Что тебе надо? Зачем подошел ко мне?' (665) ['What do you want? Why have you come?' (151)] and pleads with him for Dismas, crucified next to him: 'Дай попить ему' (665) ['Give him a drink' (151)]. In his final moments Yeshua speaks only to respond to what is happening around him. In other words, the readers, together with the procurator, have to rely on Afranius for these new details of the execution.

Afranius, of course, has privileged access to information in Yershalaim and the institutional nature of his report also guarantees its veracity. The procurator accepts his words as the truth, grimacing in dismay as he contemplates Yeshua's ordeal. He also subsequently quotes what he believes to be Yeshua's words to Levi: 'он перед смертью сказал, что он никого не винит, — Пилат значительно поднял палец' (767) ['"before he died, he said that he didn't blame anyone," — Pilate raised his finger meaningfully' (280)]. The careful attention Pilate pays to Yeshua's words can be explained by his urgent need for forgiveness. If Pilate's face and voice betray his feelings, one can only speculate about the reasons for Afranius's decisions to include or omit certain details of the execution based on the effect they have on his interlocutor. If one looks closely, each of Afranius's replies about Yeshua induces a feeling of guilt in the procurator. There is pathos in Yeshua's refusal to drink and the claim that he sought to look into the eyes of the people around him smiling 'какой-то растерянной улыбкой' (750) ['a distracted kind of smile' (261)]. Similarly, Yeshua's alleged forgiveness for his death and his condemnation of cowardice speak to Pilate's sense of guilt for his agreement to the execution out of fear of jeopardizing his career and putting his own life in danger. Particularly interesting in this context is the moment when Afrainus pointedly refers to Yeshua without naming him, prompting Pilate to ask whom he means: 'Простите, игемон! [...] Я не назвал? Га-Ноцри' (750) ['Forgive me, Hegemon! [...] Did I not give his name? Ha-Notsri' (260)]. Afranius's dialogue with Pilate concerning Judas's fate, that follows his report, is a stunning exercise in doublespeak. Ostensibly concerned with Judas's safety, the procurator, in actual fact, orders his chief of secret police to arrange his murder. Nothing is left to chance in this politically dangerous conversation, where neither interlocutor says what he means or means what he says. For this reason, it is also important to pay attention to their conversation about the execution, used by Pilate, amongst other things, to learn about Yeshua's last moments. Afranius's omission of Yeshua's name is clearly calculated to elicit a response. It seems, therefore, that at that moment Afranius, a man described as having a 'лукавый ум' (748) ['sly intelligence' (258)], engages in a subtle game of psychological one-upmanship with Pilate, using the report to demonstrate his insight into the procurator's feelings.[26] However, all this is merely implied. Pilate's chief of secret police remains inscrutable until the very end, as befits his position.

Afranius's report is unverifiable: none of the details he shares with Pilate are depicted elsewhere in the Yershalaim text (although some, such as Yeshua's refusal to accept a drink before the execution, map onto the gospel narrative). However, its truthfulness is suggested by the coincidence of the words about cowardice, attributed by him to Yeshua, with a fragment of Levi Matvei's parchment ('[...] большего порока [...] трусость' (766) ['[...] greater vice [...] cowardice' (279)]). Incidentally, these words are later also repeated by Woland, one of the narrators of the Yershalaim text, when he refers to Pilate's loyal dog Banga: 'Если верно, что трусость самый тяжкий порок, то, пожалуй, собака в нем не виновата' (802) ['If it is true that cowardice is the most grave vice, then the dog, at least, is not guilty of it' (323)]. There is, however, an irresolvable contradiction at the heart of this reading. In spite of the apparent coincidence of the words attributed to Yeshua by Afranius with Levi's record (and their repetition by Woland), it is in actual fact impossible to tell whether they belong to him. Yeshua unequivocally rejects Levi's record: 'Решительно ничего из того, что там записано, я не говорил' (557) ['Absolutely nothing that was written there did I ever say' (16)].[27] To explain this conundrum the readers would have to assume that Yeshua lies when he denies the truthfulness of Levi's record, which would be inconsistent with his character.[28] Alternatively, the readers would need to imagine that Afranius is familiar with the parchment that includes the fragment on cowardice, which Levi shows to Yeshua but gives up only to Pilate, and even then very reluctantly. As it is, Yeshua's decisive rejection of Levi's record has a destabilising effect on Afranius's report.

A different way of looking at this *non sequitur* is to interpret it as a deliberate element of Bulgakov's narrative strategy. For this, it is useful to consider the effect of the coincidence of Afranius's and Levi's words on the way the readers perceive Yeshua. The similarity of Afranius's report and Levi's record legitimizes this competing story about Yeshua, which supplements the narrative of his execution in the Yershalaim chapters. The assumption that the words about cowardice belong to Yeshua is easily made because they read convincingly as his own.[29] The assertion that Yeshua does not blame anyone for his death recalls his extraordinary compassion even for those who hurt and betray him like Mark Ratkiller and Judas. The report that he smiled and tried to look other people in the eye brings his naiveté and vulnerability to mind. Finally, since Afranius's words about cowardice resonate powerfully with the novel's exploration of moral compromise and personal guilt in both the Moscow and the Yershalaim narrative strands, they have acquired a meaning outside of the chapter where they are first uttered by Pilate's chief of secret police. Conveyed here by a ruthless murderer, they are amongst the most iconic and frequently quoted sentences from Bulgakov's masterpiece along with Woland's famous pronouncement, 'Manuscripts do not burn'.

The distortion of narratives about Yeshua by figures in positions of authority in Yershalaim, such as Pilate, parallel the revision of the gospel narrative by the Moscow functionaries, rendering this phenomenon thematically significant for the entire novel. In addition, both Pilate and Afranius introduce either new or competing readings of Yeshua's character into the novel. It is entirely possible to see Yeshua, as Pilate does, as a philosopher and a holy fool, to believe that he considers cowardice to be one of the worst human vices and that he does not blame anyone for his death. As a final thought, positing Yeshua as an object of sympathy for two major figures in the Roman administration in Judaea keeps the reader's attention fixed on his figure even after his death.

Joseph Kaifa

If Pilate holds a key position in the secular Roman administration of Judea, the High Priest Joseph Kaifa, the author of another narrative about Yeshua, is a representative of religious authority in Yershalaim. Characters in positions of power in *The Master and Margarita* consistently fail to produce truthful narratives about Yeshua, although their motivation for doing so is very different. Kaifa fears that Yeshua might incite the Jewish people to a revolt, provoking the ire of Rome. To remove this threat Kaifa uses the help of hired spies such as Judas to circulate a narrative which depicts Yeshua as a 'обольститель народа' (567) ['rabble-rouser' (28)], leaving Pilate little choice but to have him executed.

At the interrogation false allegations made against Yeshua consistently override his own testimony.[30] Kaifa's witnesses allege that Yeshua has called for the destruction of the Yershalaim temple, a charge which he denies, prompting Pilate to accuse him of lying: 'Ты, например, лгун. Записано ясно: подговаривал разрушить храм' (557) ['And liars as well. You, for example. It is plainly written: He incited the people to destroy the temple' (16)].[31] Pilate's words are deeply ironic. Yeshua's ideas are clearly decontextualized in the witnesses' statement: 'Я, игемон, говорил о том, что рухнет храм старой веры и создастся новый храм истины' (558) ['I said, Hegemon, that the temple of the old faith will fall and that a new temple of truth will be created' (17)]. He uses the symbol of the temple to speak about the evolution of faith. However, the witnesses choose to understand Yeshua's figural language literally. By leaving out Yeshua's references to faith and truth they politicize his metaphor, misrepresenting it as a call for violence. It is difficult to tell whether they do so deliberately or whether they genuinely misunderstand Yeshua because, as he claims, they lack the critical sensitivity to appreciate his figurative speech: 'Эти добрые люди [...] ничему не учились и все перепутали, что я говорил' (557) ['Those good people [...] are ignorant and have muddled what I said' (16)]. Be it as it may, Judas commissioned by Kaifa to tease out Yeshua's views on power, intentionally politicizes Yeshua's rhetoric and recontextualizes his utopian beliefs into 'государственное дело' (563) ['a matter of state' (23)].[32] Judas's report of Yeshua's rejection of all power as 'насилие[] над людьми' (562) ['a form of violence against people' (22)] and his hope for a kingdom of truth and justice where such power would be unnecessary is calculated to be read as a direct assault on the authority of Emperor Tiberius, enough to incriminate Ha-Notsri in a breach of *laesa majestatis*.[33]

Kaifa's machinations lead to Yeshua's conviction. As a result, Pilate is forced to transmit the narrative 'authored' by Kaifa, grouping Yeshua together with Dismas, Gestas and Bar-rabban and referring to them as criminals, arrested 'за убийства, подстрекательства к мятежу и оскорбление законов и веры' (569) ['for murder, incitement to rebellion, and abuse of the laws and the faith' (30)].[34] This portrayal jars conspicuously with Yeshua's timidity and stands in stark contrast with Levi's description of him as a man 'не сделавший никому в жизни ни малейшего зла' (662) ['who had never done anyone any harm in his whole life' (148)]. Yeshua is given an equally ill-fitting label as the gentle Master, who is described by the critics as a militant Old Believer. Pilate's portrayal of Yeshua as a criminal is substantiated through an inscription on the board hung around his neck, which reads 'Разбойник и мятежник' (659) ['Outlaw and Rebel' (143)] in Aramaic and Greek, when he is transported to the place of his execution. This legend is transmitted to at least two thousand curiosity-seekers who follow the procession, accompanied by heralds who repeat Pilate's words. Yeshua exercises no control over his words after he divulges his personal views on power, which are made into a public fiction of his rebellion. He remains completely silent.

Although Kaifa and Pilate are Yeshua's contemporaries, their narratives about him are anything but objective, truthful or accurate.[35] Kaifa's belief that Yeshua represents a danger to the Jewish people is channelled into a narrative that falsely depicts him as a rebel and criminal, legitimated through Pilate's announcement and transmitted by the heralds. The representation of Yeshua, which ultimately reaches the people in Yershalaim, is subject to institutional abuse, and is a result of negotiation between figures from the secular Roman and religious Judaic authorities.

Levi Matvei

Unlike biblical Christ, Bulgakov's Yeshua has only one follower — a former tax collector called Levi Matvei who authors the last Yershalaim narrative considered here. Levi sees himself as Yeshua's student and accompanies him everywhere, constantly writing on a goatskin parchment.[36] Unlike Pilate and Kaifa, who falsify or doctor accounts about Yeshua in pursuit of specific goals, Levi has no plausible motive to distort his teacher's legacy. In spite of this, Yeshua tells Pilate that Levi writes down his words 'неверно' (557) ['incorrectly' (16)] and warns him against reading the parchment as an authentic and accurate record.[37] It is unclear exactly how distortion creeps into Levi's record but it is likely that this happens inadvertently, the result of confusion or misunderstanding.[38]

By virtue of being inspired by the gospel narrative, the Yershalaim chapters set up certain expectations, which are often undermined. Levi's parchment, in this context, inevitably invites a comparison with the gospels but a simple equation of the two should be avoided.[39] Our knowledge of the contents of the parchment is limited to just five disjointed sentences:

> Смерти нет... Вчера мы ели сладкие весенние баккуроты... [...] Мы увидим чистую реку воды жизни... Человечество будет смотреть на солнце сквозь прозрачный кристалл... [...] большего порока ... трусость... (766)

> [There is no death... Yesterday we ate sweet spring figs... [...] We shall see the pure stream of the water of life ... Mankind will gaze at the sun through transparent crystal... [...] ... greater vice ... cowardice ... (279)]

It is worth pointing out that with the exception of the sentence about death, none of these fragments refer directly either to Yeshua or to the gospel texts. The fragments about crystal and the pure stream of the water of life are, in actual fact, inspired by the Book of Revelation (22.1–3).[40] Bulgakov's novel here deliberately shies away from direct parallels with the gospels and invites the readers to examine Levi's text for what it is. In fact, the parchment with allegations against Yeshua used at the interrogation seems to contain more of his words than Levi's record, which also doubles up as his diary and is used for writing down everyday notes, representing 'несвязную цепь каких-то изречений, каких-то дат, хозяйственных заметок и поэтических отрывков' (766) ['a disconnected set of sayings, dates, household jottings, and poetic fragments' (279)].[41] This generic confusion makes it impossible to ascertain the origin of the five sentences known to the reader. The fragment about sweet figs reads like a descriptive diary entry but the readers cannot be sure that it did not originally have another, figurative meaning.[42] Another entry clearly describes Levi's personal experience of the execution, which he observes from a safe distance, too far to hear Yeshua's final words: 'Бегут минуты, и я, Левий Матвей, нахожусь на Лысой Горе, а смерти все нет! ... Солнце склоняется, а смерти нет...' (661) ['The minutes go by, and I, Levi Matvei, am here on Bald Mountain, and still death does not come! ... The sun is sinking, and still, no death' (147)]. The confusion of Levi's record reflects the immediacy of writing. He writes things down as they occur to him. Just as the protocol of the interrogation, the parchment illuminates the limitations of writing as a means of producing a comprehensive record of reality. The information in the parchment must be organized, contextualized and edited to make sense to the uninitiated.

It is tempting to attribute the three aphoristic fragments about death, the transparent crystal, and the river of life to Yeshua since they recall the register and the eloquence of his figural language during the interrogation. However, Pilate's perusal of the parchment demonstrates that this would be a precarious assumption to make. Ironically, the procurator misreads even the more or less legible section of the parchment. Unable to make out Levi's sentence about Yeshua's prolonged execution ('Солнце склоняется, а смерти нет' (661) ['The sun is sinking, and still no death' (147)]), he reads its fragment as a reference to immortality ('Смерти нет' (766) ['There is no death' (279)]).[43]

Pilate represents a crucial companion figure to the readers of *The Master and Margarita* in their effort to understand Yeshua, acting as the internal audience for all narratives about Yeshua considered here. The procurator is involved in the writing of the interrogation protocol; he is the addressee of Afranius and Kaifa's narratives, and thus also of both parchments with allegations against Yeshua. Finally, the readers see Levi's parchment in the chapter 'Погребение' ['The Burial'] through his eyes. Pilate's perusal of the text in the parchment is frustrated by the generic confusion of the recording and hampered by the illegibility of Levi's handwriting: 'Трудно было понять эти корявые строчки, и Пилат морщился и склонялся к самому пергаменту, водил пальцем по строчкам' (766) ['The scrawly lines were hard to follow, and Pilate frowned as he bent over the parchment, running his finger over the lines' (279)]. In a conversation with the procurator Yeshua expresses anxiety that the parchment could be mistaken for a record of his words, an anxiety so acute that he pleads with Levi to destroy it: 'Я его умолял — сожги ты, Бога ради, свой пергамент! Но он вырвал его у меня из рук и убежал' (557) ['I begged him, 'For God's sake burn your parchment!' But he snatched it out of my hands and ran away' (16)]. Levi's gesture of tearing the parchment out of Yeshua's hands is symbolical of his inability to control his narrative. In the end, the procurator misreads Levi's text as a record 'где записаны слова Иешуа' (766) ['where Yeshua's words are written down' (279)] and accepts Afranius's narrative about the execution as the truth. An 'inadequate interpreter,' as Avins would call him, in this way Pilate's character consolidates narratives about Yeshua which compete for the attention of the readers with his actual representation in the text.[44] The Yershalaim chapters end on a promising but inconclusive note as Levi accepts a blank piece of parchment from the procurator — but we, of course, never learn what he writes in it.

Conclusion

None of the Yershalaim characters, including Levi, perceive or portray Yeshua as anything other than human. For the Moscow characters the representation of Christ is not a theological but a political and, for the Master at least, an artistic concern. Atheism has become an integral part of state ideology and its acceptance is a political statement, a demonstration of one's allegiance. However, atheism demands a certain degree of conviction and few of Bulgakov's characters actually embrace it consciously, to borrow Berlioz's expression. The majority of the Moscow characters, who either deny the existence and the divinity of Christ or who attack his figure, paradoxically appear indifferent to questions of faith. Some, like the critics and Ivan, are complicit fellow-travellers and uncritical conformists. Others, like Mogarych, are opportunists, not militant atheists. Only Berlioz can be described as a committed atheist, and for that he is cruelly punished.

Representation of Christ and Yeshua in the public domain both in Moscow and Yershalaim is controlled by those who are, in one way or another, affiliated with the establishment.[45] Only members of the literary establishment in Moscow are licensed to publish narratives about Christ. In Yershalaim Pilate and Kaifa, representatives of the judicial system and the church, exploit their administrative privilege to manipulate the depiction of Yeshua. Berlioz and Kaifa orchestrate narratives about Christ and Yeshua that serve the 'correct' ideological line using their positions of power, and do so with utmost conviction. Their stories promote atheism and pursue the Sanhedrin's political agenda. Those like Ivan and the critics are often either bound or incentivized by the dominant cultural practices, which are reproduced in their writing.

However, it is also important to acknowledge that the motivation of Bulgakov's characters is often personal and, in fact, inconsistent with what might be expected of them. The merciless procurator Pilate unexpectedly shows that he is capable of compassion through his ambivalent actions and the narratives about Yeshua (and Judas) which he is prepared to author and circulate. The opportunistic egocentrics Mogarych and Judas implicate the figures of Christ and Yeshua in narratives that raise questions of legality. They are thus able to bring state machinery into motion but use it only for personal enrichment. In both of these cases, however, both administrative privilege and the exploitation of state apparatus merely enable and license (mis)representations of Yeshua and Christ instead of dictating them.

On the whole, *The Master and Margarita* yields a fragmented and polyphonic portrait of Christ and Yeshua thanks to the competing subjective narratives about them, which are constructed by characters who are often driven by ulterior motives.[46] Many of the narratives about Christ and Yeshua in Bulgakov's novel really are 'простые выдумки, самый обыкновенный миф' (547) ['mere fabrications, myths of the most standard kind' (5)], as Berlioz claims. Each act of falsification, distortion or subjectivization of either the canonical gospel narrative or of Yeshua's story engenders a new narrative. The figures of Yeshua and Christ are thus symbolically posited as powerful sources of poetic inspiration, implicating the Yershalaim and Moscow characters in a creative process. The dynamics of this process are examined in the next chapter, which considers all three Yershalaim fragments as the text of the Master's novel about Pontius Pilate.

Notes to Chapter 1

1. Henry Elbaum, 'The Evolution of *The Master and Margarita*: Text, Context, Intertext', *Canadian Slavonic Papers*, 37 (1995), 59–87 (p. 81).

2. Ivan regrets not asking Woland about what happened to 'Га-Ноцри' ['Ha-Notsri'] in the chapter 'Раздвоение Ивана' ['Ivan is Split in Two'] and implores the Master to tell him the conclusion of Yeshua's story in the chapter 'Явление героя' ['Enter the Hero'] (p. 621, p. 644).

3. See C. E. Pearce, 'A Closer Look at Narrative Structure in Bulgakov's *The Master and Margarita*', *Canadian Slavonic Papers*, 22 (1980), 358–71 (p. 368) and Ianovskaia, *Treugol'nik*, pp. 88–89.

4. Avins examines the role of readers, such as the fictional literary critics of the Master's novel about Pontius Pilate, who are often 'inadequate interpreters' (p. 282), for its actualization, transmission and interpretation. Carol Avins, 'Reaching a Reader: The Master's Audience in *The Master and Margarita*', *Slavic Review*, 45 (1986), 272–85. Stapanian-Apkarian addresses the significance of 'language' as a site of 'symbolic placement and as physical dis-placement of concrete reality' in *The Master and Margarita* (p. 184), focusing especially on the problems of 'false witnessing' (p. 181) and the 'discrediting of documents as authoritative texts' (p. 196). Juliette R. Stapanian-Apkarian, 'Ironic "Vision" as an Aesthetics of Displaced Truth in M. Bulgakov's *Master and Margarita*', in *Russian Narrative & Visual Art: Varieties of Seeing*, ed. by Roger Anderson and Paul Debreczeny (Gainesville: University Press of Florida, 1994), pp. 173–200.

5. Haber points out the parallels between MASSOLIT and the Russian Association of Proletarian Writers (RAPP) which 'sharply denounced Bulgakov and other writers whose works did not conform to their ideological or aesthetic views' (p. 386). Edythe C. Haber, 'The Mythic Structure of Bulgakov's *The Master and Margarita*', *Russian Review*, 34 (1975), 382–409.

6. Amert aptly calls Berlioz 'one of Ivan Karamazov's progeny' (Amert, 'The Dialectics of Closure', p. 603). Bethea writes that Berlioz has no imagination, which he sees as 'the correlative of religious faith' in the Moscow narrative (p. 389). David M. Bethea, 'History as Hippodrome: The Apocalyptic Horse and Rider in *The Master and Margarita*', *Russian Review*, 41 (1982), 373–99.

7. Maksudov refers to Berlioz and Ivan as militant godless writers (p. 237). Sergei Maksudov, '*Master i Margarita* — teatral'nyi roman v piati izmereniiakh (prostranstvo, vremia, etika)', *NovZ*, 196 (1995), 202–44. Kejna-Sharratt notes 'the belligerent atheism and materialism of the two *literati* who represent the officially approved *Weltanschauung*' (pp. 2–3). Barbara Kejna-Sharratt, 'Narrative Techniques in *The Master and Margarita*', *Canadian Slavonic Papers*, 16 (1974), 1–13.

8. Haber points out that 'in this world "truth" is not attained through strenuous spiritual and intellectual activity or, indeed, through experience but is imposed from without' (Haber, 'The Mythic Structure', p. 387).

9. For Baker, the seventh proof 'is negative, a proof of man's lack of control over his destiny: it is not in itself a proof of the supernatural, but disrupts the complacency of secular human awareness and heightens receptivity to supernatural manifestations' (pp. 56–57). Harold D. Baker, 'Socratic, Hermetic, and Internally Convincing Dialogue: Types of Interlocution in Bulgakov's *The Master and Margarita*', *Russian Review*, 57 (1998), 53–71. (Henceforth Baker, 'Types of Interlocution'). See also Ericson, 'The Satanic Incarnation', p. 24.

10. Compare with Korablev who writes that an artistic image for Berlioz is only a means for an illustration of some more or less accurate ideas (p. 168). Aleksandr Korablev, 'Khorosho produmannoe prorochestvo', *Lepta*, 5 (1991), 165–70.

11. Compare with Stapanian-Apkarian, 'Ironic "Vision"', p. 183.

12. Weeks reads this as 'an obvious allusion to the Apostle's Creed' (p. 54). See Laura D. Weeks, 'In Defense of the Homeless: On the Uses of History and the Role of Bezdomnyi in *The Master and Margarita*', *Russian Review*, 48 (1989), 45–65. Krugovoy similarly understands these words as a reference to the Nicene Creed where the words 'Lord Jesus Christ' are followed by the words 'crucified for us under Pontius Pilate (Krugovoy, 'The Jesus of the Church', p. 207).

13. Kreps believes this editor to be Berlioz and sees his commission of the antireligious poem to Ivan as a response to the Master's novel (Kreps, *Bulgakov i Pasternak kak romanisty*, pp. 102–03).

14. Podgaets argues that Latunsky symbolizes the entire literary system that was hostile to Bulgakov and that his surname has absorbed the names of Lunacharskii (People's Commissar for Enlightenment), Litovskii (the head of *Glavrepertkom*, a body that approved and censored theatre repertoires) and the critic Orlinskii (p. 18). See O. A. Podgaets, 'Bezdomnyi, Latunskii, Riukhin i drugie', *Russkaia Rech'*, 3 (1991), 13–22. Williams notes that Ariman is a personification of evil and the Lord of darkness in Zoroastrianism (Williams, 'Some Difficulties in the Interpretation', p. 246). Belza identifies Ariman as Averbakh (Belza, 'Genealogiia Mastera i Margarity', p. 224).

15. The English translation gives a different title of Ariman's article. See the discussion of the different redactions of Bulgakov's novel in the Preface.

16. Belza suggests that the word 'Pilatism' may be inspired by the article by A. Orlinskii 'Protiv bulgakovshchiny' [Contra 'Bulgakovism'] which attacked Bulgakov's play *The Days of the Turbins*

(Belza, 'Genealogiia *Mastera i Margarity*', p. 223). Gasparov writes that 'Pilatism' characterizes Lavrovich's world rather than the Master (Gasparov, 'Iz nabliudenii', 11, 92–93).

17. The derogatory word 'богомаз', translated by Burgin and Tiernan O'Connor as 'religious freak', consists of 'бог' [god] and 'маз' from the verb 'мазать' (to smear).

18. Baker points out the internal inconsistency of Lavrovich's accusation for, on the one hand, 'the Master is harassed in the press for [...] "Pilatism", as though his work depicted Pilate as an ideal,' and, on the other hand, 'the one accused of "Pilatism" is called at the same time a "God-freak"' (Baker, 'Voland's Seventh Proof', p. 21).

19. See Avins, 'Reaching a Reader', p. 275.

20. Fiene, 'A Comparison', p. 343.

21. Kolysheva's version of chapter thirteen of *The Master and Margarita* agrees with Ianovskaiia's text (Bulgakov, *Sobranie sochinenii v piati tomakh*, v, 140–42) in that it excludes the long fragment about Aloysius Mogarych's friendship with the Master, which is included in Losev (Bulgakov, *"Moi bednyi"*, pp. 747–49) and Saakiants's versions (Bulgakov, *Belaia gvardiia*, p. 559). Kolysheva, Losev and Ianovskaia's versions also exclude the section about the publication of a large fragment of the Master's novel by another editor, included in Saakiants's text (Bulgakov, *Belaia gvardiia*, p. 559).

22. The secretary 'functions as a reactor, underscoring the peculiar nature of the proceedings' (Proffer, *Bulgakov*, p. 544).

23. Stapanian-Apkarian, 'Ironic "Vision"', p. 185.

24. I am indebted to Professor Edythe C. Haber for pointing out that these are two separate episodes recounted in the gospels (Matthew 27. 34 and 27. 48). In the gospel according to Mark (15. 23 and 15. 36) Christ is offered wine with myrrh. See also Andrew Barratt, *Between Two Worlds: A Critical Introduction to 'The Master and Margarita'* (Oxford: Clarendon, 1987), p. 214.

25. Stapanian-Apkarian notes that 'the chief of the secret service creatively "edits" by reporting to Pilate that one of the criminals did not drink' (Stapanian-Apkarian, 'Ironic "Vision"', p. 196).

26. Utekhin wonders whether Afranius was one of Yeshua's followers (p. 104). See Nikolai Utekhin, 'Master i Margarita M. Bulgakova (ob istochnikakh deistvitel'nykh i mnimykh)', *Russkaiia Literatura*, 4 (1979), 89–109. Curtis argues that Afranius distorts the account of the execution 'to consolidate his power over Pilate' (Curtis, *Bulgakov's Last Decade*, p. 148). Compare with Barratt, *Between Two Worlds*, pp. 214-15.

27. In the fifth redaction of *The Master and Margarita* Yeshua clarified: 'Ведь я-то говорил иносказательно о храме, а он [Levi] понял, так же, как и другие это буквально' (503) [I spoke about the temple figuratively but, like the others, he [Levi] took my words literally]. In the final redaction Bulgakov omits these words. Bulgakov, *Master i Margarita*, I, 503.

28. Proffer writes: 'Since Yeshua is unable to lie even when it may save his life, we must conclude that he did not lie about Matvei's parchment, and that these words [...] [about cowardice] are probably not Yeshua's' (Proffer, *Bulgakov*, p. 546).

29. See Haber, 'The Mythic Structure', pp. 397–98, George Krugovoy, *The Gnostic Novel of Mikhail Bulgakov: Sources and Exegesis* (Lanham, NY: University Press of America, 1991), pp. 36–37 and Genrikh El'baum, *Analiz Iudeiskih Glav 'Mastera i Margarity' M. Bulgakova* (Ann Arbor, MI: Ardis, 1981), p. 52.

30. Liakhova writes of the worship of the written, official word and the ignoring of the personal word (p. 171). E. I. Liakhova, 'Dramatizm lichnogo slova v romane M. A. Bulgakova *Master i Margarita*', in *Literaturnoe proizvedenie i literaturnyi protsess v aspekte istoricheskoi poetiki*, ed. by Valerii I. Tiupa, Mikhail Darvin and others (Kemerovo: Kemerovskii Gosudarstvennyi Universitet, 1988), pp. 169–76.

31. El'baum argues that the authors of this parchment may be either the Judaic priests or Pilate's own agents (El'baum, *Analiz*, p. 30). Maksudov aptly writes about Bulgakov's novel: 'Наиболее серьезное преступление — слово' [The gravest crime is a word] (Maksudov, '*Master i Margarita*', p. 234).

32. Kazarkin points out that Judas's slanderous report about Yeshua represents a form of a bureaucratic utterance, which functions as the only reliable source in the mechanism of secret governance (p. 21). Aleksandr P. Kazarkin, 'Tipy avtorstva v romane *Master i Margarita*', in *Tvorchestvo Mikhaila Bulgakova*, ed. by Iuliia A. Babicheva and Nikolai N. Kiselev (Tomsk: Izdatel'stvo Tomskogo Universiteta, 1991), pp. 11–27.

33. Krugovoy reads this statement as a 'dramatization' of 1 Corinthians 15. 24 (Krugovoy. *The Gnostic Novel*, p. 36).
34. Yeshua receives an 'official' title 'Outlaw and Rebel' in Yershalaim (Gasparov, 'Iz nabliudenii', 11, 92–93).
35. Compare with Curtis, *Bulgakov's Last Decade*, p. 147.
36. Savel'eva points out the Satanic connotations of the epithet 'козлиный' [goatskin] (Savel'eva, 'Russkii apokrificheskii Khristos', p. 161).
37. Past scholarship treats Levi's parchment as an imperfect record of Yeshua's words and as 'the basis for the gospels' (Wright, *Mikhail Bulgakov*, p. 268). Proffer states that through the text of the parchment 'Matvei has already begun to manufacture the myth of Yeshua' (Proffer, *Bulgakov*, p. 541). Leatherbarrow sees Levi 'as an inspired liar, an artist whose gospel is a creative distortion of reality' (p. 38). William J. Leatherbarrow, 'The Devil and the Creative Visionary in Bulgakov's *Master i Margarita*', *New Zealand Slavonic Journal*, 1 (1975), 29–45. Haber points out that Bulgakov's portrayal of Levi's record, 'presumably the source of the Gospels and all Christian tradition', undermines 'the very foundations of [...] canonical Christianity' (Haber, 'The Lamp', p. 347). Baker argues that 'the written record of Yeshua's teachings [...] gives rise to a worldly edifice through which their essence is obscured' (Baker, 'Types of Interlocution', p. 69). Solomon writes that Matvei's parchment represents his beliefs 'and thus it is true for him' (p. 247). Howard Solomon, 'The Sin of Cowardice: The Mystery behind Bulgakov's Ambiguity', *Russian, Croatian and Serbian, Czech and Slovak, Polish Literature*, 44 (1998), 241–52.
38. Chedrova points out that Levi is not always objective (p. 181). A. Chedrova, 'Khristianskie aspekty romana Mikhaila Bulgakova *Master i Margarita*', *NovZ*, 160 (1985), 175–83.
39. Belza refers to the resemblance of Levi's record to the *logia*, the evangelists' notes (not always accurate or authentic), which were later edited and formed the basis of the gospels (Belza, 'Genealogiia *Mastera i Margarity*', p. 159).
40. Krugovoy, 'The Jesus of the Church', p. 212. For a reading of the Book of Revelation as a source for Levi's text see El'baum, *Analiz*, p. 21 and Milivoe Iovanovich, 'Evangelie ot Matfeia kak literaturnyi istochnik *Mastera i Margarity*', *Canadian-American Slavic Studies*, 15 (1981), 295–311 (p. 297). Mechik-Blank argues that the New Jerusalem in the Book of Revelation, apparently alluded to in Levi's parchment, may be seen as another component of the synonymic sequence which includes light and the resurrection, symbolically linking his text to the gospels (p. 143). See Kseniia Mechik-Blank, 'Na rassvete *shestnadtsatogo* chisla vesennego mesiatsa Nisana... (Apofatizm romana *Master i Margarita*)', in *Mikhail Bulgakov na iskhode XX veka. Materialy VIII mezhdunarodnykh Bulgakovskikh chtenii v S.-Peterburge (mai 1997 g.)*, ed by Albert S. Burmistrov, Anatolii A. Grubin and Aleksandr A. Ninov, Biblioteka Sankt-Peterburgskogo Bulgakovskogo literaturno-teatral'nogo obshchestva 2 (St. Petersburg: Rossiiskii Institut Istorii Iskusstv, 1999), pp. 134–44. Kazarkin treats Levi's parchment and the gospels interchangeably. He sees Levi's record as the start of the canonical narrative about Jesus, where he is already distant to people 'в качестве сына божьего' [as a son of God] (p. 133). See Aleksandr P. Kazarkin, '"Vechnyi siuzhet" i avtorstvo v romane *Master i Margarita*', in *Problemy istoricheskoi poetiki v analize literaturnogo proizvedeniia*, ed. by Valerii I. Tiupa, Mikhail N. Darvin and others (Kemerovo: Kemerovskii Gosudarstvennii Universitet, 1987), pp. 125–35.
41. Writing about the three conflicting descriptions of Woland in the first chapter of *The Master and Margarita*, Edwards argues the following: 'Bulgakov seems to be making an important statement about the difficulty of recording experience, of registering truth: in the nature of things it is impossible to reproduce the reality of a situation in direct and objective terms, even when witnessed [...] perception itself introduces a subjective element; memory further confuses the issue, selecting and rejecting information; and the process of recording effects a further change' (p. 153). See T. R. N. Edwards, *Three Russian Writers and the Irrational. Zamyatin, Pil'nyak and Bulgakov* (Cambridge: Cambridge University Press, 1982).
42. Krugovoy reads the sentence about figs as an allusion to the 'Tree of Life that yields the "sweet spring figs" to the denizens of the Heavenly Jerusalem where "there is no death"' (Krugovoy, *The Gnostic Novel*, p. 45).
43. Burgin and Tiernan O'Connor's translation does not reflect the exact coincidence of the words that Levi writes during the execution and the words read by Pilate in his parchment.

44. Avins, 'Reaching a Reader', p. 282.
45. Although it is Levi Matvei's narrative about Yeshua that is destined to survive, it is read only by Pilate in the Yershalaim text.
46. *The Master and Margarita* 'makes the readers aware of the contingency of their own point of view' (Lovell, p. 41). See Stephen Lovell, 'Bulgakov as Soviet Culture', *Slavonic and East European Review*, 76 (1998), 28–48. See also Pearce, 'A Closer Look at Narrative Structure', p. 368.

CHAPTER 2

❖

A Novel About Pontius Pilate

One of the most striking features of *The Master and Margarita* is its structural complexity. The Moscow narrative is interrupted three times by the novel-within-the-novel, the Yershalaim text about Pontius Pilate's encounter with Yeshua Ha-Notsri, or the four so-called 'ancient' chapters, which transport the readers back in time to an imaginary Jerusalem. The authorship, origin and status of the inserted novel present a challenge to the critics. Put simply, it is unclear who is telling Pilate and Christ's story in *The Master and Margarita*. The Yershalaim text can be read as the Master's novel, Woland's eyewitness account of Christ's interrogation, Ivan's dream, and all three of the above at the same time. In addition, each of the four chapters about Pilate and Yeshua is, in one way or another, linked to Bulgakov's Satan, complicating their status. The first Yershalaim chapter is narrated by Woland who presents it as proof of Christ's historical existence. The second fragment is dreamt by heavily sedated Ivan in a psychiatric clinic following his encounter with Woland. The final two chapters, the third Yershalaim fragment, are framed as an excerpt from the manuscript of the Master's novel about Pilate. The Master burns the manuscript but it is later restored from the ashes by Woland. Woland's role as the guarantor and narrator of the Yershalaim text is ambivalent. His superior vantage point validates it as the higher truth. However, it may also be in his interest to present as a fact the version of the Passion narrative, which can only be described as apocryphal from the perspective of the church. The connection between the inserted novel and Satan was even more pronounced in the earlier redactions of *The Master and Margarita*, where Woland explicitly called the Yershalaim narrative his gospel.[1] In the final redaction Woland still casts a long shadow over the Yershalaim text, but its status is deliberately made more ambiguous and its link to Bulgakov's Satan more tenuous.

The four Yershalaim chapters form a consequential narrative delivered in the same objective narrative voice but mediated by multiple narrators.[2] In other words they are, confusingly, a single continuous narrative and three separate fragments at the same time. The continuity of this narrative, in spite of its multiple narrators, may be explained if the process of storytelling is viewed as a mystical actualization of a pre-existing universal *urtext*, whose truth is validated by the coincidence of the Master's novel and Woland's account, a narrative strategy strikingly similar to Mann's approach to the retelling of the biblical Joseph narrative.[3] A different way to approach the conundrum of a single narrative with multiple narrators is to recognize that the Yershalaim text is always directed at two different audiences. The first 'internal' audience consists of the intradiegetic recipients of the three Yershalaim fragments. This group includes Berlioz, Ivan, Margarita and, thanks to Ivan's recapitulation of Woland's narrative in the clinic, the Master himself. Each of the fragments received by this set of characters is linked to Woland. The second group which, in contrast, receives all four Yershalaim chapters, consists of the readers of *The Master and Margarita* who witness how the story 'дописывается' [is being written up] before them, to borrow Chudakova's expression.[4] This methodological caveat will inform the analysis below.

As for their status, the Yershalaim chapters have been interpreted as a demonically inspired narrative, which deliberately portrays Christ as desacralized Yeshua.[5] Alternatively and paradoxically, the Yershalaim chapters have also been read as divine revelation or even as a reflection of historical reality, intuited by the Master's artistic genius, that is if the New Testament, one of Bulgakov's sources for the Yershalaim text, is taken to be an objective historical document.[6] This conceptually problematic reading also fails to take into account the heterogeneity of the four gospels, which, this chapter will argue, is central to the way that Christ is represented in *The Master and Margarita*. A rather different approach to the Yershalaim text does away with questions of authorship and inspiration altogether by rationalizing both Yeshua and Woland as projections of Ivan's schizophrenic imagination.[7] In contrast to these established ways of reading the Yershalaim text, this chapter explores to what extent it may be seen from a narratological perspective as the Master's narrative inspired by the Bible, paying particular attention to its ending, and how far his unorthodox representation of Christ in the ancient chapters may be motivated by the choice of Pontius Pilate as his protagonist.

The Yershalaim Text and the Master's Novel

Ambiguity of origin is crucial to the conception of the Yershalaim narrative as a whole in the final redaction of *The Master and Margarita*. Therefore, the Yershalaim chapters are considered here as the Master's text, not to the exclusion of other readings of the inserted novel mentioned above, but rather in order to bring Bulgakov's Christ figure into clearer focus as a key protagonist of a self-contained narrative about Pilate. The Yershalaim narrative seems to coincide completely with the text of the Master's novel about the fifth procurator of Judea Pontius Pilate. The Master recognizes Ivan's recapitulation of the first Yershalaim chapter (as it is told by Woland) as his own: 'О, как я все угадал!' (633) ['I guessed everything right!' (112)].[8] There is nothing in Margarita's reaction to suggest that the novel restored from the ashes by Woland differs from the Master's original as she rereads the manuscript, that is, the third and fourth Yershalaim chapters, after the ball. The second Yershalaim chapter, which is framed as Ivan's dream, provides a seamless bridge between the other two fragments. It is a part of the same text, narrated by Woland and the Master, its cohesion underpinned and made possible by the idiosyncratic poetic logic of Bulgakov's novel, which celebrates the inherent authenticity of an artist's vision. In *The Master and Margarita* the Yershalaim narrative, revealed through many agents, is presented as an incontrovertible fact. The perfect coincidence of the Master's novel with Woland's story legitimizes the Yershalaim text as the truth, albeit not the truth of the canonical gospels, from which it departs on a number of crucial issues. It is the significance of the discrepancies with the gospels that endow this familiar narrative with new meanings in Bulgakov's novel.

Both Woland and Yeshua use the word 'сочинение' to refer to the Master's novel. The verb 'сочинить' means to 'write' or to 'compose' and implies authenticity.[9] When Levi visits Moscow, he reveals that Yeshua has read 'сочинение мастера' (788) ['the Master's work' (305)] and Woland himself calls the Master the man 'сочинивший историю Понтия Пилата' (741) ['who wrote the story of Pontius Pilate' (250)]. Bulgakov's Satan also appears to be genuinely surprised by the existence of the novel about Pilate written, as he puts it, 'Вот теперь?' (737) ['In these times?' (245)].[10] He demands to see it, implying that he is unfamiliar with its contents, but, after conjuring it up, he turns it over and puts it aside without so much as opening it, appearing to 'read' the novel instead by looking intently at its author.[11] In this context the description of Woland's eyes is significant. During Margarita's first encounter with Woland she notices that his left eye is black and empty but that his right eye penetrates 'до дна души' (714) [[the] 'soul to its depths' (216)]. The intensity of Woland's gaze seems to cause the text of the novel to rise up in the Master's mind, evoking a painful instant of identification with his protagonist.[12] The Master becomes distressed and says: 'И ночью при луне мне нет покоя, зачем потревожили меня? О боги, боги...' (738) ['Even at night in the moonlight I have no peace... Why have they disturbed me? O gods, gods...' (245)]. At that moment he quotes Pilate's words from the next Yershalaim chapter that we are yet to read (another suggestion that his novel and the ancient chapters are one and the same).[13] Momentarily, the Master becomes his work, which exists both inside and outside him, in his poetic imagination and in manuscript form. He is, just like Mann's narrator, both inside and outside the story. And here the question of the Master's relationship with Pontius Pilate merits a digression.

The comparison of Pilate and the Master on the basis of their cowardice is a surprising critical commonplace, given the fact that the motivation for their decisions and the circumstances under which they find themselves making these decisions are, in fact, very different.[14] The Master is accused of cowardice by the Bulgakov critics for his failure to defend his novel, for its destruction, and for his decision to keep Margarita in the dark about his fate when he is released. The Master's concealment of the truth from Margarita, although misguided since it causes her suffering by underestimating her love for him, is, in fact, a noble and self-sacrificing act of love (at least in its intention): 'Сделать ее несчастной? Нет, на это я не способен' (643) ['Make her unhappy? No, I'm not capable of that' (124)]. The Master deserves Margarita's accusation of being a 'маловерный [...] человек' (792) ['man of little faith' (310)] for insisting she go back to her previous life after she spends a night hosting Satan's ball for him. However, it is difficult to put the Master's other cowardly acts on the same plane as Pilate's failure to release Yeshua.[15]

Pilate knowingly condemns an innocent man to death for fear of compromising his career. He is aware that he is making a choice between Caesar and Yeshua: 'Так, померещилось ему, что голова арестанта уплыла куда-то, а вместо нее появилась другая. На этой плешивой голове сидел редкозубый золотой венец' (561) ['He seemed to see the prisoner's head float off somewhere, and another head appear in its place. On top of this bald head was a gold crown with widely-spaced points' (21)]. This symbolical vision illuminates the nature of his decision. Of course, a failure to prosecute Yeshua for *laesa majestatis* can have far-reaching consequences for the Roman procurator himself. Accordingly, Pilate tells Yeshua during their face-to-face conversation that he is not prepared to take his place. However, in a dream he has after Yeshua's death, Pilate asks whether it is thinkable that the procurator of Judea 'погубит свою карьеру' (759) [[would] 'ruin his career' (272)] for a man who had committed a crime against Caesar. He also makes it clear in a frank conversation with Kaifa, when the latter refuses to free Yeshua, that he is unafraid of his complaints to the Emperor and would use the High Priest's decision to release Bar-rabban to manipulate the situation to his advantage. In spite of all this Pilate sends Yeshua to his death.

The Master also risks his life and liberty with his attempts to publish a text that unwittingly contradicts the official antireligious line of the state. This much becomes clear after it is viciously attacked in the Soviet press and he is arrested. The condemnation of the Master hinges on the implicit assumption that he has an obligation to defend a political, religious or moral agenda or truth voiced by his text. This accusation is based on a view of an artist as a figure who has a public responsibility for his work and a moral duty to society. In this context, a comparison is sometimes made between Yeshua's truthfulness in the face of death and the Master's failure to defend his novel when it is attacked in the press.[16] However, Yeshua seems to be unaware that he will pay for his thoughts with his life until the very end of the interrogation. His unwillingness to lie ('Правду говорить легко и приятно' (562) ['It is easy and pleasant to tell the truth' (22)]), and inability to speak or understand the politicized language of Pilate, Kaifa, and Judas, means that he does not recognize the gravity of his predicament. His defiance appears to be inadvertent, based on his convictions but also a lack of political consciousness, a prioritization of a completely different set of values to those around him. The Master's failure to comprehend the political language of his critics and to anticipate the reception of his novel, which he describes as 'нечто внезапное и странное' (640), mirrors Yeshua's innocence.[17] His work polemicizes against the Soviet literary establishment not deliberately but inadvertently.[18] It is a vehicle for communicating a poetic rather than a political vision (if not for the readers of *The Master and Margarita*, then for the Master himself, to return to the distinction between the two audiences of the inserted novel). He is, first and foremost, an artist and the author of a work which raises timeless issues of moral failure, courage and integrity, something that his critics fail to see, fixated as they are on the biblical context of his novel. In Yershalaim and Soviet Moscow, where political literacy is of utmost importance, the Master and Yeshua appear as mavericks whose actions are guided only by their values and an inherent sense of (poetic) truth. They simply cannot do otherwise and it is this that sets them on a collision course with the authoritarian establishment that relies on compliance and conformism, and that breeds and rewards political and artistic opportunism.

There is another obvious parallel between the procurator and the writer. Both Pilate and the Master are denied the opportunity to express their thoughts freely. Pilate feels unable to exceed his authority as the procurator and Caesar's representative and to release Yeshua. The Master finds himself in a position where defending his novel and countering the very public campaign against it, which interprets it narrowly as religious propaganda, is not an option. Unlike the establishment critics, he does not have access to the printed media.[19] The Master does, in fact, make another failed attempt to publish the novel. He mentions to Ivan that he took his manuscript 'куда-то еще' (640) ['somewhere else' (119)], although we learn that it was Margarita who 'толкала его на борьбу' (640) [[was] 'pushing him into the fray' (119)]. In the case of powerful Pilate, the repressed is externalized as anger which finds expression in intricate revenge against Kaifa and Judas; in the case of the helpless Master, it is internalized and manifested in self-destruction and the burning of the novel, the unhappy cause of the campaign against him. His burning of the manuscript, instead of keeping it 'in the drawer', is a consequence of neurasthenia, an illness, a loss of control over his mind brought about by the aggressive reception of the novel and revealed through a fear of darkness (perhaps also shorthand for the secret police who often arrive in the middle of the night in *The Master and Margarita*). The Master's act is an uncontrollable expression of a nervous breakdown: 'Я встал человеком, который уже не владеет собой' (641) ['When I got out of bed, I was no longer in control of myself' (122)]. Both the procurator and the writer suffer long-term consequences of repression that surface in Pilate's dream as a wish projection that Yeshua's execution had never taken place, and which translate into the Master's illness and panic attacks. There is no courage in the Master's burning of the manuscript and his rejection of his vocation as a writer after his novel is attacked in the press, but his is a very human reaction.[20] Unlike Pilate, the Master is on the wrong side of the establishment. He is more fragile and vulnerable than his lover, lacking Margarita's spirit and resilience. An artist divorced from the world, he is so invested in his vision that he perceives the reception of his novel as a catastrophe which, as he puts it, 'как бы вынула у меня часть души' (640) [seems to have taken a part of my soul]. It appears that at the moment when Woland stares at the Master intently, the writer identifies not so much with Pilate's moral failure as with his feeling of entrapment and mental disarray, since he cites the words which convey the procurator's longing for peace, the release from his predicament.

To return to the Master's novel, its reception by Yeshua and Woland suggests that both of them have reservations about its final text. Levi, speaking on Yeshua's behalf, asks Woland to grant the Master peace rather than light, immediately after revealing that his teacher has read the novel: 'Он прочитал сочинение мастера [...] и просит тебя, чтобы ты взял с собою автора и наградил его покоем' (788) ['He has read the Master's work [...] and asks that you take the Master with you and grant him peace' (305)]. The Master's ambiguous reward seems to be linked to his work.[21] Woland explains that the novel is incomplete: 'Ваш роман прочитали [...] и сказали только одно, что он, к сожалению, не окончен' (801) ['They have read your novel [...] and they said only one thing, that, unfortunately, it is not finished' (323)]. He points out the conflict that is left unresolved in the Yershalaim narrative by showing suffering Pilate to the Master. After Yeshua is executed Pilate is tormented by an overwhelming feeling of guilt, which is only partially assuaged by his meeting with Levi and the murder of Judas. Pilate's guilt is transformed into a terrible punishment by immortality in the narrative that frames the Yershalaim chapters in *The Master and Margarita* as he is forced to relive his moral failure anew every full moon. Both Pilate's torment and his eventual release from it are hinted at in the Yershalaim chapters in the procurator's thoughts about immortality and his dream of walking along a moonbeam next to Yeshua, but are fully realized only in the framing narrative. According to Woland, the missing conclusion, Pilate's release, has been suggested by Yeshua himself: 'за него уже попросил тот, с кем он так стремится разговаривать' (802) ['the one he wants to talk to already has' [pleaded for him] (324)].

When Woland states that the novel is incomplete, the most obvious point which springs to mind is the disjunction between the immortal Yeshua who acts as an arbiter of the writer's fate in *The Master and Margarita*, and the absence of the resurrection in the Master's novel. Moreover, perhaps by persuading the Master to end his work with, what Woland implies, is a missing act of forgiveness, a final grace, he suggests that his novel does not do full justice to Yeshua's mercy, who after all intercedes for its author and Margarita in the framing narrative (and, indeed, states that he casts no blame for the taking of his life, according to Afranius).[22] References to Yeshua in *The Master and Margarita* after his death in the Yershalaim text merit a separate discussion and are addressed in the next chapter. As for the Master's novel, it coincides with Woland's narrative in all but its ending. It initially concludes with Yeshua's death and Pilate's attempts to stifle the feeling of guilt, for which there can be no relief except for in a dream. If, as Woland states, the Master's novel is incomplete, his chosen ending is his own. The Master's reasons for the unorthodox portrayal of Jesus Christ as Yeshua Ha-Notsri, the mortal protagonist of the four chapters that form a self-contained Yershalaim narrative, are considered below.

Jesus Christ and the Master's Protagonist

The biblical prototype of Yeshua, intuited by the Master, is Jesus Christ, traditionally understood by Christians to be the Son of God and a messiah, a figure both human and divine, whose coming was foretold in the Old Testament. Christian theology holds that that his self-sacrifice and the ensuing resurrection conquered death by atoning for Adam's original sin. The biblical Christ is keenly aware of his identity and guided by his mission. In contrast, the protagonist of the Yershalaim chapters neither claims to be the divine Son of God, nor does he seem to have a messianic mission, removing the motif of atonement for sins from this version of the Passion narrative.[23] In fact, the Yershalaim text reinterprets a number of familiar details of the gospels, frequently rendering what is miraculous in the original biblical narratives entirely plausible. Christ's virgin birth is replaced with Yeshua's uncertain parentage, divine omniscience with two premonitions about the storm and Judas's fate but also by Yeshua's ostensible blindness to his own predicament. The many miracles performed by Christ become Yeshua's single act of healing. The legendary God-man and messiah Jesus Christ, who had knowingly sacrificed his life and was miraculously resurrected, is demythologized as a naive, vulnerable and idealistic man, Yeshua Ha-Notsri, who believes in the inherent goodness of man and a utopian kingdom of truth, and dies unwillingly, sentenced to death as a result of a provocation: 'А ты бы меня лучше отпустил, игемон, [...] я вижу, что меня хотят убить' (563) ['Couldn't you let me go, Hegemon? [...] I can see that they want to kill me' (23)]. The modern retelling of the Passion narrative in the Yershalaim chapters departs from the gospel texts to emphasize Yeshua's humanity. In this sense, man is the primary focus, the 'alpha and omega', to borrow the expression from *Joseph and His Brothers*, both of Bulgakov's Yershalaim text and of Mann's novel about the discovery of God.

The specificity of the treatment of the gospel material in the Yershalaim chapters lies in the portrayal of a number of iconic New Testament events as either accidental or deliberate mythologizations of reality. The Yershalaim text recasts Christ's entry to Jerusalem on an ass, greeted by the people as a prophet, as a distortion, rumour or fabrication reported to Pilate (perhaps by a Sanhedrin agent to legitimize Kaifa's demand for Yeshua's execution). Indeed, Yeshua himself claims that his arrival to Yershalaim with his only disciple was unnoticed. The protagonist of the Yershalaim narrative thus rejects what is an iconic New Testament image associated with Christ's entry to Jerusalem, as described in all four gospels (Matthew 21. 7–11, Mark 11. 7–10, Luke 19. 35–38, John 12. 13–15), and with it, implicitly, the identity of a prophet and a messiah. Without a doubt, the Master's most significant departure from the canonical texts lies in the omission of the resurrection, the central event of the New Testament, the founding cornerstone of Christianity for, as Paul famously states in his letter to the Corinthians: 'and if Christ has not been raised, then our proclamation has been in vain and your faith has been in vain' (I Corinthians 15. 14).[24] The Yershalaim text, however, concludes Yeshua's story with the removal of his body and its secret burial with the bodies of the two thieves, as Pilate puts it: 'во избежание каких-нибудь сюрпризов [...] чтобы о них больше не было ни слуху ни духу' (750) ['to avoid surprises of any kind [...] so that neither hide nor hair of them remains' (261)]. The Russian expression 'ни слуху ни духу', translated as 'neither hide nor hair' in this instance, includes the word 'слух' which means 'rumour'. Rumour-mongering functions in the Yershalaim text as a creative form of untruth and tallies with the overall representation of Christ's story as a subject of misunderstanding, distortion and mythmaking.[25] All four evangelists refer to the disappearance of Christ's body on the third day after his death and burial (Matthew 28.2–6, Mark 16.4–6, Luke 24.3–7, John 20.1–8), which, in the New Testament, serves unequivocally as evidence of his resurrection and a confirmation of his divinity. Interestingly, in the gospel according to John, whose text in places differs dramatically from the other three canonical gospels, Mary Magdalene, who has come to the burial site, mistakes Jesus for a gardener and is distressed by the removal of his body (John 20. 2 and 20.12–15).[26] Christ's fate is thus, briefly, also a subject of misunderstanding in one of the canonical gospel texts. In the gospel according to Matthew (28.11–15) the soldiers are paid by the priests to spread rumours of the disciples' theft of Christ's body. In *The Master and Margarita* Pilate, apparently concerned about Yeshua's followers, orders Afranius to arrange an immediate secret burial of the executed to avoid surprises and rumours, suggested by the word 'слух[]' in 'ни слуху ни духу' (750) ['neither hide nor hair' (261)].[27] His misgivings that Yeshua's death may yet give rise to surprises are realized in Levi's 'theft' of his body from the execution site. The Yershalaim text alludes to the different gospels and implicitly ironizes the canonical depiction of the resurrection by portraying the disappearance of Yeshua's body as a result of Levi's theft. Seen from this perspective, the Yershalaim narrative highlights something that is intrinsic to the original gospel material: contingency and heterogeneity; a certain vagueness, inconclusiveness or ambiguity, in short the particular hermeneutic quality of the biblical text which invites scrutiny and interpretation, opening up its creative potential. The reworking of Pilate and Christ's story in a secular novel form in the Yershalaim text (like Mann's poetic reimagining of Joseph's narrative) is driven by a need to fill in the blanks, to expand on the sparse biblical lines, to depict their actors as psychologically convincing protagonists. The New Testament is significant here not as a sacred Word of God, as it is for Christians, but rather as a narrative which features interesting textual variation, which the author of the Yershalaim text playfully draws out in its modern retelling.[28]

Another illustration of this narrative technique concerns the fate of Judas from Kerioth. The Yershalaim narrative turns Judas's death out of contrition for his betrayal of Christ, as it is depicted in the gospel according to Matthew, into a contracted killing of a man who had orchestrated Yeshua's arrest for money. The biblical version of Judas's death is represented in the Yershalaim text as Pilate's inspired wish projection and a rumour deliberately disseminated by him, with the help of his chief of secret police: 'Да, Афраний, вот что внезапно мне пришло в голову: не покончил ли он сам с собой? [...] Я готов спорить, что через самое короткое время слухи об этом поползут по всему городу' (763) ['You know, Afranius, something just occurred to me: couldn't he have killed himself? [...] I would argue, in fact, that in no time at all rumors to that effect will be spreading throughout the city' (276)]. The story of Judas's suicide is perhaps more entrenched in popular imagination than it is in the Scripture since only one of the four gospels mentions it (Matthew 27. 5). The allusion to the single gospel which depicts Judas's suicide in the Yershalaim text and the reinterpretation of this story as a rumour both demythologizes the biblical narrative and illuminates the disparity between the four canonical New Testament texts about Christ. Rather than capturing the spirit of the individual gospels, which are, after all, hagiographical texts dedicated to the life of the divine messiah, the Yershalaim chapters reflect the nature of the New Testament canonical gospel narrative as a whole, in other words, the corpus that consists of four heterogeneous texts. By presenting various events of Christ's life in the Bible as alternative versions of the Yershalaim 'reality' and exposing the mechanisms of narrative production, *The Master and Margarita* playfully highlights the contingency of the canonical texts.

The Yershalaim text deliberately distances itself from the canonical gospels and their protagonist Christ at several crucial narrative junctions. This process reaches its pinnacle in the description of the crucifixion. The four evangelists write about Christ's suffering at the hands of his guards who beat him, spit on him and put a crown of thorns on his head, also depicting the mockery of the spectators of the crucifixion. However, none of the gospels address the physical reality of the execution in the same graphic detail as the Yershalaim text, simply stating that Jesus was crucified (Matthew 27.34–46, Mark 15.25–37, Luke 23.33–46, John 19.18–30). The lines of the Nicene Creed, recited during liturgy, state equally laconically: 'he was crucified for us under Pontius Pilate, and suffered, and was buried, and the third day he rose again, according to the Scriptures.' The crucifixion is cast as a redemptive act ('he was crucified for us'). In contrast, the Yershalaim text describes the violence and the physicality of Yeshua's execution in vivid detail: 'Мухи и слепни [...] совершенно облепили его, так что лицо его исчезло под черной шевелящейся маской. В паху, и на животе, и под мышками сидели жирные слепни и сосали желтое обнаженное тело' (664) ['he was, therefore, so covered with flies that his face had disappeared beneath a black, heaving mask. Fat horseflies clung to his groin, stomach, and armpits, sucking on his naked yellow body' (151)]. The Master's novel focuses on the indignity of dying by emphasizing Yeshua's inability to chase away the flies preying on his body. The reference to Yeshua's private body parts, the complete exposure of his body to the eyes of the readers, emphasizes his utter defencelessness and vulnerability, lending the text an uncomfortably voyeuristic dimension.

The reworking of Christ's narrative in the inserted novel results in a defamiliarization of his figure. Its author changes the familiar manner of representation of Christ through a shift away from gospel vocabulary, which has crystallized into the language of Christian liturgy and dogma.[29] This includes the usage of a russified Hebrew version of the name 'Jesus of Nazareth' as 'Иешуа Га-Ноцри' (Ieshua Ga-Notsri), which differs from the familiar Russian 'Иисус Христос' (Iisus Khristos) derived from the Greek.[30] It also involves a consistent avoidance of words which have become enshrined in the Russian language as the vocabulary of the crucifixion and the Passion of Christ. To cite but one example, Bulgakov's Yeshua is not crucified on a cross but sentenced 'к позорной казни — повешению на столбах' (569) [to a 'shameful death of hanging on posts' (30)].

The treatment of Christ in the Yershalaim text is iconoclastic. The inserted novel fleshes out the laconic text of the Nicene Creed and the lines of the gospels which refer to the crucifixion, moving from the traditional image of Christ the Redeemer to a man of flesh and blood. The Master's focus on the physicality of Yeshua's execution markedly re-accentuates the gospel depiction of Jesus's death, transforming the familiar image of Christ the Redeemer on the cross into a disturbing and literally unrecognizable portrait of dying Yeshua, whose face is described graphically as 'лицо повешенного, распухшее от укусов, с заплывшими глазами, неузнаваемое лицо' (664) ['[b]loated from bites, and with swollen eyelids, [...] [an] unrecognizable [face]' (151)]. The horror of this vivid description is not relieved through a counter image of a glorified resurrected Yeshua at a later point in the Yershalaim narrative. The deliberate omission of the resurrection means that this major aspect of Christ's divinity is not addressed in Yeshua's character. He is not resurrected, he does not seem to anticipate his fate and when he finally realizes that he will die, Yeshua perceives his death as murder ('я вижу, что меня хотят убить' (563) ['I can see that they want to kill me' (23)]).

It is important to remember that the Master is not the fifth evangelist and his novel does not purport to be a religious treatise or a historical document. It is a work of fiction and his demythologization and defamiliarization of Yeshua is a crucial aspect of his artistic design and narrative strategy. The Master's most important departure from Scripture lies in his presentation of Christ's death not as a willing and conscious sacrifice but as an unnecessary act of violence. The Master's narrative of the crucifixion divests it of its symbolical value as a redemptive act, emphasizing the tragedy of Yeshua's death instead, the death that does not have a broader religious significance within the Yershalaim chapters. It is horrifying in its finality and is represented as an act of irrevocable destruction of human life. As such, within the Yershalaim narrative it has, first and foremost, a significance that is ethical and an impact which is deeply personal to Levi Matvei and Pilate.[31] The Master's own description of the novel suggests a possible motivation behind the decision to omit the resurrection. He refers to his work as a novel about Pontius Pilate.[32] Thus the unequivocal focal point of the Yershalaim text for him is the procurator Pontius Pilate, seen through the lens of his encounter with Yeshua Ha-Notsri. His novel explores a very human drama of cowardice and moral compromise, not the myth of the resurrection. His reluctance to address the divinity of Jesus has the effect of shifting the perspective from the familiar biblical myth of Christ's death and resurrection to the drama of Pilate's decision. The only 'resurrection' afforded to Yeshua in the Yershalaim narrative takes place in Pilate's dream and is the procurator's wish projection, which shows his inability to face the consequences of his actions. Even in dreams Yeshua's fate is subject to mythologization, subjectivization and distortion. In this context the Master's narrative technique can be seen as an attempt to expose and emphasize the human and emotional core of the gospel myth. The focal point of his novel is Pilate's inner conflict rather than his biblical role as the executioner of Christ. His decision to portray the divine Christ as a vulnerable, naive and likeable man, removing direct references to his divinity and messianic mission, increases the pathos of Yeshua's predicament and deepens the drama of Pilate's conflict.[33] The Master's depiction of Christ as Yeshua, a man whose death at the end of the Yershalaim narrative is final, is an artistic decision motivated by the psychological development of his other protagonist Pontius Pilate, where Ha-Notsri serves as a measure of the procurator's humanity and moral integrity.

Conclusion

The Yershalaim chapters, a self-contained inserted novel, reinterpret the biblical text as a universal secular narrative about the betrayal of others but also, fundamentally, of oneself. The Passion of Christ becomes a story about the devastating consequences of self-compromise, and the ways in which authoritarian societies built on fear can rob victims and but also, perhaps surprisingly, perpetrators like Pilate of their dignity. The shift from the viewpoint of the four gospel writers to Pilate's perspective reanimates the traditional account of Christ's Passion and death insofar as the readers are forced to take a more active role in the reception of Bulgakov's text by constantly negotiating the familiar and the revised narratives. This subject is explored in the next chapter, which also considers references to Yeshua made outside the Yershalaim chapters, and examines whether his apparent immortality and continued existence in the framing Moscow narrative may be interpreted as markers of his divinity.

Notes to Chapter 2

1. See Bulgakov, 'Master i Margarita', I, 80. In an early redaction of The Master and Margarita it was Bulgakov's Satan who recounted one of the Yershalaim fragments to Bezdomny in the clinic in the chapter entitled 'Евангелие от Воланда' [The Gospel according to Woland]. Bulgakov, 'Master i Margarita', I, 223.

2. See Curtis, Bulgakov's Last Decade, p. 136, Kreps, Bulgakov i Pasternak, p. 115. Weeks, 'Hebraic Antecedents', p. 240. For Amusin the Master's novel intrinsically subsumes the two other fragments' (p. 84). See Mark Amusin, '"Your Novel has Some More Surprises in Store for You" (The Specificity of the Fantastic in The Master and Margarita)', Russian Studies in Literature, 42 (2005–06), 80–91. Vulis aptly writes that The Master and Margarita is a narrative about narrators (p. 136). Abram Vulis, 'Poetika "Mastera". Kniga o knige', Zvezda Vostoka, 10 (1990), 130–36. See also Vida Taranovski Johnson, 'The Thematic Function of the Narrator in The Master and Margarita', Canadian American Slavic Studies, 15 (1981), 271–86 (p. 274).

3. Kleberg believes that the Master's text and the four Yershalaim fragments constitute separate realizations of the same urtext, which exists outside time and space and represents absolute truth (p. 121). See Lars Kleberg, 'Roman Mastera i Roman Bulgakova', Slavica Lundensia, 5 (1977), 113–25. Chudakova interprets the Yershalaim text as the Master's novel, which reproduces an existing urtext brought to the light of a contemporary conscience by his genius (Chudakova, Zhizneopisanie, p. 449). For Amusin all three 'hypostases of "Pilate's story" [...] refer, in sum to the protoreality that stands behind them' (Amusin, '"Your Novel has Some More Surprises in Store for You"', p. 84). A notable exception to the established reading of the Yershalaim text as a single narrative split into three parts belongs to Faryno, who asserts that the fragments about Pilate are not homogenous and reads them as three separate chapters (p. 43). See Jerzy Faryno, 'Istoriia o Pontii Pilate', Russian, Croatian and Serbian, Czech and Slovak, Polish Literature, 18 (1985), 43–62.

4. Chudakova, Zhizneopisanie, p. 449.

5. For a range of readings on the Yershalaim chapters as a demonically inspired story see the following: Savel'eva, 'Russkii apokrificheskii Khristos', p. 176, Ericson, 'The Satanic Incarnation', p. 26, Williams, 'Some Difficulties in the Interpretation', p. 236. Mechik-Blank argues that the Master's lottery win was a gift from the Devil and that Woland co-authors the

novel (Mechik-Blank, 'Na rassvete *shestnadtsatogo*', p. 138). Frank sees Woland as the facilitator of the Master's writing (p. 288). Margot K. Frank, 'The Mystery of the Master's Final Destination', *Canadian-American Slavic Studies*, 15 (1981), 287–94. Korablev describes Woland as being behind the Master's 'творческая одержимость' [creative possession or fervour] (p. 39). Aleksandr Korablev, 'Tainodeistvie v *Mastere i Margarite*', *Voprosy Literatury*, 5 (1991), 35–54. Also see Pierre R. Hart, '*The Master and Margarita* as Creative Process', *Modern Fiction Studies*, 19 (1973), 169–78 (p. 177).

6. For a reading of the Yershalaim chapters as a reflection of historical reality see Faryno, 'Istoriia o Pontii Pilate', p. 50, Kreps, *Bulgakov i Pasternak*, pp. 115–16, Lesskis, '*Master i Margarita* Bulgakova', pp. 52–53. Kazarkin believes that the Master's authorship is true and divinely inspired (Kazarkin, 'Tipy avtorstva', p. 13). Amusin writes that the Master's 'clairvoyance [...] issues from the artist's very nature' but also considers whether it might be divinely inspired (Amusin, '"Your Novel has Some More Surprises in Store for You"', p. 85). Taranovski Johnson offers a similar reading: 'The Pilate-Ieshua story has a dual existence in Bulgakov's novel, both as an artistic creation — the Master's novel — and as historical fact whose occurrence in the past is indisputable because of its multiple narrative sources and its objective chronicle-like narration' (Taranovski, 'The Thematic Function', pp. 275–76).

7. Matt F. Oja, 'The Role and the Meaning of Madness in *The Master and Margarita*: The Novel as a Doppelgänger Tale', in *Bulgakov: The Novelist-Playwright*, ed. by Lesley Milne, Russian Theatre Archive, 5 (Luxembourg: Harwood, 1995), pp. 142–54 (pp. 142–43). See also Riitta H. Pittman, 'Dreamers and Dreaming in M. A. Bulgakov's *The Master and Margarita*', in *Bulgakov: The Novelist-Playwright*, ed. by Lesley Milne, Russian Theatre Archive, 5 (Luxembourg: Harwood, 1995), pp. 157–70 (p. 163).

8. Avins notes that the Master 'regards the Jerusalem text, while no less his creation, as existing beyond him and as being both true and sacred' (Avins, 'Reaching a Reader', p. 276).

9. Faryno writes that after reading the Master's novel Woland seems to deliberately stress the independent and authentic ('авторский') nature of the Master's work (Faryno, 'Istoriia o Pontii Pilate', p. 48).

10. Kazarkin notes that it transpires that Woland did not know what the Master's novel is about (Kazarkin, 'Tipy avtorstva', p. 11). Ianovskaiia argues that Woland is 'слишком масштабен' [too great] to stoop to lying (Ianovskaiia, 'Pontii', p. 62). Vulis writes that Woland curiously seems to combine omniscience and ignorance (Vulis, 'Poetika "Mastera"', p. 133).

11. In the fifth redaction Woland reads the novel by turning the pages of the manuscript with supernatural speed: 'Воланд проглядел роман с такой быстротой, что казалось, будто вращает страницы струя воздуха из вентилятора. Перелистав манускрипт, Воланд [...] уставился на мастера' [Woland looked through the novel with such speed that it seemed as if the pages were turned by a stream of air from the ventilator. Having looked through the manuscript Woland [...] turned his gaze to the Master]. Bulgakov, '*Master i Margarita*', I, 759.

12. Fiene writes that the Master also 'represents Pilate when he uses virtually the exact words of the latter' (p. 125). See Donald M. Fiene, '"Pilatism" in Mikhail Bulgakov's *Master i Margarita*', in *Bulgakov: The Novelist-Playwright*, ed. by Lesley Milne, Russian Theatre Archive, 5 (Luxembourg: Harwood, 1995), pp. 125–39.

13. Taranovski Johnson interprets 'the unexplicated and unmotivated narrative commentary' as 'an expression of deep physical and spiritual torment' which unites Ivan and the Master with Pilate and 'the narrator-author in their suffering' (Taranovski Johnson, 'The Thematic Function', p. 285).

14. Talbot sees the grounds for the Master's identification with Pilate in 'remorse for having bowed down in the face of adversity' (p. 190). Nathalie Mahieu Talbot, 'Giving the Devil His Due: The Register of Voices in *The Master and Margarita* and in York Höller's Operatic Adaptation of the Novel', trans. by Julie A. E. Curtis, in *Bulgakov: The Novelist-Playwright*, ed. by Lesley Milne, Russian Theatre Archive, 5 (Luxembourg: Harwood, 1995), pp. 187–200. Naiman argues that the Master's destructive act is 'the cowardly betrayal by the artist of his own morality and talent, whether by pandering to the state or falling silent through fear' (p. 82). Eric Naiman, 'The Morality of Punishment and Execution in *The Master and Margarita*', *Russian, Croatian and*

Serbian, Czech and Slovak, Polish Literature, 18 (1985), 63–90. Proffer writes '[bo]th the Master and Pilate have been men of little faith' (Proffer, *Bulgakov*, p. 532). See also Edwards, *Three Russian Writers and the Irrational*, p. 171 and Bruce A. Beatie and Phyllis W. Powell, 'Bulgakov, Dante, and Relativity', *Canadian-American Slavic Studies*, 15 (1981), 250–70 (p. 265). Frank asserts that the Master gives in to his fears like Pilate: 'He does not put up a Faust-like fight for publication, a fight that matters, for his novel is, after all, a tale of individual courage and Christian implications amid the Stalinist atheism and terror' (Frank, 'The Mystery', p. 290). Also see Haber, 'The Mythic Structure', p. 399. In contrast, Ianovskaiia praises the Master's courage as a writer (Ianovskaiia, 'Pontii', p. 9) and Pokrovskii notes that critics forget that the thought about cowardice being the greatest sin is uttered on the pages of the Master's novel and that he is the source of that thought (p. 145). Boris Pokrovskii, 'O chem besedoval Voland s Berliozom: Filosofskie problemy romana Bulgakova *Master i Margarita*', *Transactions of the Association of Russian-American Scholars in the USA*, 24 (1991), 143–62.

15. Curtis argues that 'the extent and nature of this cowardice is surely of a different order' but asserts that the Master 'is cowardly in that he fails to defend his art, his love, and himself when persecuted by the small minded' (Curtis, *Bulgakov's Last Decade*, p. 143).

16. Proffer writes that '[i]nstead of continuing to speak the truth in the face of danger as Yeshua does, the Master burns his novel' (Proffer, *Bulgakov*, p. 539).

17. The English translation leaves out the last part of the quotation: 'something sudden and strange.'

18. Compare with Riitta Pittman, *The Writer's Divided Self in Bulgakov's 'The Master and Margarita'* (London: Macmillan in association with St. Antony's College, Oxford, 1991), p. 105. Henceforth Pittman, *The Writer's Divided Self*.

19. The Master's situation is a poignant echo of Bulgakov's own predicament, whose works, such as his play *The Days of the Turbins*, were viciously attacked in the Soviet press. Bulgakov would eventually find publication in Soviet Russia impossible. See Bulgakov, *Sobraniie sochinenii v vos'mi tomakh*, VIII: *Zhizneopisanie v dokumentakh* (2004), pp. 279–81.

20. Bulgakov's thoughts on a writer's integrity are revealing here. In a diary entry from 26 October 1923 he laments his publications in *Nakanune* (*On the Eve*), which he believes compromise him as a writer, adding: 'Нужно быть исключительным героем, чтобы молчать в течении четырех лет, молчать без надежды, что удастся открыть рот в будущем. Я, к сожалению, не герой' [One has to be an exceptional hero to be silent for four years, to be silent without a hope that one will be able to speak in the future. Unfortunately, I am not a hero] (Bulgakov, *Sobraniie sochinenii v vos'mi tomakh*, VIII: *Zhizneopisanie v dokumentakh* (2004), p. 78). Although Bulgakov destroyed an early draft of *The Master and Margarita*, he would carry on his tenacious clandestine work on his last novel for as long as he could, writing it 'for the drawer'. See Bulgakov, *Sobraniie sochinenii v vos'mi tomakh*, VIII: *Zhizneopisanie v dokumentakh* (2004), p. 285.

21. Kreps echoes a number of critics when he argues that the Master is granted peace because of his weakness rather than cowardice, his 'неспособность к стойкости, а также и пассивная добродетель' [failure to be steadfast as well as passive virtue] (Kreps, *Bulgakov i Pasternak*, p. 84). Chudakova points out in this context that the Master has chosen to turn to the Devil for help and that his fate is therefore linked with him from that moment onwards. That is why, she writes, he does not deserve the light (Chudakova, *Zhizneopisanie*, p. 382). See also Barratt, *Between Two Worlds*, p. 256, p. 291.

22. Mechik-Blank suggests that Woland's act, which prompts the Master to conclude his novel with Pilate's release rather than Yeshua's resurrection, is a brilliant final temptation (Mechik-Blank, 'Na rassvete *shestnadtsatogo*', p. 138).

23. For Savel'eva, Yeshua's suffering is unwilling and he does not have a mission that justifies it (Savel'eva, 'Russkii apokrificheskii Khristos', p. 171). Chedrova argues that Yeshua's view that there are no wicked people contradicts the Christian belief in the real existence of evil in the world and the original sin. That is why for her Yeshua's suffering has no expiatory significance (Chedrova, 'Khristianskie aspekty romana', p. 176).

24. See Bruce M. Metzger and John Barton, eds, *The Holy Bible Containing the Old and New Testaments. New Revised Standard Version. Anglicized Text. Cross-Reference Edition* (Oxford: Oxford University Press, 2003), p. 189.

25. Leatherbarrow notes that Pilate 'arranges the assassination of Judas and then propagates two myths: firstly, that Yeshua had a large band of disciples and was thus a much greater threat than he actually was, and secondly that Judas took his own life' (Leatherbarrow, 'The Devil and the Creative Visionary', p. 39).

26. For a discussion of St. John's gospel as a source for *The Master and Margarita* see Donald B. Pruitt, 'St. John and Bulgakov: The Model of a Parody of Christ', *Canadian-American Slavic Studies*, 15 (1981), 312–20.

27. In the fifth redaction of *The Master and Margarita* the link between Yeshua's death and rumour-mongering was more pronounced with Pilate expressing fears that Ha-Notsri's grave would become [an] 'источник[] нелепых слухов' (774) [a source of extravagant rumours]. Bulgakov, *'Master i Margarita'*, I, 774.

28. Bulgakov's interest in the issue of synoptic gospels is evident in an earlier draft of the novel which describes Ivan's attempts to learn more about Pilate from the Bible: 'Но Матфей мало чего сказал о Пилате, и заинтересовало Ивана только то, что Пилат умыл руки. Примерно то же, что и Матфей, рассказал Марк. Лука же утверждал, что Иисус был на допросе не только у Пилата, но и у Ирода, Иоанн говорил о том, что Пилат задал вопрос Иисусу о том, что такое истина, но ответа на это не получил' (220) [But Matthew had said little about Pilate. The only thing that piqued Ivan's interest in his account was that Pilate had washed his hands. Mark had said roughly the same things as Matthew. As for Luke, he had stated that Jesus was interrogated not just by Pilate but also by Herod. John had written that Pilate asked Jesus about the nature of truth but received no answer]. Bulgakov, *'Master i Margarita'*, I, 220.

29. Ianovskaiia argues that Bulgakov wanted to look behind the great legend, to see, hear and show the way that the events described in it took place (Ianovskaiia, 'Pontii', p. 44). Belza writes that Bulgakov had interpreted the Passion narrative by trying to extract from it the seeds of historical truth, contained in the *logia*, and by clearing away the accretions (Belza, 'Genealogiia', p. 169).

30. See Ianovskaia, 'Pontii', p. 41. Elbaum points out that 'From the third redaction (1932–1936) on [...] the Greco-Russian names of Christ stop being used, and the wandering philosopher from Galilee is invariably called by his russified Hebrew name *Ieshua Ga-Notsri*' (Elbaum, 'The Evolution of *The Master and Margarita*', p. 81).

31. I am grateful to Professor Edythe C. Haber for this observation.

32. Compare with Curtis: 'the overriding difference of emphasis in the Master's text lies in the central significance of Pilate in the story' (Curtis, *Bulgakov's Last Decade*, p. 154).

33. Kreps highlights that the conflict at the heart of the Yershalaim narrative centres on a man and his conscience, rather than the man who condemned a God. However, he interprets the Master's novel as a historical text (Kreps, *Bulgakov i Pasternak*, p. 117). Compare with Barratt, *Between Two Worlds*, p. 180.

CHAPTER 3

❖

Reading Between the Lines

There are many ambiguities and incongruities inherent to the way Yeshua's story is told and retold in *The Master and Margarita*. The most important of these has to do with the way that Bulgakov's novel approaches the divinity of Christ. There is no contradiction in Christian theology between the humanity and the divinity of the biblical Jesus, who represents a perfect synthesis of both aspects. However, Bulgakov's demythologization and secularization of the gospel material and, crucially, his omission of the resurrection, the central event of the New Testament, problematizes Yeshua's relationship to his divine biblical prototype. At the same time, the Yershalaim chapters, which ostensibly read as a desacralized version of the gospel narrative, incorporate a discourse on the resurrection by including numerous allusions to immortality. Yeshua's representation in the novel as a whole is also contradictory. He features in the inserted novel, set two thousand years ago, where his death is represented as final, and outside it, in Soviet Moscow, when Levi Matvei conveys a message to Woland from a figure he refers to as his teacher. With few exceptions, past scholarship either fails to address the contradictions in Yeshua's depiction or sees his 'resurrected' hypostasis as divine.[1] Whether or not immortality should be equated with divinity and whether Yeshua's resurrection outside the Yershalaim narrative has any religious significance is explored below. More broadly, the ambiguity of the Yershalaim text and of Yeshua's character are considered an integral part of the novel's poetic design, and a crucial part of Bulgakov's narrative strategy for engaging the reader into an active exploration of the idea of the divine, although perhaps not in the most orthodox sense of that word.[2]

God in *The Master and Margarita*

It is impossible to address the question of Yeshua's identity and representation without at some point turning to Bulgakov's depiction of God in the Judeo-Christian tradition in the novel. Bulgakov had famously conducted extensive research dedicated to Christ and the Devil but, although there is a section entitled 'God' in his notebook with materials for the novel, it was left blank.[3] Unlike Woland, God does not feature in the novel as a character, nor is there any explicit evidence of divine intervention in the text.[4] Under these circumstances, the devil's presence in Moscow in *The Master and Margarita* has sometimes been taken 'as the seventh proof of the existence of God'.[5] Indeed, God is prominent in the novel only by His absence.

There are few significant references to God in *The Master and Margarita* outside of Woland's theological discussion with Berlioz in the first chapter. Moscow characters use God's name 'in vain', as an emphasizer: casually and conversationally, breaking one of the Ten Commandments (Exodus 20. 7).[6] The religious significance of the word 'God' is obvious in Levi's speech, where it is capitalized so long as he calls on an omnipotent God, an entity he believes in and to whom he appeals: 'О Бог' (663) ['Oh, God!' (149)], 'он [...] потребовал у Бога немедленного чуда' (663) ['he demanded that God send a miracle right away' (149)].[7] In contrast, it is not capitalized when Levi is referring to other deities or cursing his God: 'существуют другие боги и религии' (663) ['there were other gods and religions' (149)], 'Ты бог зла' (663) ['You are the God of evil' (149)].[8]

Only an obvious and frightening manifestation of the demonic forces can make Muscovites like the boorish Nikanor Ivanovich use God's name appropriately. Black magic, which transforms Korovyov's bribe to Nikanor Ivanovich into foreign currency and leads to his arrest, prompts him to sanctimoniously reflect on God's involvement: 'Господь меня наказует за скверну мою' (650) ['The Lord is punishing me for my sins' (133–34)]. On the whole, however, the word 'God' has become simulacral for the Soviet people in the novel, divested of its original sacral signification thanks either to the adoption of a new, atheist system of beliefs or to the indifference and ignorance of characters such as Ivan. Profanation of God's name is especially significant in the novel where words have a magical performative effect and must be used with utmost caution as the functionary Prokhor Petrovich finds out when his throwaway remark 'черти б меня взяли' (671) ['the devil take me' (159)] is realized unexpectedly and literally. Perhaps one of the most ironic nuances of Bulgakov's narrative here is that it is Satan and his retinue who take the word 'God' and the sign of the cross extremely seriously, while Muscovites fail to do so.[9]

The most meaningful references to God in *The Master and Margarita* are made by Yeshua and Levi Matvei in the Yershalaim chapters. Yeshua declares to Pilate simply and powerfully: 'Бог один [...] в него я верю' (563) ['There is one God [...] I believe in Him' (23)]. His statement 'перерезать волосок уж наверно может лишь тот, кто подвесил' (560) ['the thread can only be cut by the one who hung it' (19)] also testifies to his faith in the existence of a God.[10] Levi's passionate demand that God spare Yeshua further suffering and send him death shows that he sees Him as a force that can change and shape the material world. Indeed, a storm that arrives suddenly, as if in response to Levi's prayers, does bring about Yeshua's death, as the guards hurriedly finish the execution and rush back to the city. Levi understands his invocation of God as a dialogue with a real interlocutor. For him the storm is an unequivocal sign of divine intervention and he bitterly regrets his rash curses, convinced that 'теперь Бог не послушает его' (664) ['Now God would not listen to him' (150)]. However, the storm merely suggests God's involvement.[11] Of course, in contrast to atheist Moscow, appeals to the deities are to be expected in Yershalaim. It is a city decorated with idols and steeped in an apocalyptic mood, where rumours of the impending coming of the messiah are circulating amongst the Jewish believers. For Levi, faith is a condition for interpreting natural phenomena as divine interventions. This is also true for *Joseph and His Brothers*, where God accompanies those who believe in Him.

God's presence in *The Master and Margarita* is predicated either by a horizon of personal belief, as is true for Levi and Yeshua, or by logic, if we take Woland's appearance in Moscow as proof of His existence. In spite of Yeshua's statement of faith, he is neither explicitly linked to God, nor is he called the Son of God in the Yershalaim text. What connects Yeshua and God, if anything at all, is their very elusiveness, the silences, lacunae and absences in the narrative, where the readers, thanks to their knowledge of the biblical context of the novel, might expect a more active presence.

Beyond the Text: Immortality and Resurrection

Christ's death and resurrection in the canonical gospels are a manifestation of his divine nature. Yeshua Ha-Notsri makes several appearances both in Yershalaim and in Moscow after his death in the ancient chapters. Whilst this fact may imply immortality and divinity, most of his 'posthumous' appearances are in fact ambiguous, since they are mediated by other characters and resonate suspiciously with the desires that drive them.[12] For this reason, it is important not to simply take them at face value.

Following the execution on the Bald Mountain, Pilate's troubled mind conjures up a fantastic dream in which he walks with Yeshua along a moonbeam. This is Yeshua's first appearance in the Yershalaim text after his death and, on the textual level, it is framed in *The Master and Margarita* as a fragment of the Master's novel read by Margarita. His next 'posthumous' appearance takes place in the epilogue and is linked to Bezdomny, whose dream of Gestas's execution marks the anniversary of his encounter with Woland every spring. This traumatic vision is always followed by a dream of a man recognizable as Pilate walking towards the moon and beside him: 'какой-то молодой человек в разорванном хитоне и с обезображенным лицом' (811) ['a young man in a torn chiton with a disfigured face' (334)]. Pilate implores this man (clearly Yeshua) to swear that the execution never took place, and his interlocutor obliges smiling to himself. 'Resurrection' ritualistically follows execution in this recurrent dream sequence but it takes place in an imaginary moonlit world and recycles fragments of two previous Yershalaim chapters, one of which is framed as Ivan's dream at Stravinsky's clinic and the other, mentioned above, is Pilate's wish projection, a product of his guilty subconscious. Far from being an authentic event, Yeshua's 'resurrection' in Bulgakov's novel is filtered by two dreaming minds, Pilate and Ivan's, and is, in both cases, a response to the trauma of the execution, an attempt to 'undo' and to 'unsee' it.[13] Each new reference to Yeshua's resurrection affirms it, but the multiple framing of this narrative or *mise en abyme* also creates a distance to his figure.

These visions ultimately reveal more about Pilate and Ivan, both of whom are seeking closure in the form of a continuation to Yeshua's story, than about Yeshua himself. Indeed, Yeshua's description in Ivan's dream is vague, underscoring his inaccessibility. Yeshua is unnamed and his image is quite literally eroded as the adjective 'обезображенное' can be broken down into 'без' ['without'] and 'образ' ['image']. It is a face of a man who had died in Yershalaim, the tortured protagonist of the Master's novel, not the resurrected Christ of the gospels. Bulgakov's focus on Yeshua's disfigured face represents a shift away from traditional Christian iconography, where it is the body of Christ that carries the stigmata and a graphic wound from the spear. The injuries to his face are presumably caused by the mass of flies that cover him as he hangs on the post. His face and torn clothes are stark reminders of his violent death. On the whole, his appearance in this dream sequence has a narrative, rather than a religious significance. By denying that the execution took place, Yeshua provides forgiveness and mercy, closure and a conclusion to Pilate's narrative, the missing end of the Master's novel, not redemption through resurrection in the dogmatic sense of that word.

However, the crux of the narrative logic of *The Master and Margarita* is that it does not preclude something just because it is rationally impossible. In fact, the whole novel is built on the premise that the impossible is often poetically necessary. Despite Pilate's urgent desire to the contrary, the execution had, in fact, taken place while the resurrection had not. And yet, in spite of all this, Levi's conversation with Woland in Moscow testifies to Yeshua's continued existence outside of dreams and the pages of the Master's novel. Yeshua's immortality in *The Master and Margarita* is a narrative fact and fact, according to Woland, is one of the most stubborn things in the world. There are, nevertheless, some important differences between the Master's protagonist, the subject of Pilate and Ivan's dreams, and the immortal Yeshua of the Moscow text. This 'resurrected' Yeshua dwells in light, not in the nightmarish moonlit space haunted by another Master's character — Pilate. In contrast to the graphically visualized Yeshua of the Yershalaim chapters, Levi's sender is anonymous and distant, accessible only through Woland and Levi's words. There is something majestic in Yeshua's absence in the Moscow narrative and an indisputable gravity in Levi's simple words: 'Он прислал меня' (788) ['He sent me' (305)]. No further explanation is needed. Neither Woland, nor Levi name Yeshua in their conversation, using only the laconic 'Он' ['He'].

Yeshua's intercession in the Moscow text results in the Master's death and his journey to a fantastical lunar world beyond.[14] Bulgakov scholars often interpret this moonlit place of Pilate's confinement and the Master's resting place by drawing on the terminology and the imagery of Christian eschatology, specifically, the notions of heaven, hell, and purgatory.[15] However, Christian categories 'heaven,' 'hell' or 'limbo' should be used here with utmost caution since Bulgakov's characters Woland and Levi operate with less concrete terms of light and shadow, good and evil. Of course, light and darkness are also standard elements of Christian eschatological imagery but Bulgakov's deliberate movement away from religious vocabulary should be respected rather than ignored. The word 'hell' features only twice in *The*

Master and Margarita and both times in a trivial context.[16] Bulgakov's decision not to use it elsewhere in the novel suggests that the meaning of this fantastical world may extend beyond the obvious parallel with hell or limbo.

The lunar world is also often linked to the Master's identity as a writer and interpreted as meta-fictional or literary in nature.[17] It is a liminal ambiguous space populated by his characters and envisioned in poetic rather than religious terms. It exists outside time, beyond life and death and on the border between Moscow reality and his fiction. The Master undergoes a symbolical transformation as he travels to this world. A cloaked horseman with long braided hair, he lives on after his death only in a hypostasis of an idealized Romantic artist, the essence of his character.[18] He is rewarded with peace rather than light. His final abode is an attractive collage of Romantic clichés conjured up by Woland: blossoming cherry trees, Schubert's music, writing with a quill by candlelight.[19] If Yeshua represents creativity insofar as he is posited as a stimulus for narrative production in the novel, Woland's reward only reflects the creative life of an artist but does not embody it. He offers the writer a future spent creating imitation or artificial life, a homunculus, a far cry from the Master's vivid and vital novel about Pilate.

The Master's vision of suffering Pilate, whom Woland refers to as 'выдуманный вами герой' (803) ['the hero you created' (324)] and who speaks in the Yershalaim idiom, calling Yeshua 'арестант[]' ['the prisoner'] and Levi 'оборванны[й] бродяг[а]' (802) ['the ragged wanderer' (323)], not Christ and his disciple, suggests that he is both inside and outside the text of his novel at the same time in a space that allows for self-conscious reflection on the creative process. This space is linked to the Master's imagination and is malleable only to his words, since Margarita's plea for Pilate fails to break the spell he is under. Her speech, invested with the power to release Frieda, loses its magical performativity here.[20] The Master frees Pilate and changes the ending of his novel by simply shouting: 'Свободен!' (802) ['Free!' (324)]. As previously discussed, the Master seems to identify with Pilate's feeling of entrapment, which is literalized in this fantastical space. It seems appropriate that it is only after the Master himself escapes from the nightmare of Soviet reality that his protagonist, who mirrors his predicament, can also be freed.

The topography of this fantastical space is mutable and dependent on the Master's imagination, which is vividly illustrated by the destruction of the moonlit landscape after he releases Pilate:

> Горы превратили голос мастера в гром, и этот же гром их разрушил. Проклятые скалистые стены упали. Осталась только площадка с каменным креслом. Над черной бездной, в которую ушли стены, загорелся необъятный город с царствующими над ним сверкающими идолами над пышно разросшимся за много тысяч этих лун садом. Прямо к этому саду протянулась долгожданная прокуратором лунная дорога. (802)

> [The mountains transformed the Master's voice into thunder, and the thunder destroyed them. The accursed rocky walls caved in. The only thing that remained was the summit with the stone chair. Above the black abyss where the walls have vanished, blazed a vast city dominated by glittering idols that

> towered over a garden gone luxuriantly to seed during these thousands of
> moons. The path of moonlight long awaited by the procurator led right up to
> the garden. (324)]

Mountains collapse abruptly in this stunning vision. Their destruction reflects
the immediacy with which the Master's thoughts are translated into images.
The unstable landscape of the fantastical chapter illuminates the inception and
actualization of an image in the mind's eye and its disappearance when attention
is diverted to a new subject. Everything in this vision is unstable, all the changes
are sudden and absolute. Yershalaim suddenly lights up in the darkness when the
Master frees Pilate and is extinguished at a wave of Woland's hand. This process
parallels the way in which the city, the fruit of the Master's imagination, is
obliterated by the storm in his novel: 'Пропал Ершалаим, великий город, как
будто не существовал на свете' (691) ['Yershalaim — the great city — vanished
as if it had never existed' (188)].[21] Similarly, when the Master remembers Moscow,
it instantly materializes behind him like a mirage: 'соткался в тылу недавно
покинутый город с монастырскими пряничными башнями, с разбитым
вдребезги солнцем в стекле' (803) ['the city they had just left displayed itself with
its gingerbread monastery towers and its sun broken into smithereens in the glass'
(324)]. The Russian word 'соткался' (translated here as 'displayed itself') refers to
weaving or creative handiwork and suggests that the readers are seeing a projection,
not the city itself. The events of this chapter unfold at night in the moonlight
and yet the image of Moscow is lit up by the sun and the city rises not from the
distance behind but from the Master's imagination and memory, as it was captured
in the moment of departure, which coincided with the sunset. This testifies to the
imaginary nature of the two cities, Yershalaim and Moscow, envisioned by the
Master here as alternative destinations for himself. This Yershalaim, conjured up by
the Master's imagination, is what Ivan sees in the clinic by virtue of having been
touched by Pilate's story: 'город странный, непонятный, несуществующий'
(771) ['a strange, incomprehensible, non-existent city' (285)].

Yeshua's continued existence in *The Master and Margarita* is inextricably linked
to the way the Yershalaim narrative is enmeshed with the Moscow text and the
concluding fantastical chapter. In this liminal meta-fictional space Woland treats
the Master's protagonist and Levi's teacher, who has read the Master's novel, as one
and the same:

> Тот, кого так жаждет видеть выдуманный вами герой, которого вы сами
> только что отпустили, прочел ваш роман [...] то, что я предлагаю вам, и
> то, о чем просил Иешуа за вас же, за вас, еще лучше. (803)[22]
>
> [The one whom the hero you created and just released so yearned to see has
> read your novel [...] I assure you that what I am offering you, and what Yeshua
> has requested for you, is better still. (324)]

Yeshua is simultaneously a character invented by the Master in the novel and
transcends it, he is the Master's creation but he also determines the writer's fate. He
is, as Mann's narrator and Yahweh in *Joseph*, both inside and outside the (Yershalaim)
narrative at the same time, its subject and reader, a paradox, a contradiction. This

narrative situation amounts to metalepsis or a 'paradoxical contamination between the world of the telling and the world of the told'.[23] The Yershalaim and the Moscow realities co-exist on this fantastical plane of reality next to and part of each other. It is an ability to bring together the illogical and the irrational in an organic whole that is shared by religious and poetic sensibilities, both of which are abstract and figurative in nature.[24] Both require a suspension of disbelief, a certain degree of 'faith' in a logically impossible narrative that is poetically explored in *The Master and Margarita* and integral to the fabric of Bulgakov's text. Yeshua's presence inside and outside the Yershalaim narrative produces two irreconcilable readings or an Aporia, which dramatizes the inaccessibility of Bulgakov's Christ figure.[25] The narrative logic of *The Master and Margarita* allows life and death, literary and extra literary realities to co-exist on the same meta-fictional plane not as contradictory but as complementary categories, categories such as light and shadow, categories that are, moreover, not fixed but fluid and contingent. It is the very literary nature of this place that allows for an exploration of the divine, not in a conventional theological sense but thanks to the possibilities afforded by the poetic imagination. The divine, if it is understood as logically impossible and incomprehensible to the human mind (there is, after all, no logic that can explain Christ's miracles and the resurrection in the Bible), exists in the liminal space between these categories.

The language of the fantastical chapter holds a promise of a revelation as the light of a crimson moon that illuminates the characters strips away 'все обманы' (800) ['all illusions' (321)]. The relationship between the 'realistic' Moscow chapters and the fantastical chapter is thus symbolically reversed, the poetic reality, revealed by the moonlight, is posited as more true than the Moscow reality.[26] The moon is, however, a staple trope both for poetic imagination and distortion and a contradictory symbol in *The Master and Margarita*. It illuminates 'Professor' Woland in his Mephistophelean guise in the beginning of the novel when Ivan momentarily sees him with a rapier instead of a walking stick: 'в лунном, всегда обманчивом свете' (575) ['In the moonlight, which is always deceptive' (39)]. By playfully referring to the moon as an agent of both distortion and revelation Bulgakov implies that the truth unveiled in the poetic lunar world may be contingent and ambiguous.

Woland's transformation under the moon may tell us something about Yeshua since Bulgakov's Satan sets himself up as equal and opposite to him, as shadow and darkness are to light, in his rooftop conversation with Levi. There are, in fact, many allusions to Woland's identity in the Moscow text and they point towards a literary or musical rather than a biblical genealogy, a genealogy uniquely appropriate to the fantastical meta-fictional space he disappears into at the end of the novel.[27] However, these allusions are a performance of sorts, a joyful mystification that Muscovites fail to see through. Only Bulgakov's artist-hero the Master, who has a privileged narrative perspective, immediately identifies Satan in his poetic guise and names him Woland, when he hears about Ivan's encounter at the Patriarch's Ponds. Incidentally, he, too, uses a work of art, Gounod's opera *Faust*, rather than the Bible, as a point of reference.[28] Woland's true essence is revealed by the crimson moon:

Воланд летел тоже в своем настоящем обличье. Маргарита не могла бы сказать, из чего сделан повод его коня, и думала, что возможно, что это лунные цепочки, и самый конь — только глыба мрака, и грива этого коня — туча, а шпоры всадника — белые пятна звезд. (801)

[Woland, too, was flying in his true aspect. Margarita could not have said what his horse's reins were made of and thought they might have been moonbeam chains, and his horse — just a clump of darkness, and the horse's mane — a cloud, and the rider's spurs — the white specks of stars. (322)]

We are promised a revelation of Woland's true identity but he turns out to be indescribable.[29] Woland merges with the darkness of the night, the very fabric of the fantastical narrative, which erases his features. There is something imposing about the cosmic scale of this depiction, which gives so little away, just as there is something majestic in Yeshua's failure to appear in Moscow, when he sends Levi instead of himself. Margarita's recourse to metaphors to describe Woland points to a failure of language. This is the poetic truth revealed in the lunar world: Woland, like Yeshua, is elusive and unknowable. *The Master and Margarita* playfully mocks and defies all attempts to impose a neat identity on its supernatural protagonists. Both are ultimately inscrutable, just out of our reach, ineffable. For all the abundance of allusions in the Moscow narrative, we are none the wiser about Woland's 'true' appearance.[30] Bulgakov dramatizes both the divine and the demonic as the unknowable.

In this context, the ambiguous embedding of the Yershalaim text into the framing Moscow narrative as three separate fragments, mediated by different characters, which, for all appearances, also coincide with the Master's novel, may be interpreted as an integral part of Bulgakov's narrative strategy. The Yershalaim narrative simultaneously represents the Master's novel, the Devil's eyewitness account of Jesus's interrogation, and a dream of ambiguous origin. The text of *The Master and Margarita* is thus deliberately organized in a way which precludes a prioritization of one possible explanation of the origin and status of the narratives about Yeshua over the other, symbolically emphasizing his elusiveness.

The Master and Margarita posits the lunar world linked to the Master's artistic imagination as the truth in relation to the Moscow reality but does not lend this truth any religious meaning. Nor does the immortal Yeshua have any clearly defined religious significance. Bulgakov's novel deliberately and systematically eschews Christian dogma in its retelling of the Passion story, whilst imaginatively exploring the poetics that underpin its narrative, such as the dissolution of boundaries between life and death by the divine Christ, made possible in the fantastical chapters. Yeshua exists both inside and outside the Yershalaim narrative, mortal and immortal at the same time, producing a narrative tension, an irreconcilable contradiction or an Aporia. The divinity of Christ is dramatized in *The Master and Margarita* through Yeshua's inaccessibility of sorts, thanks to the many, often contradictory, frames through which his image is refracted and distorted, in spite of the vividness of his character in the Yershalaim chapters. An inspiration for a series of conflicting narratives in Yershalaim, he is inaccessible in the abstract reality where he dwells, denoted only as light, manifesting himself only once in Moscow, and even then, through Levi Matvei. His other appearances after death play out in the imagination of the characters who desire a continuation to his story and have a narrative rather than a religious significance.

Parallel Text in the Yershalaim narrative

The Yershalaim text demythologizes the gospel narrative and depicts the Son of God Jesus Christ as a man, Yeshua Ha-Notsri. Nevertheless, a certain degree of ambivalence about Yeshua's identity remains unresolved in the narrative thanks to Bulgakov's contradictory narrative strategy. The Yershalaim chapters include several prominent allusions to immortality, resurrection and the messiah. These allusions form a parallel text that relies on the readers' knowledge of the gospels as the essential context to the novel and that creates uncertainty about Yeshua's character.

To explain what is meant by a parallel text, it is useful to turn to Levi's parchment one more time. Thanks to the author's illegible handwriting, Pilate misreads the section of the parchment that refers to Levi's dismay at Yeshua's suffering: 'Солнце склоняется, а смерти нет' (661) ['The sun is sinking, and still, no death' (147)]. All that the procurator can make out of that fragment is the short sentence 'Смерти нет' (766) ['There is no death' (279)]. The decontextualization of Levi's words invests them with a completely different meaning, creating an allusion to the New Testament doctrine of the resurrection of the dead, inextricably linked to Jesus's messianic mission and his divine identity. Yeshua never speaks about immortality during his interrogation. This explains why Pilate does not pay quite as much attention to these words as to the sentence about cowardice, which resonates painfully with his moral failure. It also suggests that the actual addressee of the allusion to immortality is the reader of *The Master and Margarita*. The 'parallel' text, which addresses the resurrection, however allusively and fleetingly, capitalizes on the readers' knowledge of the gospels and plays to their expectations. In other words, in the narrative situation created in the Yershalaim text, that is, Pilate's interrogation of Yeshua, the readers' anticipation of the resurrection, based on their knowledge of the gospels, must be inevitably reanimated by this remark. Pilate's misreading, which constructs a parallel text, is representative of the way in which the resurrection discourse is embedded into the Yershalaim text. Bulgakov also alludes to certain subjects, such as immortality, in the Yershalaim chapters by either denying or deliberately diminishing their significance, using another strategy of Aesopian expression.[31] This is exemplified particularly well by Pilate's conversation with Afranius. Ostensibly, Pilate informs his chief of secret police about a plot to kill Judas and asks him to prevent a murder:

> кто-то из тайных друзей Га-Ноцри, возмущенный чудовищным предательством этого менялы, сговаривается со своими сообщниками убить его сегодня ночью, а деньги, полученные за предательство, подбросить первосвященнику с запиской: "Возвращаю проклятые деньги." (752)

[One of Ha-Notsri's secret friends, outraged by this money-changer's monstrous
betrayal, has conspired with accomplices to kill him tonight, and to send the
money he received for his betrayal back to the high priest with a note saying:
'I am returning your accursed money.' (262)]

Pilate's choice of emotionally charged epithets leaves little doubt that he condemns
Judas's betrayal in the strongest possible terms. The information about an attempt
on Judas's life, which Pilate passes on to Afranius as intelligence is, in fact, an
elucidation of his own plan of revenge for Yeshua's death. The exchange between
Pilate and Afranius is characterized by deliberate displacement and creation of
parallel and opposite meaning by both interlocutors. Afranius upholds the game by
promising to do everything in his power to prevent the killing, before setting out to
arrange the murder. By investing exactly the opposite meaning into their words the
procurator and his chief of secret police arrange the murder of the provocateur who
had procured evidence of Yeshua's *laesa majestatis*, without ostensibly compromising
their allegiance to the Caesar.[32]

Similarly, all allusions to the resurrection, immortality and the messiah in the
Yershalaim text are presented either as inconsequential asides or in a displaced
context.[33] Bar-rabban is symbolically 'resurrected', when Yeshua dies in his place:
'человек, который уже был в руках смерти, вырвался из этих рук' (570) ['a
man who was already in the hands of death, had been torn from its grip' (31)].[34]
Gestas's song about grapes, albeit not directly linked to Yeshua, can be read as an
allusion both to 'vine,' the symbol Jesus uses in the New Testament to refer to
himself as the Son of God, but also to Communion wine, which symbolizes the
sacrificial blood of Christ.[35] Afranius does connect the idea of the resurrection with
that of a messiah, but only conversationally when he says that Judas: 'встанет [...]
когда труба Мессии, которого здесь ожидают, прозвучит над ним' (764) ['will
arise [...] when the trumpet of the Messiah, whom they await here, sounds above
him' (276)]. Pilate's casual complaint to Afranius about a messiah, 'которого они
вдруг стали ожидать в этом году' (749) ['who they've suddenly started waiting
for this year!' (259)], links messianic and apocalyptic expectations in Yershalaim to
Yeshua's narrative in *The Master and Margarita* but not directly to his person. Indeed,
just one set of allusions to immortality in the Yershalaim text marries it specifically
to Yeshua; it has to do with a sudden bout of overwhelming depression experienced
by Pilate when he understands that Ha-Notsri's death is inevitable:

Все та же непонятная тоска, что уже приходила на балконе, пронизала
все его существо. Он тотчас постарался ее объяснить, и объяснение было
странное: показалось смутно прокуратору, что он чего-то недоговорил с
осужденным, а может быть, чего-то недослушал.
Пилат прогнал эту мысль, и она улетела в одно мгновение, как и
прилетела. Она улетела, а тоска осталась необъясненной, ибо не могла
же ее объяснить мелькнувшая, как молния, и тут же погасшая какая-
то короткая другая мысль: 'Бессмертие ... пришло бессмертие...' Чье
бессмертие пришло? Этого не понял прокуратор, но мысль об этом
загадочном бессмертии заставила его похолодеть на солнцепеке. (566)

[The same incomprehensible anguish, which had come over him on the balcony, pierced his entire being once again. He immediately tried to explain this anguish, and the explanation was strange: the procurator had the dim sense that there was something he had not finished saying to the condemned man, or perhaps something he had not finished listening to.
Pilate dismissed the thought, and it flew away as fast as it had flown in. The thought flew away, and the feeling of anguish remained unexplained, for it could not be explained by a second brief thought that flashed like lightning and immediately died out, 'Immortality... immortality has come...' Whose immortality has come? The procurator did not understand this, but the thought of that mysterious immortality made him turn cold despite the broiling sun. (26)]

Here the word 'immortality' is repeated three times in one paragraph in a context directly linked to Yeshua's impending death. It becomes clear to the readers retrospectively that this reference is also displaced, since Pilate's premonition is realized in a punishment by immortality for his moral failure in the fantastical chapter rather than in Yeshua's resurrection in Yershalaim. However, in the Yershalaim chapters, if they are read as a self-contained narrative, Pilate's premonition of immortality is contextualized only through references to Yeshua's death. In the gospels Christ's death after the crucifixion, sanctioned by Pilate, leads to his resurrection. In the Yershalaim text this biblical context emerges, voiced but unfulfilled, through Pilate's confused thoughts as the text invites the readers to contemplate his question: 'Whose immortality has come?'

Although this moment of involuntary introspection results in an overpowering experience for the procurator, it is downplayed and dismissed as momentary, 'incomprehensible' and 'strange'.[36] It is significant that Pilate's thoughts about immortality are presented as irrational, emotional and apparently unmotivated, thanks to their confusion and lack of structure. They are coupled only with an undefined doubt about Yeshua. Pilate senses that there is something that transcends appearances and evades definition in his interlocutor. The word 'недослушал' ['had not finished listening to'] implies an imperfection or defectiveness of perception but also a lack of mimetic clarity, which feeds into Bulgakov's representation of Yeshua as elusive. To a certain extent Pilate's doubt and discomfort are reflected in the readers' experience as they negotiate Bulgakov's contradictory narrative strategy. His Christ figure is uncanny, familiar and unfamiliar at the same time. The Yershalaim text demythologizes Christ as Yeshua whose death is final and is not followed by a resurrection. However, this narrative is subverted through multiple allusions to resurrection and immortality, which, in the context of Bulgakov's retelling of Christ's narrative, cannot but raise the subject of Yeshua's divinity. These allusions are displaced, merely introducing dissonant notes into the narrative. Nevertheless, they invite the readers to actively engage with Bulgakov's text and to negotiate its biblical context. The tension between the text and the context evokes a lingering feeling of uncertainty. Through Pilate's doubt about Yeshua and a series of references to immortality Bulgakov encodes and dramatizes the very essence of faith into his narrative, if faith is understood as irrational and defined as doubt, based on uncertainty rather than certain knowledge.

Further uncertainty in the text is created by Yeshua Ha-Notsri himself who combines contradictory and apparently incompatible character traits.[37] His inability to recognize a paid provocateur or to understand Pilate and Judas's politicized language suggest naiveté, a lack of awareness and control over his fate. This impression is consolidated by his body language during the interrogation, as he looks at Pilate 'с тревожным любопытством' (555) ['with anxious curiosity' (14)], 'всем существом выражая готовность отвечать толково, не вызывать больше гнева' (556) ['demonstrating with all his being his readiness to answer sensibly, and not to provoke more anger' (15)], 'весь напрягаясь в желании убедить' (557) ['straining every nerve in his desire to be convincing' (16)]. However, Yeshua's ostensible naiveté and simplicity are belied by his perceptiveness, quick intelligence, repartee and knowledge of Latin, Greek and Aramaic. His insight into unseen phenomena, such as Pilate's headache, introduces another dissonant note into the narrative, as does his casual allusion to the storm, which, judging by the suddenness of its arrival later in the narrative, should be impossible to predict at this point. Yeshua's premonition about Judas's death, another example of his clairvoyance, is perhaps self-fulfilling. He inadvertently suggests Judas's murder to the frustrated procurator. In spite of this, his throwaway remark about the storm in the novel functions as a prophecy of the future execution, which is accompanied by a storm in the Bible, and, in this limited sense, raises the idea of prophecy fulfilment. Yeshua's concern for his legacy is also out of kilter with his apparent lack of self-awareness. He anticipates that his words will have a long-term impact and is anxious about the way in which they may become misrepresented and misinterpreted:

> Эти добрые люди [...] ничему не учились и все перепутали, что я говорил. Я вообще начинаю опасаться, что путаница эта будет продолжаться очень долгое время. И все из-за того, что он неверно записывает за мной. (557)
>
> [Those good people [...] are ignorant and have muddled what I said. In fact, I'm beginning to fear that this confusion will go on for a long time. And all because he writes down what I said incorrectly. (16)]

To Pilate Yeshua's words sound like an attempt to exonerate himself, whereas for the readers the word 'confusion' may resonate with the discussion about the different ways of interpreting the gospels in the beginning of the novel. They also highlight the uncertainty principle at the heart of Yeshua's representation in the novel, which gives a powerful impetus to the proliferation of conflicting narratives about him. Although these dissonant notes in the narrative should not be overemphasized, together they destabilize Yeshua's representation. His clairvoyance and inexplicable insight suggest that it is those around him, like Pilate, who are in actual fact unaware of the long-term significance of their actions.

This impression is reinforced by Yeshua's strange haste to reach Yershalaim without the cannier Levi who might have recognized and stopped Judas's provocation. The urgency of Yeshua's departure suggests an unrevealed underlying purpose: 'Но Иешуа почему-то заспешил, сказал, что у него в городе неотложное дело' (661) ['But for some reason Yeshua had suddenly started to hurry, said he had urgent business in the city' (147)]. The coincidence of Levi's strange illness ('Какая-то неожиданная и ужасная хворь' (662) ['a sudden and terrible illness' (147)]) with Yeshua's departure and his equally sudden recovery at the moment when he can only play the role of a witness begs at least a nod to either divine providence or fate, which sets in motion a series of events that will bring about the execution. Levi leaves for Yershalaim tormented 'каким-то предчувствием беды' (662) [by 'forebodings of disaster' (147)]. For Levi the illness is a tragic coincidence, which prevents him from saving Yeshua. For the readers, Yeshua's resolve to reach Yershalaim and Levi's incapacitating illness contribute to the feeling of uncertainty about Bulgakov's protagonist. Bulgakov's choice of words is important here. Like the description of Pilate's premonition of immortality, the passage describing Yeshua's departure for Yershalaim is full of indefinite words, such as 'почему-то' ('for some reason') and 'каким-то' ('some'), which invite speculation by drawing attention to what is left unsaid. One cannot help but wonder if Yeshua's mysterious 'urgent business' is not, in fact, a meeting with Judas, if he is not hurrying to meet his fate in Yershalaim.

The Yershalaim text never provides an explanation for the single miracle performed by Yeshua, the curing of Pilate's headache, which recalls Christ's miracles in the Bible.[38] If other incongruous textual instances merely suggest that there is more to Yeshua than meets the eye, this act is unambiguously subversive of the secularizing thrust of the Yershalaim text. There is no rational explanation for it. It is, without a doubt, a miracle.

Yeshua is a likeable, naive and idealistic man who is in the wrong place at the wrong time and whose unnecessary violent death unexpectedly traumatizes and changes the cruel procurator of Judea, Pontius Pilate. But then again, he is somehow more than just that. It seems appropriate to conclude by repeating Kaifa's question to Pilate: 'Неужели ты скажешь мне, что все это [...]. вызвал жалкий разбойник Вар-равван?' (567) ['Are you really telling me that all this [...] was caused by that miserable outlaw Bar-rabban?' (28)].

Conclusion

Uncertainty is the lynchpin of Bulgakov's representation of Yeshua Ha-Notsri. Bulgakov's Christ is never depicted as divine, however, the ambiguity of his portrayal creates a lingering feeling of doubt. An uncanny character, both familiar and unfamiliar, mortal and immortal, inside and outside the Yershalaim text, its subject and reader, he evades straightforward categorization. Divinity in the novel is thematized primarily as Yeshua's elusiveness, symbolized by the proliferation of conflicting narratives about him and encoded into the narrative as doubt. Finally, it is explored as an Aporia, a contradiction that is essentially irreconcilable but true and logical to a poetic and a religious sensibility.

The Yershalaim narrative is not a hagiographical devotional text about Christ, nor is it a historical account of his last days, in spite of its historical verisimilitude. In a certain sense, *The Master and Margarita* poetically engages with both these modes of representation and invites the readers to make their own decisions about Yeshua's identity.[39] The novel celebrates and dramatizes the divine as the unknowable and ineffable, alluded to, hinted at but never explicitly addressed in the Yershalaim chapters. The divine comes into play on the meta-fictional level of the text, between the lines, as a result of the tension created by Bulgakov's contradictory narrative strategy, which encourages the readers to participate actively in the construction of meaning by negotiating the text of the novel and its biblical context. In this way the novel challenges prescription of any single interpretation and constitutes a transformative experience for the readers who, in the process of interpreting Yeshua's character, practise a reading strategy based on critical engagement.

Notes to Chapter 3

1. Lesskis differentiates between Yeshua's material, human hypostasis as the protagonist of the Master's novel and his mystical transcendental hypostasis as the protagonist of the entire novel and Woland's antagonist (Lesskis, 'Master i Margarita Bulgakova', p. 56). Amert believes that the 'resurrected' Yeshua in Ivan's dream is 'all-powerful, immortal Ieshua', 'the living Truth affirming itself to Pilate, the mysterious smile in [his] eyes a sign of divine grace' (Amert, 'The Dialectics of Closure', p. 612). Bethea writes that Yeshua is divine at the conclusion of the novel (Bethea, 'History as Hippodrome', p. 394). For Frank, 'Ieshua appears in divine guise only outside the Master's novel' (Frank, 'The Mystery of the Master's Final Destination', p. 291). Zlochevskaia considers the two manifestations of Yeshua as depictions of one and the same figure and argues that he turns out to be the ruler of the universe (p. 212). See Alla Zlochevskaia, 'Paradoksy Zazerkalia v romanakh G. Gesse, V. Nabokova i M. Bulgakova', Voprosy Literatury, 3 (2008), 201–21. For Ericson, Yeshua at the end of the novel 'no longer exhibits any of the faults which were evident in the apocryphal, sublunary accounts. He is now the glorified Lord' (Ericson, 'The Satanic Incarnation', p. 26). Faryno reads Woland and Yeshua as real figures who exist outside the Master's novel, witnesses and participants of the events narrated in it, concluding that 'они читают роман о самих себе' [they are reading a novel about themselves] (Faryno, 'Istoriia o Pontii Pilate', p. 50). Zigelis argues that 'the characters of the Master's novel often become actualized outside of it. It transcends itself' (p. 128). Andrew Zigelis, 'Bulgakov's Master i Margarita: Three Types of Reductive Ambiguity', Russian Language Journal, 30 (1976), 119–30. Amusin explains Yeshua's existence outside the inserted novel by attributing a powerful generative quality to the Master's work that ' "creates" reality [...] that [...] is external to and inclusive of [his] opus' and sees Yeshua in the Moscow narrative as 'an offshoot of the Master's creative imagination' (Amusin, ' "Your Novel has Some More Surprises in Store for You" ', p. 86). Longinović's Gnostic reading posits the existence of 'the transient from Nazareth' and 'heavenly Christ [...] the liberator of the soul' in Bulgakov's novel (Longinović, Borderline Culture, pp. 55–56).
2. On Bulgakov's strategies for engaging with the Soviet reader see also Maria Kisel, 'Feuilletons Don't Burn: Bulgakov's The Master and Margarita and the Imagined "Soviet Reader" ', Slavic Review, 68 (2009), 582–600.
3. Ianovskaia, Tvorcheskii put', p. 249. Very little has been written about God in The Master and Margarita. For Baker, 'God's only effectivity lies in the moral and compassionate impulses of human actors' (Baker, 'Types of Interlocution', p. 59). Ianovskaiia highlights Bulgakov's attitude to God as one of the most complex questions of his personality and points out that, as yet, there is no study of God as an active character in The Master and Margarita. She defines God in the novel as '[к]акое-то отстраненное присутствие, над-присутствие' [some detached presence, a sur-presence] (Ianovskaiia, Treugol'nik, p. 95) and a 'божественное присутствие и предопределенность судьбы' [divine presence and the determinism of fate] (Ianovskaiia, 'Pontii', p. 55). Pokrovskii argues that God features in the novel. However, he bases this assertion only on the fact that Bulgakov had read the article entitled 'God' in the Brokgauz Efron Encyclopaedia (Pokrovskii, 'O chem besedoval Voland s Berliozom', p. 148 and p. 150). For

Kushlina and Smirnov, Woland's antipode plays the role of a passive observer rather than an active and omnipotent creative source. However, his assumed relationship with Woland forms the background to the entire novel (Kushlina and Smirnov, 'Magiia slova', p. 164). Ericson, in contrast, argues that 'it is God's doing that Satan comes to Moscow' (Ericson, 'The Satanic Incarnation', p. 24).

4. Ianovskaia, *Tvorcheskii put'*, p. 249.

5. Ericson, 'The Satanic Incarnation', p. 24. Kazarkin, 'Tipy avtorstva', p. 26.

6. For example, 'Слава Богу!' (670) ['Thank God'! (158)], 'оставь ты меня, Христа ради' (684) ['leave me alone for Christ's sake' (170)], 'Господи Боже мой!' (682) ['Oh, my God!' (174)].

7. Fiene, 'A Comparison', p. 337. Ianovskaia pays close attention to the capitalization of the word God in *The Master and Margarita* (Ianovskaia, *Sobranie sochinenii v piati tomakh*, pp. 174–75). She sees this as an indication of God's clear and powerful presence as an active figure in the novel (Ianovskaia, *Treugol'nik*, p. 95). The inconsistent capitalization is not always reflected in O'Connor and Burgin's translation.

8. See also 'Ты черный бог' (663) ['You are a black God' (149)], 'бог разбойников' (663) ['God of outlaws' (149)], 'Проклинаю тебя, Бог!' (663) ['I curse you, God!' (149)], 'Ты не всемогущий Бог' (663) ['You are not an omnipotent God' (149)].

9. For example, Bengalsky's head is returned to him at the Variety theatre after a woman in the audience shouts: 'Ради Бога, не мучьте его!' (627) ['Stop torturing him, for God's sake!' (104)] (Compare with Curtis, *Bulgakov's Last Decade*, p. 159). Ianovskaia notes that Woland's retinue finds the sign of the cross unpleasant but that it is also strangely and consistently not associated with the crucifixion in the novel (Ianovskaia, 'Pontii', p. 38).

10. Compare with Solomon, 'The Sin of Cowardice', p. 246.

11. Ianovskaia believes that Yeshua's death ('жестокое избавление Иешуа от страданий' [the cruel end to Yeshua's suffering]) is caused not by God or by the Devil but only by Pilate (Ianovskaia, *Treugol'nik*, p. 96). Kushlina and Smirnov, in contrast, point out that the storm in Yershalaim arrives from the West, the part of the world associated with the Devil. They also speculate that Levi inadvertently addresses Woland rather than God when he is asking for Yeshua's death because that lies outside of his jurisdiction (pp. 290–91). Olga Kushlina and Iurii Smirnov 'Nekotorye voprosy poetiki romana *Master i Margarita*', in *M. A. Bulgakov — Dramaturg i khudozhestvennaia kul'tura ego vremeni*, ed. by Aleksandr A. Ninov and Violetta V. Gudkova (Moscow: Soiuz teatral'nykh deiatelei RSFSR, 1988), pp. 285–303.

12. Haber mentions that Yeshua 'never appears in the novel in actuality, but only through the mediation of the "messenger" Woland, the dreams of Ivan Bezdomnyi, the artistic intuition of the Master' (Haber, 'The Mythic Bulgakov', p. 356).

13. Amusin notes that '[t]his episode is an almost verbatim reiteration of Pilate's own dream in chapter 26 and, accordingly, in the Master's novel' (Amusin, ' "Your Novel has Some More Surprises in Store for You" ', p. 88). Amert reads Ivan's dream of Yeshua as 'a glimpse of resurrected Yeshua' but asserts that 'by framing it as Ivan's dream he [Bulgakov] veils from the reader its full significance' (Amert, 'The Dialectics of Closure', p. 610).

14. Proffer writes in this context that 'Yeshua himself is not the god figure ... for how could he intercede with himself?' (Proffer, *Bulgakov*, p. 557).

15. Ericson argues that through their belief in the Devil, the Master and Margarita 'implicitly profess[] faith in the reality of the Deity' and that they thus attain 'redemption' through 'grace' (Ericson, 'The Satanic Incarnation', p. 31). Frank believes that they are 'denied entrance to heaven' and are left in a limbo for the Master 'did not raise the human Ieshua to divine Christ status' (Frank, 'The Mystery of the Master's Final Destination', pp. 292–93). For Fiene, the Master and Margarita 'settle in a place symbolic of purgatory — approximately parallel to the limbo to which Pilate had been assigned for so long' (Fiene, 'Pilatism', p. 136). Beatie and Powell contextualize the ending of the novel through a reference to Dante's Garden of Eden in *La Divina Commedia* (Beatie and Powell, 'Bulgakov, Dante and Relativity', p. 264). Allen Lubkemann interprets the fantastical chapter and the epilogue as 'the writing of the novel through Bezdomny's imagination' which 'verbally' resurrects the Master 'who seems to follow Pilate, his fictional creation, along the moonbeam into a Dantesque refractive paradisal space'

(p. 64). Sharon Allen Lubkemann, 'From the Grotesque to the Sublime: Logos and Purgatorial Landscape of *Dead Souls* and *Master and Margarita*', *Slavic and East European Journal*, 47 (2003), 45–76. Utekhin reads the fantastical space as a Dantesque purgatory (Utekhin, '*Master i Margarita* M. Bulgakova', pp. 103–04). Milne argues that the Master remains in a 'pagan Elysium' or 'Limbo in the First Circle of Dante's *Inferno*' because of the failure of his imagination which she also interprets as faith (p. 25). Lesley Milne, '*The Master and Margarita*'. *A Comedy of Victory*, Birmingham Slavonic Monographs, 3 (Birmingham: Birmingham University Press, 1977). For Bethea, the Master and Margarita are 'left in a timeless present, the one that is both free from the pain of the past and the promise of the future' (Bethea, 'History as Hippodrome', pp. 397–98). Ianovskaia writes that Margarita's words 'Вечный дом' ('eternal house') for the eternal abode is also a Jewish name for a tomb, referring to N. L. Makkaveiskii *Arkheologiia istorii stradanii Gospoda Iisusa Khrista* (1891) which was consulted by Bulgakov (Ianovskaia, *Treugol'nik*, pp. 53–54).

16. It is used to describe the revelry at the Griboedov after Berlioz's death and the 'hell' that awaits an unfaithful husband in Nikanor Ivanovich's dream.

17. Leatherbarrow interprets the Master's escape as 'the flight of the inspired from a vulgar world' which 'illustrates the traditional elitist view of the artist, the view that the imagination is somehow a divine thing that can seek only divine rewards' (Leatherbarrow, 'The Devil and the Creative Visionary', p. 41). Zlochevskaia understands this world as a meta-fictional space which recreates the life of an author's creative conscience that strives to penetrate into the hidden transphysical meaning of life beyond the material world (Zlochevskaia, 'Paradoksy Zazerkalia', p. 205). Finally, Amusin interprets all that is fantastic in *The Master and Margarita*, including Yeshua and Woland, as 'purely literary in nature' (Amusin, '"Your Novel has Some More Surprises in Store for You"', p. 89). However, the reality of Woland's appearance in Moscow is fundamental to the artistic design of Bulgakov's novel.

18. Compare with Amert who argues that the Master's poisoning 'blatantly dramatizes the personal, literal immortality of the writer' (Amert, 'The Dialectics of Closure', p. 605). Liakhova believes that the word of the Master the man ('Мастера-человека') in the fantastical chapter has died and only the immortal word of the Master the creator ('Мастера-творца') remains (Liakhova, 'Dramatizm lichnogo slova', p. 176).

19. See Longinović: 'By placing the Master and Margarita in an environment derived from the literary commonplaces of the romantic tradition, Bulgakov defines his archetypal lovers as the artefacts that are produced and contained by the literary tradition itself' (p. 50). This 'transcendental realm' is 'built out of romantic clichés' (Longinović, *Borderline Culture*, p. 53). Gasparov notes that the Master's abode is overly idyllic and oversaturated with literary attributes of sentimental happy endings (Gasparov, 'Iz nabliudenii', 1, 78–90 (p. 84)).

20. See Curtis: 'The release of Pilate is a matter of artistic truth' (Curtis, *Bulgakov's Last Decade*, p. 184).

21. Gasparov reads the apparition of Moscow in the fantastical reality as a mythical phenomenon (Gasparov, 'Iz nabliudenii', 11, 96). He compares the motif of a sinking and perishing city with the Russian legend of the mythical city of Kitezh which disappeared to the bottom of a lake when it was attacked (Gasparov, 'Iz nabliudenii', 12, 119).

22. In the second redaction of *The Master and Margarita* (1932–1936) Woland explicitly equates the Master's protagonist and the immortal Yeshua: 'Ты награжден. Благодари бродившего по песку Ешуа, которого ты сочинил, но о нем более никогда не вспоминай. Тебя заметили, и ты получишь то, что заслужил' (357) [You have been rewarded. Thank Eshua [Bulgakov's spelling] who wandered on sand and whom you have invented, but never think of him again. You have been noticed and you will be granted what you deserve]. Bulgakov, '*Master i Margarita*', I, 357. See also Marietta Chudakova, 'Tvorcheskaia istoriia romana M. Bulgakova *Master i Margarita*', *Voprosy Literatury*, 20 (1976), 218–53 (pp. 242–43).

23. Peter Hühn, John Pier, Wolf Schmid and Jörg Schönert, eds, *Handbook of Narratology* (New York, NY: De Gruyter, 2009), p. 190.

24. For an interesting discussion of the importance of artistic expression in *The Master and Margarita*, see Krugovoy, *The Gnostic Novel*, pp. 3–4.

25. See Ianovskaia: 'Между читателем и этим персонажем — дистанция. И, при всей зримости образа, — его недоступность' [There is distance between the reader and this character. For all the visibility of his image, he is inaccessible] (Ianovskaia, 'Pontii', p. 60). Taranovski Johnson notes that 'Ieshua is a passive, even peripheral figure whose consciousness the narrator, and therefore the reader, never penetrates' (Taranovski Johnson, 'The Thematic Function of the Narrator', p. 276). For a discussion of Aporias in the context of reading *The Master and Margarita* as either a modern or a postmodern text see Gary Rosenshield, '*The Master and Margarita* and the Poetics of Aporia: A Polemical Article', *Slavic Review*, 56 (1997), 187–211.

26. Gasparov notes that both Moscow and Yershalaim turn out to be parables in relation to the epilogue (Gasparov, 'Iz nabliudenii', 12, 109).

27. Zerkalov notes that Woland stems from a dozen of literary characters and artistic depictions of the Devil (p. 49). Aleksandr Zerkalov, 'Voland, Mefistofel' i drugie. Zametki o "teologii" romana M. Bulgakova *Master i Margarita*', *Nauka i religiia*, 8 (1987), 49–51.

28. For parallels between Gounod's Mephistopheles and Woland see David Lowe, 'Gounod's *Faust* and Bulgakov's *The Master and Margarita*', *Russian Review*, 55 (1996), 279–86 (pp. 281–84). Gasparov notes that Schubert's romance 'Starrender Fels, mein Aufenthalt' recalls Rubinstein's operatic Demon (Gasparov, 'Iz nabliudenii', 1, 80). Woland evokes the fantasies of Hoffmann, Goethe and Gogol (Maksudov, '*Master i Margarita*', p. 204), and resembles the 'Karamazov devil' (Pittmann, 'Dreamers and Dreaming', p. 160). Goethe's *Faust* is the source of inspiration for Woland's name ('Junker Voland'), the cane with a decorative poodle's head, his ability to produce any brand of cigarettes at will, his rapier (Belza, 'Genealogiia *Mastera i Margarity*', pp. 186–88).

29. Compare to Belza who argues that Woland leaves Moscow in the guise of 'владыки-Люцифера' [Lord Lucifer] who sheds his Mephistophelean attributes (Belza, 'Genealogiia *Mastera i Margarity*', p. 196).

30. Compare with Krugovoy, *The Gnostic Novel*, p. 181.

31. Gasparov highlights that the canonical gospel text is constantly present in the novel through negation and allusion (Gasparov, 'Iz nabliudenii', 1, 83–84). See also Stapanian-Apkarian: 'By means of irony as shift, the novelist questions "real" images and logocentric signs of truth to show Reality and Truth as primary texts that are persistently edited. As a result, absolutes are traced, ironically, from their continual potential for displacement' (Stapanian-Apkarian, 'Ironic "Vision"', p. 173). The dialogue between Afranius and Pilate is in some ways also a reflection on the Soviet communication culture in the 1920s and the 1930s. In what reads as an apt description of this dialogue Irina Sandomirskaja writes that the politics of Aesopian language produces 'a grey zone of collaboration, between challenging the power of censorship and conforming to it — in what appears to be one and the same linguistic gesture' (p. 64). See Irina Sandomirskaja, 'Aesopian Language: the Politics and Poetics of Naming the Unnamable', in *The Vernaculars of Communism. Language, Ideology and Power in the Soviet Union and Eastern Europe*, ed. by Petre Petrov and Lara Ryazanova-Clarke, Routledge Studies in the History of Russia and Eastern Europe, 21 (London: Routledge, 2015), pp. 63–88.

32. Baker defines the exchange between Afranius and Pilate as 'Hermetic' or as 'privileged communication' (Baker, 'Types of Interlocution', p. 61) which 'depends on a deep context of shared knowledge between the interlocutors, proceeds by hints or even by a kind of private code' (ibid., p. 55). Bulgakov engages in just such a Hermetic dialogue with his readers, drawing on their knowledge of the gospels.

33. Compare with Amert: 'references to resurrection are either oblique, as in the intimations of immortality that plague Pilate; or figurative, as when Pilate is about to proclaim Bar-Rabban free [...] or negated, as when Pilate inquired with irony about Iuda, whose murder he ordered: "So of course he will not arise?"' (Amert, 'The Dialectics of Closure', p. 604).

34. See Mechik-Blank for the recurrent motif of travestied resurrection in the Moscow strand (i.e. the resurrection of the dead at Satan's Ball) (Mechik-Blank, 'Na rassvete *shestnadtsatogo*', p. 139). Beatie and Powell see a displaced reference to the resurrection in a description of Archibald Archibaldovich which features a reference to Adam's head on the pirate flag. They cite the Legend of the Cross from the apocryphal *Gospel of Nicodemus* according to which Adam's skull

was placed at the foot of the cross on which Jesus was crucified. Jesus's blood 'flowed down onto Adam's skull beneath the hill, thus freeing Adam from the sin incurred when he signed a pact with the devil in order to be allowed to till the earth after his expulsion from Paradise' (pp. 234–35). See Bruce A. Beatie and Phyllis W. Powell, 'Story and Symbol: Notes Toward a Structural Analysis of Bulgakov's *The Master and Margarita*', *Russian Literature Triquarterly*, 15 (1978), 219–38.

35. Savel'eva interprets this line as an allusion to John 15. 1, a blasphemous parody of the prayer uttered by Gestas's biblical counterpart before his death (Savel'eva, 'Russkii apokrificheskii Khristos', p. 163).

36. For an interesting linguistic analysis of the function of the words 'for some reason' in *The Master and Margarita* see Elena P. Senichkina, 'Aktualizator vyskazivaniia "POCHEMU-TO" i ego rol' v khudozhestvennom tekste. (Na materiale romana M. Bulgakova *Master i Margarita*'), in *Khudozhestvennaia rech': obshchee i individual'noe*, ed. by Olga I. Aleksandrova and others (Kuibyshev: Kuibyshevskii gosudarstvennii pedagogicheskii institut imeni V. V. Kuibysheva, 1980), pp. 78–97. Senichkina argues that the word 'почему-то' [for some reason] stimulates co-creation as the reader is forced to explain 'неопределенность, актуализированную почему-то' [the indeterminacy actualized by the words <u>for some reason</u>] (p. 85).

37. Compare with Ianovskaia who writes that there is no duplicity to his behaviour (Ianovskaia, 'Pontii', p. 57).

38. Baker notes that '[c]ritics have shown remarkable stubbornness in refusing to recognize that this cure is a miracle' but for him this 'detail could be read [...] as a reminder of the mass of miraculous material which has been removed' (Baker, 'Types of Interlocution', p. 67).

39. It is interesting in this context that although Ianovskaia sees Yeshua as human, she also wonders if Woland was in Yershalaim on the day of the execution because he knew *what* would happen there on the fourteenth of the spring month of Nisan, he knew *who* Yeshua Ha-Notsri really was and he wanted to see *how* it would happen (Ianovskaia, 'Pontii', p. 68). Ianovskaia's emphasis.

CHAPTER 4

❖

Inventing God

Biblical text is treated idiosyncratically in *Joseph and His Brothers* as historical reality that can be animated and replayed in real time, witnessed by the readers as it unfolds (similar to the way that the Yershalaim chapters magically bring the Passion narrative to life in *The Master and Margarita*). This is made possible thanks to the feast of storytelling, a narrative strategy that hinges on the actualization of biblical stories as they are being re-enacted in the novel, providing the ultimate experience of what the novel calls 'dabei gewesen zu sein' (1229) [being present].[1] In other words, the telling of the story in *Joseph* functions ingeniously as its own confirmation and proof. At the same time the scripture is also scrutinized and interrogated by Mann's narrator as a formalized narrative, a literary text with a history of editorial interventions, which is subject to critical exposition and hermeneutic analysis.

Mann's modern narrator has a privileged perspective on the narrative, immanent to it and transcending it at the same time, whereby he is in a position to provide a tongue-in-cheek critical commentary on the re-enactment of the biblical story in *Joseph* as it is being told. This dual narrative strategy, which humorously combines the telling with the exegesis, is driven by a desire to produce a plausible and psychologically convincing rendition of the ancient corpus of mythical texts in a modern secular form of a novel. In this spirit *Joseph* returns to Abraham's narrative at least three times in the chapters 'Hauptstück Höllenfahrt' ['Descent into Hell'], 'Zwiegesang' ['Duet'] and 'Wie Abraham Gott entdeckte' ['How Abraham Discovered God'], and tells it differently each time.

The existence of God is the underlying premise of the Old Testament, its cornerstone and the fact that gives impetus to its narrative. In contrast, in Mann's novel Abraham discovers God in at least one version of the biblical story, which is foundational for Joseph's faith community. The novel makes the juxtaposition of these two competing narratives about the Jewish God one of its starting points, setting it up as a conceptual framework for the exploration of mankind's spiritual emancipation through its engagement with the notion of the divine. In what follows, the stories about God's first manifestation to Abraham in the novel are examined side by side with particular attention paid to their discrepancies and similarities, which are traced to their sources and narrators.

In Abraham's Footsteps

The first prelude 'Höllenfahrt' tells two different stories of Abraham's journey from the city of Ur, side by side and just a page apart. In the first story Abraham's journey is driven by doubt, and in the second — his path is guided by God. Abraham's narrative is one of many told in 'Höllenfahrt' in a search for the origins of mankind. The search fails as all known beginnings prove to be contingent and many of the sources the narrator consults turn out to be either fictional or inauthentic. As for the patriarch himself, he is portrayed as a mythical figure with an uncertain open-ended identity.[2] Abraham is deliberately nameless in the first prelude, identifiable only thanks to the reference to his travelling companion, his 'sister-wife' Sarai.[3] Instead, he is given a symbolic identity as a moon-wanderer, the man of Ur or 'Ur-Mann' (10) ['Ur man' (6)] (a wordplay on the first or original man), de-familiarized as a 'Mahdi' ('messiah' in the Islamic tradition).[4] Time in the tetralogy often follows a cyclical pattern which means that Abraham is also confused with his namesakes, both ancestors and descendants, who walk in his mythical footsteps through playful identification and imitation.[5] Given that the biblical narrative is framed in the tetralogy as mythologized and contingent from the very beginning, what becomes important is not so much the authenticity of Abraham's story, of which there are several different versions even in Joseph's time, but its reception by his descendants in faith.

The readers first see Abraham in Joseph's mind's eye as his ancestor and the founder of his spiritual community, the protagonist of his tutor Eliezer's 'Überlieferungen' (9) [narratives]. In Eliezer's stories Abraham leaves Ur because of doubt, a crisis of faith manifested in his displeasure at King Nimrod's ostentatious worship of the deities Sin and Marduk. Abraham's rejection of the extant religious practices creates a space for reflection and reassessment of his spiritual values. In Mann's writing the abstract often translates into the literal. Doubt, an undecidedness of belief, restlessness because of the loss of spiritual coordinates, becomes a dynamic and creative force motivating Abraham to undertake a journey, described anachronistically as a 'hegira' (Mohammed's flight from Mecca to Medina) with an uncertain goal.[6] He sets out from Ur 'da mit zweifelnder Seele nicht gut stillsitzen ist' (9) ['since it is not easy to sit still with doubt in one's soul' (5)]. He first travels north to Haran, then west and, finally, south. Abraham's erratic journey suggests a lack of direction. His apparently aimless wanderings are a symbolic expression of existential angst.

In stark contrast to this narrative, in the second, mythical account of Abraham's journey which follows it and is ascribed to tradition or 'Die Überlieferung', the trajectory of his path from Ur in Chaldea to the promised land and from the present into the distant future is clear, linear and divinely inspired:

> Die Überlieferung will wissen, daß ihm sein Gott, der Gott, an dessen Wesensbild sein Geist arbeitete, der Höchste unter den anderen, dem ganz allein zu dienen er aus Stolz und Liebe entschlossen war, der Gott der Äonen, dem er Namen suchte und hinlängliche nicht fand, weshalb er ihm die Mehrheit verlieh und ihn Elohim, die Gottheit versuchsweise nannte [...] ihm ebenso weitreichende

wie fest umschriebene Verheißungen gemacht hatte, des Sinnes nicht nur, er, der Mann aus Ur, solle zu einem Volke werden, zahlreich wie Sand und Sterne, und allen Völkern ein Segen sein, sondern auch dahingehend, das Land, in dem er nun als Fremder wohne und wohin Elohim ihn aus Chaldäa geführt hätte, solle ihm und seinem Samen zu ewiger Besitzung gegeben werden. (10)

[Tradition has it that his God — the God on whose essential image his mind was hard at work, the highest among all the others [...] the God of the eons, for whom he had sought a name and finding none to his satisfaction, had assigned him a plural, tentatively calling him Elohim, the Godhead [...] had made him both far-reaching and tightly circumscribed promises to the effect that not only would he, the man of Ur, become a nation numberless as sand and stars and a blessing to all nations, but also to the effect that the land in which he now dwelt as a stranger and to which Elohim had led him from Chaldea would be given to him and to his seed as an eternal possession. (6)]

Abraham's conceptualization of the God of gods is a concrete project which endows his life with a sense of purpose. However, it is unclear whether God first manifests himself only after the patriarch discovers him in this mythical account. His name and contours are negotiated, concretized and shaped by Abraham rather than revealed to him, positing God as a passive object of the patriarch's intellectual endeavour, if not his invention. Mann creates a unique conceptual vocabulary in *Joseph* which is used to shape and structure the narrative. Abraham's experience of God in this context is idiosyncratically defined by the narrator as a form of an anticipation: specifically, an expectation that his doubt and the need to fill the resulting vacuum, or 'Gottesnot' (10) ['a need for God' (7)], will be shared by many others and that it will bear the seed of the future. The origin of Abraham's vision is described ambiguously as his sense of self, where his anticipation is expressed symbolically as a promise from his 'neuerschauten' (10) ['newly discerned' (7)] God that his restlessness will bring him countless proselytes. Abraham's doubt is an indeterminate but powerful anticipation projected into the future, much like Pilate's premonition of immortality in *The Master and Margarita*, and in *Joseph* it also belongs to the same associative chain as the idea of the divine. In Mann's modern reading of the Old Testament, God becomes a metaphorical expression of Abraham's doubt, its dynamic emanation.

The narrative about Abraham's discovery of God is recounted one more time in fine discourse by Jacob and Joseph in the chapter 'Zwiegesang'. Fine discourse or 'Schönes Gespräch' in the tetralogy is stylized dialogue, a form of recital that commemorates and consolidates the history of Abraham's community. Together, father and son rehearse a familiar story in which God commands Abraham to travel to the land of the Amurru from Haran after he leaves the city of Ur and makes a covenant with him when he reaches Egypt:

Da fiel ein Schlaf über ihn, der war nicht wie andere, und faßten ihn Schrecken und Finsternis. Denn der Herr redete zu ihm im Schlaf und ließ ihn sehen die Fernen der Welt und das Reich, das ausging aus seines Geistes Samen und sich ausbreitete aus der Sorge und Wahrheit seines Geistes [...] Und ging hindurch in der Nacht als eine Feuerflamme auf den Weg des Vertrages zwischen Opferstücken. (85)

> [And a sleep came over him that was like no other, and he was seized with terror and darkness. For the Lord spoke to him in that sleep and let him see the distant places of the world and the nation that would go out from the seed of his spirit and grow large out of the truth and vigilance of his spirit [...] And in the night passed like a flame of fire along the path of the covenant between the pieces of the sacrifice. (90)]

The Jewish God is represented as an impressive and powerful figure who manifests himself as a flame of fire and inspires awe and terror. This version of Abraham's narrative largely coincides with and expands the mythical account in the first prelude. They are variants of one and the same narrative, recounted in full in fine discourse and paraphrased and interpreted by the narrator in the first prelude. In this account God is once again posited as an object of Abraham's endeavour. Abraham's discovery precedes God's first manifestation, who appears when the patriarch is in a highly ambiguous state, a sleep like no other, a projection of his dreaming mind. The function of fine discourse is to consolidate and confirm rather than to interrogate the narrative heritage of Abraham's descendants, and father and son validate their recital as the truth by using affirmative rhetoric: 'So war es in Wahrheit [...] Du sagst es recht' (85) ['In truth that is how it was [...] You have told it rightly' (90)]. However, in spite of their truth claims, the novel returns to Eliezer's 'Höllenfahrt' narrative of Abraham's discovery to tell it differently one more time.

Joseph's tutor Eliezer, Jacob's half-brother and steward, is one of the key narrators of stories about Abraham in the tetralogy. In Abraham's story, as it is told by Eliezer in 'Wie Abraham Gott entdeckte', his discovery develops out of the attempt to situate human beings in the universe. Central to that quest is his unique self-consciousness, articulated in the commitment to serving only the highest: 'Ich, Abram, und in mir der Mensch, darf ausschließlich dem Höchsten dienen' (310) ['I, Abraham, and, in me, humankind, may serve only what is highest' (344)].[7] In his search for a worthy object of veneration, a rigorous intellectual pursuit that grows out of active contemplation of the world, Abraham considers and rejects the earth, the sky, the sun, the moon and the stars.[8] Using logic as a guiding principle, he concludes that the highest can only be conceptualized as a superior universal prime cause (reminiscent of the Aristotelian Unmovable Mover), the origin of the natural world and human experience.[9] His conception of God is a brilliant intellectual construct, which requires a thinking counterpart for its realization, possible only 'in der Erkenntnis des Menschen' (311) ['in the minds of men' (345)]. God's features emerge thanks to Abraham's contemplation of the world and of what is posited in the tetralogy as its opposite — his self. It is a deeply subjective experience that relies on a subconscious projection of his ego and results in the perfect consonance of God and the patriarch's traits:

> Er hatte ihn erschaut und hervorgedacht, die mächtigen Eigenschaften, die er ihm zuschrieb, waren wohl Gottes ursprüngliches Eigentum, Abram war nicht ihr Erzeuger. Aber war er es nicht dennoch in einem gewissen Sinne, indem er sie erkannte, sie lehrte und denkend verwirklichte? (312)

> [He had discovered Him and thought Him into being. Those mighty attributes

that he ascribed to Him were surely God's original property, Abram was not
their originator. But by recognizing them, teaching them, and realizing them
in his own thought, was he not His father in a certain sense? (346)]

The Jewish God is paradoxically both Abraham's creator and his creation which
sublimates his being, a figurative embodiment of the highest state of spiritual
emancipation achievable to man.[10] The process of emancipation is projected into
the future, with a utopian promise of a full realization, described in metaphorical
terms as God's apotheosis as the King of Kings. God's features, his loneliness,
jealousy of man's loyalty and transcendence, logically emerge from the patriarch's
definition of Him as the highest. If God is the highest, there can be no other being
like him. Since God is alone he is lonely and jealous of man's loyalty to him. God
is transcendent because, as the source of all creation, he is greater than His works
and is necessarily outside them. Abraham's God shares this property with *Joseph*'s
narrator. They are both a part of the universe they created and transcend it, moving
freely inside and outside the story. This quality is also inherent to Bulgakov's artist-
narrator the Master and his divine protagonist Yeshua, who are able to traverse the
line between fiction (as it is posited in *The Master and Margarita*) and reality.

Eliezer's Abraham eventually arrives at what is a monotheist and a monistic
concept of God as 'nicht das Gute, sondern das Ganze' (314) ['not what is good, but
what is all (348)], and thus also 'unheimlich, gefährlich und tödlich' (314) ['uncanny,
dangerous, deadly' (348)]. However, in Eliezer's stories Yahweh, conceptualized
by Abraham as abstract and all-embracing, is also curiously depicted as a folksy
comical personified figure who observes the patriarch unseen from on high, kissing
his fingertips for joy at being discovered and exclaiming: 'Bisher hat kein Mensch
mich Herr und Höchster genannt, nun werde ich so geheißen!' (310) ['Until now
no man has called me Lord and the Most High, but so will I now be called!' (344)].
The register of God and Abraham's speech in Eliezer's stories occasionally shifts
to casual and conversational, markedly different from the mythical 'Höllenfahrt'
and 'Zwiegesang' narratives, where Yahweh uses the language of command and
prophecy and the patriarch silently obeys. Eliezer's Abraham, in contrast, also uses
a colloquial idiom to address God: 'Höre, Herr [...] so oder so, das eine oder das
andere! Willst du eine Welt haben, kannst du nicht Recht verlangen' (313) ['Hear
me, Lord [...] yes or no, one way or another! If You want to have a world, You
cannot demand justice' (347)]. Eliezer's narrative is transgressive in its subversion
of the injunction against visualizing God. The gesture of kissing His fingertips
in delight, a very human expression of excitement, lends God's figure physicality,
rendering him an anthropomorphous and emotive entity. It reduces an abstract
voice or a flame of fire to a body which can be delimited and visualized.

Joseph depicts God's first manifestation to Abraham, a defining and unique
historical event in the canonical biblical text (Genesis 12.1), through a number of
disparate narratives. The reiteration of his story in the tetralogy recalls the ritual
repetition of familiar narratives in fine discourse, but instead of confirming, it draws
attention to the contradictions in Yahweh's representation. In the different versions
of Abraham's narrative in the novel God is depicted as a disembodied voice, a flame

of fire and a personified comical figure, but also as a metaphorical expression of man's striving for self-perfection, his daring and inspired projection, which imposes a meaning and an order onto the chaotic world, narrativizing it as an issue of a single prime cause. Yahweh emerges in the tetralogy in the process of storytelling as fine discourse crystallizes into the biblical tradition; the many 'Überlieferungen', passed down as oral lore, become a single definitive 'Überlieferung', a written quotable text. This process and the evolution of God's story and iconography in the novel are addressed below.

A Play with Sources

Abraham's story, its plot, style and register in *Joseph* change depending on who is speaking and these shifts in the narrative voice can often be traced back to the ways in which Mann synthesizes and integrates different source materials into the novel. For the purposes of this study the textual composition of Abraham's narrative in the tetralogy is as important as its content.

The 'Zwiegesang' and the mythical 'Höllenfahrt' narratives belong to the same shared pool of ancestral memories, the communal tradition about Abraham's descendants in faith, based originally on the patriarchs' stories and passed down in shepherds' fine discourse. As a collection of patriarchal narratives fixed in a written form in the future, tradition in *Joseph* represents the basis for the Hebrew Bible.[11] In fact, the 'Zwiegesang' and 'Höllenfahrt' narratives largely coincide with Abraham's story as it is told in the Book of Genesis, with one crucial exception: in the Old Testament God is not discovered by the patriarch; His existence is unambiguous.[12]

Doubt is a major operative part of Mann's narrative strategy in his treatment of the biblical text in the novel. The narrator polemicizes against the tradition which he is deeply sceptical about, arguing that it reinterprets, distorts and mythologizes Abraham's story, accusing it of imprecision, fabrication and conflation. In particular, he argues that Abraham's personal experience of God (recounted in the mythical 'Höllenfahrt' account), his ambitious expectation projected into the distant future, metamorphizes in the tradition into prophecies of fabulous spiritual posterity, to which a promise of land is opportunistically added at a later date to legitimize his descendants' claims to the Amurru territory.[13] In a parallel to Berlioz, who sees Tacitus's reference to Christ as a fraudulent addition, the narrator critiques God's prophecies of land to Abraham as a deliberate later interpolation into the biblical narrative that serves the purpose of justifying 'politische Machtverhältnisse, die sich auf kriegerischem Wege hergestellt' (10) ['political arrangements established [...] by force of arms' (6–7)]. He draws attention to Abraham's detour to Egypt en route from Ur, apparently ignored by the tradition, as evidence that the patriarch did not initially envisage the land of the Amurru as his final destination. Another serious indictment of the tradition relates to the narrative about Jacob's disastrous stay at Shechem, which fails to mention that his camp intended to settle matters by means of war from the start, 'überzeugt von der Erlaubtheit solcher epischer Reinigung der Wirklichkeit' (115) ['being convinced that it has been given permission to purify reality on an epic scale' (124)]. The deliberate distortion of the chronology of the Shechem narrative in fine discourse, according to the narrator, means that the brothers' plan to pillage the city is presented as a later development, motivated and justified by the kidnapping of their sister Dina. The story is edited in order to show Abraham's descendants in a better light. In this context, editorial responsibility for the narrative becomes an ethical concern. On this account the narrator criticizes the format of fine discourse, the precursor of the tradition, a sequence of questions and affirmative answers designed to validate its narratives as the truth, as deceptive formulae: '"Weißt du davon?" — "Ich weiß es genau." Mitnichten wußten es Israels Hirten noch genau, wenn sie es später am Feuer zum Gegenstand "Schöner" Gespräche machten' (119) ['"Do you know of this?" — "I know it well." Israel's shepherds knew nothing of the sort when they later made it the subject of "fine discourses" by the fire' (128)]).[14] The impressive tribal God who guides Abraham to the land of the Amurru appears as the protagonist of a deeply problematic and unreliable oral tradition, retrospectively edited in by anonymous redactors. To a certain extent, this narrative situation echoes the tension between authorial intention and scribal error, which is evident in the way that Yeshua's narrative is recorded by Levi Matvei in *The Master and Margarita* and underscores what both novels portray as the unstable nature of the canonical biblical text.

In contrast to the tradition, Eliezer's narrative about Abraham's discovery of God, recalled by Joseph in the first prelude and told in full in 'Wie Abraham Gott entdeckte', is a collage of stories from Micha Josef bin Gorion's compilation of Midrashic exegesis *Die Sagen der Juden*.[15] Midrash refers to detailed verse analysis of the biblical text and means to 'to seek out, inquire, demand.'[16] *Die Sagen der Juden* is an anthology of haggadic Midrashim — rabbinic commentary which interprets and expounds the non-legal parts of the Hebrew Scriptures and includes myths, legends and 'fanciful stories, some the product of the Jewish imagination and "wisdom," and others remnants of the folklore treasury of nearby and faraway people, which had become judaized in the course of time.'[17] In other words, Eliezer's narratives about God in the tetralogy in this case are based on haggadic exegesis, which is characterized by legendary illustration. The internal incoherence and the variation of register in 'Wie Abraham Gott entdeckte' is explained by Mann's interweaving of several different midrashic stories from bin Gorion's anthology.[18] So, for example, Eliezer's depiction of Abraham's search for the prime cause, his urge to serve only the highest and the exposition of God's transcendence originate in two separate fragments in bin Gorion's compilation.[19] Eliezer's portrayal of an anthropomorphic God in 'Wie Abraham Gott entdeckte' as well as all of his other stories in 'Der Unterricht' ['The Lesson'] and 'Höllenfahrt' are also based on Mann's (often verbatim) borrowing from rabbinic exegesis.[20] Eliezer recounts these stories to Joseph along the lines of 'hebräischen Kommentaren zur Urgeschichte' (34) ['Hebrew commentaries on the stories of the beginning' (33)], introducing a specifically Jewish perspective on the figure of God in the tetralogy. In fact, Mann acknowledged that *Joseph* often reads as 'eine Thora-Exege und — Amplification, wie ein rabbinischer Midrasch' [a Torah exegesis and amplification, a rabbinic Midrash].[21] In accordance with rabbinic exegesis in *Die Sagen der Juden*, in Eliezer's narratives God is depicted as a personified figure, a King in a heavenly court who presides over an angelic entourage and finds himself in a comically antagonistic relationship with it.[22] The main object of contention between God and the angels, which provokes their jealousy and offends their sensibility, is mankind, both good and evil, and favoured by God in spite of its propensity for sin.[23] Eliezer's depiction of God represents a comical antithesis to his portrayal in the tradition as an omnipotent Lord who directs the course of the sun and the stars, introducing a joyful incoherence into his representation in the novel.

The first prelude implicitly juxtaposes 'Überlieferung' and 'Überlieferungen', the tradition, based on fine discourse, and Eliezer's narratives, playing on the tension between orality and textuality.[24] However, the stories about Yahweh and Abraham, which have been treated here as distinct, are not, in actual fact, clearly demarcated as such in Mann's dizzyingly complex and rich text. The portrayal of Yahweh as a flame of fire follows his depiction as a metaphorical emanation of Abraham's doubt in the first prelude. God is represented as a prime causal force and a comical anthropomorphic figure within one and the same story told by Eliezer in 'Wie Abraham Gott entdeckte'. The implication of Mann's creative and, crucially, indiscriminate inclusion of sources different in register, style and intention, is that an equal weight is given to the tradition, which is based on the canonical Old Testament, and Eliezer's fabulous narratives that humorously interpret it. The result of the interweaving of stories about the Jewish God that originate in completely different sources, an important part of the novel's narrative strategy, is a relativization of the canonical biblical texts. Both the tradition and Eliezer's midrashic stories are treated as entertaining narratives used for Joseph's edification, the sharpening of his critical faculties. Man, rather than God, and, specifically, man who is also a masterful storyteller, is the alpha and omega of Mann's novel. The ways in which two key storytellers, Eliezer and the narrator, shape the depiction of the divine in the tetralogy is the subject of the next section.

Eliezer and the Narrator

Joseph and *The Master and Margarita* are highly self-conscious novels that reflect on the conventions and dynamics of narrative production and the role of narrators in this creative process. Eliezer, one of the most important narrators of stories about God in *Joseph*, is consistently posited in the tetralogy as a purveyor of fiction. God and the angels often appear in a number of patriarchal narratives thanks to his lively imagination and his propensity to ornament the stories of Joseph's ancestors with fabulous detail.

Eliezer primarily uses fables which feature divine protagonists to exercise Joseph's mind and memory and to prepare him for the reception of more challenging material.[25] Such stories include the narrative of Ishchara's escape from the lascivious angels and the three reasons why God had created man last (transcribed verbatim from bin Gorion). A particularly interesting example of his narrative style is the tale about the angel Semhazai's pursuit of maid Ishchara, which Eliezer combines with the story of Jacob's dream of the heavenly ladder at Beth-El in chapter 'Der Unterricht' ['The Lesson'].[26] Semhazai is not mentioned in Jacob's dream in the novel.[27] However, Eliezer humorously claims that the angel was unable to ascend to heaven after Ishchara's escape and had to wait for Jacob's dream to use the ladder in order to return home. In another story in 'Wie Abraham Gott entdeckte' Eliezer turns the absence of an answer that greets Abraham's tirade about Sodom into a 'wohlwollendes Schweigen' ['benevolent silence'], a sign that God 'es gut aufnahm' (313) ['had taken it well enough' (347)], interpreting it creatively as a form of a response. In the same chapter he mythologizes the secular narrative of Abraham's journey in the first prelude, by suggesting that it may have been God's cunning that had secretly inspired restlessness and doubt in the patriarch, paving the way for His discovery. Unlike the anonymous redactors, criticized by the narrator for purposefully enshrining a dubious claim to the land of the Amurru in the tradition, Eliezer pursues no ulterior motive when he engages in myth making. He delights in the very activity of creative storytelling and his God and the angels are subjects of joyful and pleasurable fiction.

As the most educated member of Jacob's household, Eliezer consciously plays with myths, de-constructing them as fictions and delighting in telling them at the same time. This means that he often tells the same story in two different ways, one mythical and the other demythologized. This is how Abraham's God becomes either the patriarch's projection and construct or a personified anthropomorphic figure in the tetralogy. Similarly, Abraham's journey from Ur is variously either driven by doubt or by Yahweh, depending on the version of the story Eliezer is telling.

Eliezer is associated with three metaphors for fictional narration in the tetralogy: the rolling sphere, the double tongue and lunar grammar.[28] The metaphorical rolling sphere that governs Eliezer's storytelling consists of an upper heavenly and a lower earthly hemisphere which form a whole in such a way:[29]

> daß, was oben ist, auch unten ist, was aber in Irdischen vorgehen mag, sich im Himmlischen wiederholt [...] es wandelt sich auch, kraft der sphärischen Drehung, das Himmlische ins Irdische, das Irdische ins Himmlische, und daraus erhellt, daraus ergibt sich die Wahrheit, daß Götter Menschen, Menschen dagegen wieder Götter werden können. (138)

> [that what is above is also below and whatever may happen in the earthly portion is repeated in the heavenly [...] thanks to spherical rotation the heavenly also turns into the earthly, the earthly into the heavenly, clearly revealing, indeed yielding the truth that gods can become human and that, on the other hand, human beings can become gods again. (151)]

This programmatic passage represents Mann's exposition of his poetic design, a methodological blueprint for his narrative strategy with regards to the dichotomy of the divine and the earthly in *Joseph*.[30] The metaphor of the rolling sphere emphasizes that the divine, the miraculous and the supernatural in Eliezer's stories is a reflection and mythologization of the earthly and the secular and vice versa.

In this context, Eliezer operates as a Hermes figure who mediates between the heavenly and the earthly spheres through his narratives.[31]

Another principle that shapes Eliezer's storytelling is the so-called lunar grammar, which involves a substitution of indirect speech for direct quotation, third-person for first-person reference and relies on an openness to mythical thinking. In this spirit Eliezer tells Joseph the story of Rebecca's courtship by Abraham's eponymous servant Eliezer, who had lived twenty generations before him, as his own. Joseph listens to him with a delight unaffected by 'die grammatische Form' (89) ['the grammatical form' (94)] in which the story is told. Storytelling in a lunar key is functionally similar to narration with a double tongue in the tetralogy. Both enable Eliezer to play with the narrative perspective and to tell the same story in two different ways. In one such story Eliezer first speaks of Abraham as a man who had discovered God:

> Aber unversehens spaltete diese Zunge sich im Reden und redete auch noch anders von ihm, auf eine andere Weise. Es war immer noch Abram, der Mann aus Uru oder eigentlich Charran, von dem die würdige Schlangenzunge redete, — und sie nannte ihn Josephs Urgroßvater. (317)

> [But even as he spoke his tongue might suddenly fork, and he would speak differently about him, in other terms. It was still Abram, the man from Uru (or actually, Haran), about which the venerable serpent's tongue spoke — calling him Joseph's great-grandfather. (352)]

Eliezer mythologizes Joseph's great-grandfather Abraham and projects his figure onto an older narrative of a man from Ur, which he reinterprets and 'judaizes' as Joseph's family history. Both Eliezer and Joseph know that his great-grandfather and the eponymous Abraham who had lived twenty generations before him and who had discovered God, are not one and the same person:

> Aber es gab über mehr noch ein Auge zuzudrücken zwischen ihnen als nur über diese Ungenauigkeit; denn der Abraham von dem die Zunge nun redete, zwischendrein, hin und her wechselnd, zwiespältig, war auch der nicht, der damals gelebt und Sinears Staub von den Füßen geschüttelt hatte, sondern vielmehr eine Figur, die wiederum tief hinter jener sichtbar wurde und für die jene durchscheinend war. (318)

> [But they shared a wink over more than just this imprecision; for the Abraham of whom this tongue now spoke, alternating on occasion, moving back and forth in its forked fashion, was likewise not the one who had lived back then and had shaken the dust of Shinar from his feet, but rather a figure who came into view far behind him and for whom he grew transparent. (352)]

In Eliezer's stories the prototypical figure for Abraham, the man who had discovered God, the 'Unbekanntes der Vorzeit' (291) ['venerable unknown out of the primal past' (322)], is entirely submerged and obscured under later superimpositions, which include both the man from Ur and Joseph's great-grandfather.[32] The rolling sphere and Eliezer's forked tongue are metaphors for a process of mythologization whereby Joseph's great-grandfather Abram becomes a legendary figure, a hero of the tradition (and of Eliezer's narratives) inscribed into the conscience of the emerging Judaic community as the man who had 'discovered' their God. Thanks to this device, the mythical and demythologized accounts complement rather than contradict each other. The rolling sphere does not resolve the earthly and the heavenly dichotomy in favour of one or the other but represents both as an integral part of the organic whole, for both belong to the *Weltanschauung* of Mann's characters.

Eliezer's propensity for mythologization, his repertoire of midrashic anecdotes, which serve as legendary illustration to Joseph's family history, and his narration in a lunar key make him an epitome of a narrator of fiction. As such, Eliezer stands in an apparently antagonistic relationship to the narrator of the tetralogy, who explicitly dissociates himself from the role of an inventor of stories who can 'im stillen Einvernehmen mit dem Publikum, [...] Lügenmärlein für einen unterhaltenden Augenblick wie Wirklichkeit aussehen [...] lassen' ['merely for the sake of momentary entertainment and with the tacit agreement of our audience [...] lend the appearance of reality to spurious fables'], and be accused of having 'den Mund zu voll von Fabel' (206) ['been carried away by the plot' (226)].[33] He rejects the kind of contract with the audience which exists between Joseph and Eliezer, when the latter presents Joseph's great-grandfather as the man from Ur which, both know, cannot be true, or when he tells him about Rebecca's courtship in the first person with Joseph's silent and delighted consent. Indeed, the only occasion in the novel when the contract between a storyteller and his audience is broken is associated with Jacob's exhortation to reason, which echoes the narrator's rhetoric and results in a demystification of a legendary narrative.[34] Jacob refuses to uphold his part of the bargain and accept Eliezer's story of his courtship of Rebecca when he learns about Joseph's death:

> Es ist wahrhaftig erbaulich, wie du mich schiltst und läßt einfließen, daß du mit Abram die Könige vertrieben habest, was glattweg unmöglich ist; denn nach der Vernunft bist du mein Halbbruder von einer Magd, geboren zu Dimaschki, und hast den Abraham so wenig mit den Augen gesehen wie ich selber. [...] Ich war rein, aber Gott hat mich in Kot getunkt über und über, und solche Leute halten es mit der Vernunft, denn sie wissen nichts anzufangen mit frommer Beschönigung, sie lassen die Wahrheit nackend gehen. Auch daß dir die Erde entgegengesprungen sei, bezweif_e ich hiermit. Es ist alles aus. (471)

> [It is truly edifying that you scold me and remind me how you drove off those kings with Abram — which is patently impossible. For reason tells me that you are my half brother by a handmaid, born in Dimashki, and never beheld Abram with your own eyes any more than I. [...] I was pure, but God has drenched me in dung, over and over, and such people hold fast to reason, for they can make nothing of the guise of pretty piety and they let truth go naked. And I declare my doubts as to whether the earth leapt up to greet you. It is all over. (524)]

Jacob and the narrator's insistence on the naked truth is juxtaposed to the notion of 'die Wahrheit, daß Götter Menschen, Menschen dagegen wieder Götter werden können' (138) ['the truth that gods can become human and that, on the other hand, human beings can become gods again' (151)] which characterizes the metaphorical rolling sphere and Eliezer's storytelling. The poetic in both *The Master and Margarita* and *Joseph* is often a truth unto itself. Indeed, the relationship between truth and fiction, the factual and the poetic in the tetralogy is complicated. Eliezer's 'Schlangenzunge' recalls the biblical serpent. Narration in a lunar key is described as being conducive to leading astray: 'Was uns verführt, ist die Natürlichkeit, mit der er "ich" sagte' (307) ['What seduces us is the natural ease with which he said "I" ' (340)]. In this context Serach's song about Joseph serves as a useful point of comparison to Eliezer's narratives about God and the angels.[35] Serach, one of Mann's artist figures, mythologizes the narrative of Joseph's life in a song she composes to help his brothers disguise their role in his disappearance. To Jacob, Serach's song appears to be a divine revelation to an innocent child, although he cautions her that the allure of poetry is 'ein gefährliches, schmeichlerisch-verführerisch Ding' (1245) ['dangerous and flattering' (1400)] (in German, literally 'flattering-seductive'). Indeed, in a parallel to Eliezer's stories, Serach's song actually represents a creative palimpsest and appropriation, in this case, of a resurrection narrative of the fertility deity Tammuz. The 'resurrections' of both Tammuz and Joseph are engineered, the first — by the women, who use a wooden figure to represent the deity in an annual resurrection feast, the second — by Serach who mythologizes and aestheticizes Joseph's story to represent his homecoming as a symbolical return from the dead.

The complex relationship between fiction and fact is mirrored in the connection between Eliezer, the inventor of stories, and the narrator, the self-proclaimed arbiter of the truth in the novel. The narrator repeatedly stresses the importance of truth and reason as the principles which underpin his narration, calling for 'die nüchterne Anschauung der Tatsachen' (46–47) ['sober observation of fact' (47)], promising a 'wahrheitsgetreuen Darstellung' (131) ['factual presentation' (142)] of the events 'so, wie sie sich in Wirklichkeit zutrugen' (111) ['as they really happened' (119)], anxious for imagination not to get the better of his readers. However, his reliable and objective self-presentation is ironic and tongue-in-cheek and he actually performs a role that is functionally similar to that of Eliezer.[36] Although the narrator adopts the personas of a historian and an essayist in the first prelude, his sources, the basis of his claim to objectivity, are deliberately de-concretized in the text, including the anonymous 'Gerücht und Gedicht' (46) ['hearsay and poetry' (46)], 'Lied und Legende' (46) ['song and saga' (46)], 'Die morgenländische Überlieferung' (46) ['Oriental tradition' (47)], a 'Referat' (30) ['the source' (29)], 'Ein persischer Sänger von besonderer Autorität' (46) ['A Persian bard of great authority' (47)]. The narrator's truth claims are also frequently based on self-validating rhetoric, which ironically emulates the formulae of unreliable fine discourse: 'so war es' (105) ['That was how it had gone' (112)], 'und so geschah' (119) ['And thus it was' (128)], 'In Wahrheit' (146) ['In truth' (160)]. In addition, some of his confident pronouncements are built on rather whimsical premises. He asserts that Joseph was thirty years old when he was elevated in Egypt because it is 'ein Axiom, das keines Beweises bedarf' (601) ['an axiom that requires no proof' (670)] that this is the right age for that stage of life.[37] If Eliezer narrates in the lunar key, the storyteller's star in *Joseph* is the moon. Both *Joseph* and *The Master and Margarita* link narration in a lunar key to poetic imagination. The moon is also the storyteller's star in Bulgakov's novel, where Yeshua and Pilate walk along a moonbeam on the pages of the Master's novel. The light of the moon dissolves barriers between fiction and reality, as well as temporal barriers in both texts. This allows the Master to participate in the events that had taken place two thousand years ago as if he had witnessed them first-hand in the fantastical chapter and illuminates the narrator's journey into the well of the past in *Joseph*.

One of the most ironic stratagems used to uphold the narrator's authority in *Joseph* hinges on his claim that the readers are eye witnesses of the narrative.[38] The narrative validates itself as it is being told, unfolding in the present as if for the first time. This is made possible by Mann's ingenious dramatization of narration in *Joseph* as a 'Fest der Erzählung' (39) ['Feast of storytelling' (40)], a ritual repetition or actualization of the (biblical) story. The narrator provides an immersive mimetic experience of 'dabei gewesen zu sein' (1229) [being present] for his readers. However, Eliezer, ostensibly the narrator's opposite, furnishes a similar experience when he 'remembers' his namesake's search for a bride for Isaak as his own narrative. He knows that story 'haargenau bis auf die kleinen Monde und Mondsicheln, die an den Hälsen seiner zehn Dromedare geklingelt [...] hatten' (89) ['in exact detail, down to the little moons and crescents that had jingled from the necks of his ten dromedaries' (94)]. Eliezer's mythical identification with Abraham's servant enables him to set himself up as an eyewitness of Rebecca's courtship and to convey the experience of 'dabei gewesen zu sein' [being present] to Joseph.[39] It allows him to pose as a witness to the events long embedded in the collective memory of Jacob's household as fine discourse. By assuming the perspective of Abraham's steward Eliezer also adopts the narrator's position, for he is both in the story and outside it. Even Eliezer's attention to the most insignificant and mundane details, such as the ornaments on the dromedaries and Rebecca's exact purchase price, is reminiscent of the narrator's pedantic style, since he devotes entire chapters to determining the exact number of years Jacob spent in Laban's service ('Wie lange Jaakob bei Laban blieb' ['How Long Jacob Remained with Laban']), or the number of family members who followed him to Egypt ('Ihrer siebzig' ['Seventy in All']). The narrator's implicit juxtaposition with Eliezer, the narrator of fables about God, Abraham and the angels and his polemics with the tradition are not to be taken too seriously. On the last page of the novel the narrator refers to 'die schöne Geschichte und Gotteserfindung von *Joseph und seinen Brüdern*' (1324) ['this invention of God, this beautiful story of *Joseph and his brothers*' (1492)].[40] He retrospectively identifies the story he has been telling as a form of fine discourse which features God as its character but also, ambiguously, as its author. By citing the title of the tetralogy in the last line, the narrator underscores its fictitiousness and highlights his own role as a narrator of fiction.[41]

In fact, the narrator participates in the invention of God in the novel on a par with Eliezer by interpreting natural events, such as Rachel's death at childbirth, as an expression of Yahweh's jealousy of Jacob and presenting this reading of the Old Testament as a fact: 'Rahel starb. So wollte es Gott' (273) ['Rachel died. It was God's will' (303)].[42] More importantly Eliezer's narratives often appear in the novel in free indirect speech and it is frequently difficult to separate his voice from the voice of the narrator, leaving the ultimate responsibility for his narratives ambiguous. Eliezer's mythologization of God's silence as a response to Abraham in 'Wie Abraham Gott entdeckte,' discussed above, can be read both as the narrator's report of Eliezer's story and as his humorous commentary on it.

Another notable example of the ambiguity surrounding the narrator of a story about God in *Joseph* is the Gnostic narrative about the romance of the soul in 'Höllenfahrt'. In this narrative the soul falls in love with matter and God, moved by compassion, comes to its aid and creates the world of forms which makes their union possible. The romance of the soul is ostensibly told by the narrator but is immediately followed in the novel by Eliezer's comical translation of this Gnostic narrative into midrashic terms.[43] Eliezer recasts God's assistance to the soul which results in the creation of the world of forms, as an expression of his love for mankind, which angers the angels.[44] It is hard to tell where Eliezer's story begins and whether it encompasses the Gnostic narrative. Here the image of Eliezer's double tongue can also be read as an allusion to the overlap between his voice and that of the narrator. This narrative situation recalls the confusion that surrounds the attribution of the pronouncement about cowardice to Yeshua in *The Master and Margarita*.

Eliezer appears to be the narrator's parodic likeness and counterpart, who reflects back on his own storytelling. An inventor of stories, he symbolizes a 'Mund zu voll von Fabel' (206) [mouth too full of fables], an embodiment of a narrator *par excellence*. In this context, the following description of Eliezer is important:

> [seine] Augen [waren] so geartet, daß die oberen und unteren, fast wimperlosen Lider, schwer und gleichsam geschwollen, wie Lippen wirkten. [...] Der Ansatz des Bartes an den Wangen [...] war ganz besonders ebenmäßig, so daß man den Eindruck gewinnen konnte, als sei dieser Bart an den Ohren befestigt und man könne ihn abnehmen. Ja, noch mehr, das ganze Gesicht erweckte die Vorstellung, es sei abnehmbar, und darunter möchte erst Eliezers eigentliches Gesicht sich befinden. (291–92)

> [the almost lashless eyelids, both the upper and lower, were so heavy and somehow swollen that they looked like lips [...] There was such regularity about the starting point of the beard on his prominent cheeks [...] that one might have had the impression it was attached at his ears and easily removable. Indeed, the whole face left one imagining it could be removed, and that only then would Eliezer's true face be discovered. (322)]

Eliezer's face is visualized grotesquely as having three pairs of lips, three mouths, his 'real' face concealed underneath a fake beard. This detail is repeated in the chapter called 'Der Geläufige' ['The Fleet-Footed Runner'], where, upon seeing Joseph in the ill-fated *ketônet passim*, Eliezer prophetically warns him of the fatal dangers of unveiling 'mit so unbewegtem Gesicht, daß es aussah, als könne man es abnehmen und es wäre vielleicht ein andres darunter' (354) ['with a face so immobile that it looked as if you could remove it and might find another beneath' (394)]. A fake beard and a mask are a means of disguise. On the one hand, Eliezer is a concrete individual, Jacob's servant, his half-brother and Joseph's teacher. On the other hand, his three mouths make him quite literally a mouthpiece, a grotesque embodiment of a telling voice. The reductive metonymic reference to Eliezer as a 'Zunge' (318) ['tongue' (352)] or a 'Schlangenzunge' (317) ['serpent tongue' (352)] in 'Der Herr des Boten' ['The Messenger's Master'] belongs to the same cluster of imagery.

Conclusion

Both *The Master and Margarita* and *Joseph* poetically and playfully explore the tension created when ancient biblical myths are read from a modern, secular perspective as *bona fide* historical records. The first prelude in *Joseph* suggests that all beginnings, including those of the Old Testament myth, are conditional, evoking an image of a vista of shifting sand dunes that conceal an ever-retreating line of the horizon. This image perfectly encapsulates the search for the origin of the narrative about Abraham's discovery of God (which, as was mentioned above, is already extant in many variants in Joseph's time in the novel), expressed in the narrative through a series of *mise en abyme*. Eliezer's stories are reported by the narrator, whilst it is Eliezer who teaches Joseph about Abraham's conceptualization and discovery of God. His Abraham, however, is based on an unknown protagonist of some ancient narrative, whose beginnings are concealed in the darkness of the apparently bottomless well of the past.

Although God is consistently demythologized by the narrator as a construct, a human projection and a subject of fiction, this does not make the idea of Him less important or compelling. Mann's characters use stories about God and the angels to shape their lives and to present them as divinely intended. In this context it is illuminating that Eliezer, Mann's roguish narrator, tells entertaining fables about God only when he teaches Joseph. In contrast, when Jacob rails against Yahweh at the news of Joseph's death, Eliezer assumes the role of a defender of God.[45] In admonishing Jacob not to blaspheme, Eliezer suggests that God is incomprehensible and unfathomable: 'Willst du verstehen, was dir zu hoch ist, und das Leben ergründen nach seinem Rätsel, daß du drüber hinfährst mit deinem Menschenwort und sprichst: "Es ist nichts für mich, und heiliger bin ich denn Gott"?' (471) ['Are you determined to understand what is too high for you and fathom the riddle of life, riding roughshod over it with human words and saying: "It's nothing for me, and I am holier than God?"' (524)]. For Mann's characters, including Eliezer, who narrates Yahweh into existence in several of his stories, a transcendent, spiritual and all-embracing God remains an idea to be reckoned with. Their contemplation of the divine is the subject of the next chapter.

Notes to Chapter 4

1. Compare with Jan Assmann who writes that all 'Geschehen' [that happens] is a fulfillment, an 'Ur-Schrift' [Ur-text] precedes all history and is fulfilled as it unfolds (p. 138). Jan Assmann, 'Zitathaftes Leben. Thomas Mann und die Phänomenologie der kulturellen Erinnerung', *Thomas-Mann-Jahrbuch*, 6 (1994), 133–58.
2. Murdaugh, *Salvation in the Secular*, p. 43.
3. See Elizabeth Drave, 'Strukturen jüdischer Bibelauslegung in Thomas Manns Roman *Joseph und seine Brüder*: das Beispiel Abraham', in *Bibel und Literatur*, ed. by Jürgen Ebach and Richard Faber (Munich: Fink, 1995), pp. 195–213 (pp. 206–07).

4. Jeremias points out that the moon is the wanderer everywhere in myth and that the characterization of Abraham as a wanderer allows the biblical narrator to introduce moon motifs into his narrative (Jeremias, *Das Alte Testament im Lichte des Alten Orients*, p. 182). 'Early German writing on race' was characterized by a search for 'an *Urheimat*, a primordial homeland of nation, culture, and Volk' (Heschel, *The Aryan Jesus*, p. 29). In the tetralogy the narrator's search for the historical and the symbolical 'Ur' becomes a quest for the origins of mankind as a whole.

5. Marquardt notes Mann's mystification and withdrawal of that which has just been told, which renders the depiction of Abraham's character imprecise (p. 192). See Franka Marquardt, *Erzählte Juden: Untersuchungen zu Thomas Manns 'Joseph und seine Brüder' und Robert Musils 'Mann ohne Eigenschaften'*, Literatur — Kultur — Medien, 4 (Münster: LIT, 2003).

6. Jeremias calls Abraham a leader or a 'Mahdi' on 'eine Art Hedschra' [a kind of hegira] (Jeremias, *Das Alte Testament im Lichte des Alten Orients*, p. 181).

7. Swensen argues that Abraham's reading of the world results 'in the creation' of a superior being 'who validate[s]' his 'personal stories by intending them' (Swensen, *Gods, Angels and Narrators*, p. 107).

8. Abraham's work on God has been described as a process of continuous transcendence of mythical certainties. Borchmeyer writes that God is no longer the immanent 'divine' that manifests itself in many mythical deities. Instead He is a unique transcendent deity, a persona saying 'I' (p. 22, p. 23). See Dieter Borchmeyer, ' "Zurück zum Anfang aller Dinge." Mythos und Religion in Thomas Manns "Josephsromanen"', *Thomas-Mann-Jahrbuch*, 11 (1998), 9–29.

9. 'The first principle of primary being is not moveable either in itself or accidentally, but produces the primary eternal and single movement' (Ackrill, p. 349). See John Lloyd Ackrill, ed, *A New Aristotle Reader* (Oxford: Clarendon, 1987). Beck sees Abraham's God here as a dialectically conceived 'unholy' notion (Beck, 'Thomas Manns Josephstetralogie', p. 23).

10. Hamburger, *Thomas Manns biblisches Werk*, p. 100.

11. Swensen: 'the Bible appears to be a late and simplified redaction of the material presented here in full and original form' (Swensen, *Gods, Angels and Narrators*, p. 122). Murdaugh: 'although the novel purports to be a dramatization, a mere "filling in of details" of the biblical account, it is in fact a contradiction, a correction, a humanistic improvement of the biblical story' (Murdaugh, *Salvation in the Secular*, p. 93). Jäger understands fine discourse as Mann's reference to the Bible and notes that the novel occasionally presents itself humorously as the original and the true version of the biblical story (Jäger, *Humanisierung des Mythos*, p. 129, p. 107).

12. For points of intersection with the 'Zwiegesang' and 'Höllenfahrt' narratives about Abraham see the Book of Genesis 11.31–32; 12.1–3; 12. 7; 15.12–17; 17.

13. Marquardt notes that *Joseph* retells not only the story of the books of Pentateuch but also the story of their narration in fine discourse; she writes that Mann juxtaposes the biblical narrators, an anonymous monoperspectival source to the modern polyperspectival self-reflexive narrator (Marquardt, *Erzählte Juden*, p. 110 and p. 120). Reiss calls this 'dargestellte[] Hermeneutik' (p. 148) [represented hermeneutics] where the process of interpretation and understanding itself becomes the 'novel' (p. 165). See Gunter Reiss, *'Allegorisierung' und moderne Erzählkunst. Eine Studie zum Werk Thomas Manns* (Munich: Fink, 1970).

14. Beck wonders in this respect if the narrator seeks to draw the attention to the uncertainty of the historical tradition which rests only on the human ability to remember (Beck, 'Thomas Manns Josephstetralogie', p. 48).

15. Lehnert, 'Thomas Manns Vorstudien', pp. 471–74. Eliezer, a key narrator of stories about Yahweh in the tetralogy, is conventionally and almost exclusively interpreted as the epitome of an open mythical personality. Berger sees Eliezer as an archetype of the oldest servant (Berger, *Die mythologischen Motive*, p. 54). Hughes interprets Eliezer as an example of 'the predominance of mythical identification over the awareness of personal identity' (p. 26). See Kenneth Hughes, 'Theme and Structure in Thomas Mann's *Die Geschichten Jaakobs*', *Monatshefte*, 62 (1970), 24–36. Murdaugh reads his figure as 'a voice of the unconscious in its positive aspects of innocence, harmony with nature, and tradition', and as a representation of 'a primitive human type which embodied the Will ... in its most serene manifestation, as the principle of permanence and repetition' (Murdaugh, *Salvation in the Secular*, p. 39). Fischer compares Eliezer to the narrator

insofar as neither clearly differentiates between himself and those he speaks about (p. 179). Bernd-Jürgen Fischer, *Handbuch zu Thomas Manns "Josephsromanen"* (Tübingen: Francke, 2002).

16. See Alan Levenson, 'Christian Author, Jewish Book? Methods and Sources in Thomas Mann's *Joseph*', *German Quarterly*, 71 (1998), 166–78, (p. 166). For a detailed definition of midrash see Jacob Neusner and Alan J. Avery-Peck, eds, *Encyclopaedia of Midrash: Biblical Interpretation in formative Judaism*, 2 vols (Leiden: Brill, 2005), I, pp. 520–27.

17. See the section on 'Folkloristic Aggadah' in Fred Skolnik and Michael Berenbaum, eds, *Encyclopaedia Judaica*, 2nd edn, 22 vols (Detroit, MI: Macmillan Reference USA in association with the Keter Publishing House, 2007), I, 455–57 (p. 455). Bulgakov's Yershalaim chapters have also been described as a sort of midrash. See Malcolm Jones, 'The Gospel According to Woland and the Tradition of the Wandering Jew', in *Bulgakov: The Novelist-Playwright*, ed. by Lesley Milne, Russian Theatre Archive, 5 (Luxembourg: Harwood, 1995), pp. 115–24 (p. 116).

18. Berger mentions Mann's technique of cryptographic citation, coded allusions and syncretic play with religious, mythological and literary traditions which creates something new out of his sources (Berger, *Die mythologischen Motive*, pp. 2–3). He calls *Joseph* a compendium of heterogeneous religious, historical and mythological stories (p. 14).

19. For Abraham's search for the highest, the prime cause see Micha Josef bin Gorion, *'Die Sagen der Juden': Mythen, Legenden, Auslegungen gesammelt von Micha Josef bin Gorion*, 3rd edn (Berlin: Schocken, 1935), pp. 193–94. For the definition of God's transcendence as 'Makom' see bin Gorion, *'Die Sagen der Juden'*, p. 310. Lehnert points out that although Mann emended the biblical stories about Abraham according to *Die Sagen der Juden*, the compiler of the midrashic text was very far from interpreting the patriarch's 'discovery' in its full sense (Lehnert, 'Thomas Manns Vorstudien', p. 473).

20. This cycle in *Joseph* includes stories about the prediction of Abraham's birth, Nimrod's slaughter of the infants in an attempt to murder him, Abraham's fabulous childhood in a cave suckled by an angel, the assertion that Eliezer was given to him by Nimrod and that Abraham was thrown into a limekiln, Abraham's proselytizing in prison and, finally, Eliezer and Abraham's victory over the kings (pp. 306–08 [pp. 339–42], pp. 318–19 [pp. 352–54]). See bin Gorion, *'Die Sagen der Juden'*, p. 183, pp. 187–89, p. 199, pp. 203–04, p. 223. Berger notes that all of the stories, which appear in the chapter 'Der Unterricht' ['The Lesson'], are variants of the biblical patriarchal stories conveyed in the Talmud, Midrash and Julius Braun's *Naturgeschichte der Sage* (Berger, *Die mythologischen Motive*, p. 65). To give an example, for mythical narratives about Abraham's birth and their origins see Julius Braun, *Naturgeschichte der Sage*, 2 vols (Munich: Bruckmann, 1864–65), I (1864), pp. 279–80.

21. *GW*, XI, 663. For Mann's use of Midrash in *Joseph* see Terry R. Wright, *The Genesis of Fiction: Modern Novelists as Biblical Interpreters* (Aldershot: Ashgate, 2007), pp. 133–48. Wright mentions that Midrash plays a 'significant role' in 'the textual montage' of the tetralogy' (p. 133) but points out that the 'pervasiveness of midrashic material in *Joseph and His Brothers* is still a fairly well-kept secret' (p. 146). Levenson writes that the 'very method Mann employs draws on rabbinic techniques' (Levenson, 'Christian Author, Jewish Book?', p. 166) and calls *Joseph* 'a distinctly Jewish commentary on the Bible' (pp. 168). He is echoed by Appelfeld who writes that Mann 'sought to fill in what was missing or unsaid in the story' like 'the Jewish Sages [...] in earlier generations' (p. 67). See Aharon Appelfeld, 'The Bible and Thomas Mann', in *Vom Weitläufigen Erzählen*, ed. by Manfred Papst and Thomas Sprecher, Thomas-Mann-Studien, 38 (Frankfurt a.M.: Klostermann, 2008), pp. 63–71. On this subject see also Fred S. Heumann, 'Some Major Biblical Sources in Thomas Mann's *Joseph* Tetralogy', *Notre Dame English Journal*, 14 (1982), 87–112 (p. 89) and Evelyn Bukowski, 'Jüdisches Erzählen und mythische Erinnerung in Thomas Manns *Joseph*-Romanen', in *Thomas Mann (1875–1955)*, ed. by Walter Delabar and Bodo Plachta, Memoria, 5 (Berlin: Weidler, 2005), pp. 159–80 (pp. 170–71). Marquardt, in this context, argues in contrast that it is dubious whether Mann's irreligious or even multireligious invention of God can be read as a rabbinic Jewish novel (Marquardt, *Erzählte Juden*, p. 92).

22. Compare with Hamburger who writes that Mann exploits the Jewish mythical tradition to humorously depict the invisible God of the Old Testament in humanly comprehensible terms,

as a King of a court of the hosts of angels with whom he finds himself in a strained relationship (Hamburger, *Thomas Manns biblisches Werk*, p. 97).

23. See bin Gorion, '*Die Sagen der Juden*', p. 56.
24. Nolte asserts that 'the style' of 'Wie Abraham Gott entdeckte' 'is spoken, rather than written language, and it is marked by a naïve quality, which we immediately associate with Eliezer and certainly not our narrator' (Nolte, *Being and Meaning*, p. 133).
25. See bin Gorion, '*Die Sagen der Juden*', p. 62.
26. See bin Gorion, '*Die Sagen der Juden*', pp. 130–31.
27. Murdaugh writes that Joseph recounts this story to his father who knows it cannot be true (Murdaugh, *Salvation in the Secular*, p. 48). However, she misreads the text, for Joseph never finishes telling this story to his father, nor does he mention Semhazai. Indeed, Jacob is absorbed in his thoughts and is not listening to Joseph at that point.
28. Vogelmann also notes the correlation between Eliezer's double tongue and lunar grammar (p. 70). See Katharina Vogelmann, *Konstellationen von Mythos und Erzählen in Thomas Manns 'Josephs'-Romanen: unter besonderer Berücksichtigung der Figur des Jaakob*, Studien zur Germanistik, 15 (Hamburg: Kovač, 2005).
29. From Jeremias, Mann takes one of the main ideas of the pan-Babylonian system, the perfect harmony of the above and below, heaven and earth, as a narrative device of the rolling sphere (Berger, *Die mythologischen Motive*, p. 46). Jeremias writes 'alles, was auf der Erde sich zieht und geschieht, geschieht auch im Himmel' [everything that takes place on earth also takes place in heaven] (Jeremias, *Das Alte Testament im Lichte des Alten Orients*, p. 8).
30. Feuerlicht writes that the narrator lets the reader see him at work (p. 423). See Ignace Feuerlicht, 'Der Erzähler bei Thomas Mann', *German Quarterly*, 43 (1970), 418–34. McDonald sees the revolving sphere as a master trope, 'at once a structural principle, thematic subject, and nascent theory of narrative' (p. 249). See William E. McDonald, 'Deep is the Well of the Past. Should we not call it Bottomless' in *Third Person: Authoring and Exploring Vast Narratives*, ed. by Pat Harrigan and Noah Wardrip-Fruin (Cambridge, MA: MIT Press, 2009), pp. 243–51.
31. Gisela Bensch, *Träumerische Ungenauigkeiten: Traum und Traumbewusstsein im Romanwerk Thomas Manns: 'Buddenbrooks' — 'Der Zauberberg' — 'Joseph und seine Brüder'* (Göttingen: V & R Unipress, 2004), p. 127.
32. Hamburger notes that the Genesis stories are narrated mythically and that Mann develops a psychology of mythical thought linked with the research of the pan-Babylonian school for this purpose (Hamburger, *Thomas Manns biblisches Werk*, p. 32).
33. John E. Woods does not translate either of these expressions literally. 'Geschichtenerfinder' means 'an inventor of stories,' 'Mund zu voll von Fabel' — a 'mouth too full of fables.' Beck argues that the narrator expressly distances himself from being seen as the author of a novel (Beck, 'Thomas Manns Josephstetralogie', p. 42). Hamburger notes the irony of Mann's narrator, for a biblical fiction is just as much a version of the biblical narrative as a historical fiction is a version of the historical reality, where the biblical narrative represents a reality in relation to the biblical fiction, but differs from the historical reality in that it has no documentation other than itself. Hamburger writes that it has this in common with every mythical narrative (Hamburger, *Thomas Manns biblisches Werk*, p. 11).
34. Beck writes that in his anger Jacob admits that his stories about God are just variants of the fine discourse (Beck, 'Thomas Manns Josephstetralogie', p. 16). Murdaugh argues that 'Jacob rises above himself and his myth and openly denies the possibility of eternal recurrence, thereby achieving the first major breakthrough into the overt expression of historicity. In his despair, he finally addresses Eliezer as an individual and bitterly attacks the latter's assertion of a mythical identity' (Murdaugh, *Salvation in the Secular*, p. 48).
35. Hughes points out that Serach's song symbolically enables Joseph's fulfilment (p. 132). See Kenneth Hughes, 'The Sources and Function of Serach's Song in Thomas Mann's *Joseph, der Ernährer*', *Germanic Review*, 45 (1970), 126–33. Fischer notes that Serach's song is prefigured in the chapter 'Adonishain' ['The Grove of Adoni'] and originates in *Die Sagen der Juden* and in *Sefer ha-Yaschar* (Fischer, *Handbuch*, pp. 753–54).
36. Bond writes that 'there is more than a suspicion' that the narrator 'is making it all up' (p. 84).

See Greg Bond, '"Der Brunnen der Vergangenheit": historical narration in Uwe Johnson's *Heute neunzig Jahr* and Thomas Mann's *Joseph und seine Brüder*', *German Life and Letters*, 52 (1999), 68–84. Feuerlicht states that the pseudo academic narrator's references to evidence are simply a joke (Feuerlicht, 'Der Erzähler bei Thomas Mann', p. 426). Marquardt argues that under his authoritative mask the narrator is always unreliable; he speaks from the very beginning with several voices and from different directions at the same time (Marquardt, *Erzählte Juden*, pp. 105–06). Nolte writes that although the narrator 'never tires of asserting his own competence and objectivity, or the absolute integrity of his sources and observations', the novel 'often enough ... makes a mockery of precisely this enlightened attitude which it claims to celebrate. This arises for instance from the narrator's serious consideration of what is obviously metaphorical or mythical language' (Nolte, *Being and Meaning*, pp. 138–39). In this context, she mentions the natural parallels that arise 'between the narrator and the figure of Eliezer, who is also a teller of stories' (p. 140). Swensen echoes Nolte: 'In its visible details, the narrative that the narrator weaves may be that of a scholar or researcher, but in its overall substance, its contours reveal it to be the narrative either of a story-teller whose abilities exceed human bounds, or of one who fabricates his story' (Swensen, *Gods, Angels and Narrators*, p. 62). Beck notes that a peculiarity of Mann's irony lies in the fact that although he depicts the events as they could have happened in reality, he also indicates to the reader that his convincing retelling is nevertheless only *one* version 'des "Es-hätte-so-sein-Können"' [of 'it-could-have-happened-like-this'] (Beck, 'Thomas Manns Josephstetralogie', pp. 36–37).

37. Compare with Feuerlicht, 'Der Erzähler bei Thomas Mann', p. 426.

38. Feuerlicht, 'Der Erzähler bei Thomas Mann', pp. 420–21. Beck aptly remarks that Thomas Mann claims the air of reality for his literary reproduction (Beck, 'Thomas Manns Josephstetralogie', p. 57). The narrator equates 'Historisches Geschehen und literarische Wiederholung' [historical events and literary reproduction] (Beck, 'Thomas Manns Josephstetralogie', p. 57).

39. Nolte points out that Eliezer presents himself 'as an eyewitness, describing everything in minute detail and thus giving it authenticity', and sees a parallel to the narrator also typified by 'the assumed eyewitness status, the absolute knowledge which can describe even the innermost feelings of a character.' She argues that '[t]his particular narrative style' is 'part of the mythical consciousness' (Nolte, *Being and Meaning*, p. 140).

40. Ort notes the ambiguity of the German word 'Gotteserfindung' [invention of God/God's invention]: God invents stories and their characters invent God (p. 264). See Claus-Michael Ort, 'Körper, Stimme, Schrift: semiotischer Betrug und "heilige" Wahrheit in der literarischen Selbstreflexion Thomas Manns', in *Die Erfindung des Schriftstellers Thomas Mann*, ed. by Michael Ansel, Hans-Edwin Friedrich and Gerhard Lauer (Berlin: de Gruyter, 2009), pp. 237–71.

41. Ann Lawson, '"Die schöne Geschichte": a corpus-based analysis of Thomas Mann's *Joseph und seine Brüder*', in *Working with German Corpora*, ed. by Bill Dodd (Birmingham: University of Birmingham Press, 2000), pp. 161–80 (p. 175). Marquardt writes that *Joseph* draws the attention of the readers to its artifice (Marquardt, *Erzählte Juden*, p. 48). See also Jürgen Hohmeyer, *Thomas Manns Roman 'Joseph und seine Brüder'. Studien zu einer gemischten Erzählsituation*, Marburger Beiträge zur Germanistik, 2 (Marburg: Elwert, 1965), p. 68, p. 70.

42. Cunningham writes that the narrator 'chooses to insert such suggestions of divine intervention' at various points in the narrative (specifically in Joseph's narrative) 'where one would not normally have expected them. [...] In contrast, at precisely those points where the given events of the story appear 'unnatural', and where divine intervention would therefore appear to be a more plausible explanation, this view is discredited' (p. 185). See Raymond Cunningham, *Myth and Politics in Thomas Mann's 'Joseph und seine Brüder'*, Stuttgarter Arbeiten zur Germanistik 161 (Stuttgart: Heinz, 1985). Von Rad emphasizes how secular *Joseph*'s narrative is in the Old Testament, far more secular than Mann's retelling, where characters constantly orient themselves using mythical-divine mysteries (p. 143, p. 147). See Gerhard von Rad, 'Biblische Josephserzählung und Josephsroman', in *Joseph: Bilder und Gedanken zu dem Roman 'Joseph und seine Brüder' von Thomas Mann*, ed. by Gisela Röhn (Hamburg: Witting, 1975), pp. 141–49.

43. Lehnert cites Hans Heinrich Schäder's essay *Die islamische Lehre vom vollkommenen Menschen, ihre Herkunft und ihre dichterische Gestaltung* (1925) as a source for this narrative (Lehnert, 'Thomas

Manns Vorstudien', p. 506); he notes that the creation of the world is treated in terms of Gnostic speculation in the romance of the soul (p. 507).

44. Hamburger writes that Mann humorously integrates the Jewish mythical motif of God's preference for the first man into the Gnostic narrative about the soul (Hamburger, *Thomas Manns biblisches Werk*, p. 97).

45. This chapter in the novel is modelled on the Book of Job, where Jacob performs the role of the grieving Job and Eliezer stands for his interlocutors (Tumanov, 'Jacob as Job', p. 291). Eliezer also quotes God's words from the Book of Job almost verbatim (Tumanov, 'Jacob as Job', p. 294).

❖

CHAPTER 5

High Silence and Man's Telling Word

Mann's modern readers and the protagonists of biblical narratives in his novel have different conceptions of time. In the tetralogy, Abraham is as far removed in time from Joseph and Jacob as Yeshua is from the Master in Bulgakov's novel. His narrative is inherited by the patriarchs, who live many generations after him in the novel but understand themselves to be both his direct and symbolical descendants. In other words, for the patriarchs, the discovery of God is a distant ancestral memory of an uncertain origin, a narrative that provides a framework for their daily lives and shapes their worship practice. As will be demonstrated below, the depiction of Yahweh is constructed in the novel in the process of telling and elucidation of patriarchal narratives but also through mythologization of personal experience as divinely intended, a result of a conscious interpretative effort.

Jacob's God: A Voice from Within

God in *Joseph* is revealed and actualized through man, the result of a conscious effort to understand the natural world and human life as created and infused with divine meaning. Jacob has more visions of God than any other character in the novel. God speaks to the patriarch in a holy voice that comes 'von innen' (102) [from 'within him' (109)] and that 'seine Seele' (1261) ['his soul' (1419)] needs to hear. Conveniently, his divine visions always resonate perfectly with his practical and psychological needs. When Jacob needs reassurance and protection, God commands him to travel to Beth-El, a place of refuge: once, as he is fleeing the Shechem massacre perpetrated by his sons, and another time after he escapes his nephew Eliphaz. Beth-El provides a shelter and serves as the site where God restores Jacob's dignity by renewing Abraham's covenant with him in a dream. God's prophecies to Jacob in the novel are depicted as self-fulfilling, realized by the patriarch himself, who believes that they cannot come true 'ohne des Menschen Zutun' (199) ['unless a man does his part as well' (219)]. With this in mind, he uses what he sees as an obligation to fulfil God's promise of wealth to him to retain some of the profit he generates for Laban. On more than one occasion Jacob simply writes God into his stories for his own advantage. He revises the story of a humiliating encounter with his teenage nephew Eliphaz, which concludes with him begging for his life, into a fabulous heroic narrative. In the updated version of the story, that Jacob tells to all who will listen in return for food as he travels to Laban, God helps him defeat

Eliphaz by destroying his sword. Jacob also lies to Laban to magnify the power of his blessing, claiming that Yahweh had appeared in a dream to the merchant Belanu, ordering him to sell corn at a better price, in spite of telling Rachel's father on a different occasion that his God does not manifest Himself to those outside of his community. In a sense, Jacob's propensity for inspired fabrication is part and parcel of practising his faith in Abraham's God, which, for him, operates as a conceptual framework for understanding and representing his life as divinely intended. This religious *Weltanschauung* requires his active participation and relies on a sustained creative interpretative effort.

Jacob is skilled at endowing the ordinary and the mundane, indeed, everything that happens to him, with transcendental significance. This is how he mythologizes Joseph's disappearance as an Abrahamic human sacrifice exacted by God forcibly and through guile: 'gewollt, erlaubt, mit einem Worte *getan* hatte Gott das Gräßliche' (469) ['God had willed, permitted, or, in a word, *done* the horrible deed' (522)]. By giving a supernatural explanation and meaning to this tragedy, Jacob ignores his own moral cowardice, his failure to admit that it was his unapologetic favouritism that had provoked the brothers' attack. Most of God's manifestations to Jacob in the novel, too many to list here, are emotionally-motivated wish projections, which help him achieve his practical, often opportunistic goals, or compensate for moments of weakness and moral failure, functioning as an elaborate psychological defence mechanism against the trauma of the outside world.[1]

In spite of his many visions, Jacob complains that he is weary of Abraham's legacy because, as he puts it, God is not 'deutlich' (75) ['clear' (79)] to him.[2] The lack of clarity arises from his inability to reconcile what he sees as God's conflicting aspects into a coherent whole: 'Möge immerhin sein Anlitz zu sehen sein wie das Anlitz der Milde, so ist es doch auch zu sehen wie Sonnenbrand und wie die lohe Flamme [...] Die fressende Flamme ist er' (75) ['And even though one may behold His countenance as the face of gentleness, it is also like the fire of the sun and like a blazing flame [...] He is the devouring flame' (79)]. God's aspect as the 'devouring flame', a capricious, dangerous and jealous deity, comes to the fore in the novel through the narrative about Jacob's relationship with his favourite wife Rachel and their son Joseph.[3] According to the tradition, God makes Leah fruitful and Rachel barren out of spite and jealousy, because Jacob loves the younger sister with the abandonment reserved only for Yahweh himself. Jacob interprets Rachel's death, as well as Joseph's disappearance, as a sin of God, His 'guilt'. On the night when Rachel dies, Jacob directs his raw grief at God, crying out: 'Herr, was tust du?' (281) ['Lord, what are you doing?' (313)]. Jacob's contemplation of the divine is, in many ways, a search for, if not reciprocity, then transparency and accountability in man's dealings with God.[4] He eventually accepts that God takes a man's life when it suits Him, 'ohne Erläuterung' (1137) 'without explanation' (1277)]. The process of coming to terms with man's mortality begins on the night that Rachel dies, when Jacob rejects the magical rituals performed by the members of his household to delay or prevent her death, to compel the 'starke und unverständige Mächte zum menschlich Wünschenswerten' (282) ['the terrible and foolish powers to follow human wishes' (313)]. Jacob's cry goes unanswered but, at that moment, he sees 'die Majestät des Unbegreiflichen' (281) [the 'majesty of what is incomprehensible' (313)], understanding that a *quid pro quo* relationship between God and man contradicts the hierarchy devised by Abraham, where man serves only the highest, and not vice versa. This budding insight is later obscured by an overwhelming sense of injustice at Joseph's disappearance. It is only when Jacob is forced to let Benjamin, the last link to his beloved Rachel, go on a dangerous journey to Egypt much against his will that he grudgingly begins to come to terms with the nature of his God and the inevitability of death. After Joseph is restored to him from the 'dead', Jacob symbolically begins to interpret Yahweh as 'der Gott des Lebens' ['the God of Life'] who expresses Himself 'nur annähernd' (1267) ['only in approximate terms' (1425)], celebrating rather than questioning His inscrutability. This allows Jacob to give a new meaning to his son's disappearance. He no longer sees it as a sacrificial killing, but as an event that forms part of a long-term divine plan, which ultimately leads to the preservation of his community. After they are reunited, Jacob accepts what Joseph knew in his heart from the beginning: 'Gott kannte keine Schuld [...] Der Mensch trägt Gottes Schuld' (719) ['God knew no guilt [...] Man bears God's guilt' (803)]. The contradictions which Jacob perceives in God's nature are resolved in a consensus with Abraham's definition of God as all-embracing: 'der Allgott war Er allhiervon, denn aus Ihm kam es' (1260) ['He was the universal God, it all came from Him' (1417)].

Death and the divine are linked in Jacob's religious imagination and it is symbolic that his insight about God's nature coincides with his first reference to the 'Good Shepherd', an allusion to Jesus Christ, who in Christian theology takes away the sin of the world and grants mankind immortality. At this point in *Joseph*, in an anachronistic allusion to the New Testament, Jacob describes God in Trinitarian Christian terms as a threefold unity, made up of the Father, the Good Shepherd and the Angel.[5] The figure of Christ emerges in the narrative as a symbol of Jacob's reconciliation with his God. In words that abound in Christological and Eucharistic allusions Jacob prophesies the coming of Shiloh from his bloodline, the Anointed One, the figure of promise, the link between the past and the future, who (like Christ) will enter his city riding on an ass and whose blood he refers to as 'Weinblut' (1308) ['the blood of the wine' (1473)].[6] Far from being a divine revelation, Jacob's prophecy is the outcome of a thought process that has lasted 'ein halbes Leben lang' (1131) ['half his life' (1270)]: Shiloh is a figure whom he 'sich [...] ausgesonnen hatte' (1131) ['had contrived' (1270)] and whom he has already mentioned to Tamar. In the tetralogy man's ability to harness the creative potential of language for naming thus bringing an object into existence, forges an affinity with God. Jacob's invention of Shiloh, the salvation, for whom he 'seit langem einen Namen suchte und einen vorläufigen gefunden hatte' (1123) ['had long sought to put a name and [...] had in fact found a provisional name' (1260)], also echoes Abraham's conceptualization of God, 'dem er Namen suchte und hinlängliche nicht fand' (10) ['for whom he had sought a name and [found] none to his satisfaction' (6)] in the tradition. Jacob believes Shiloh's coming to be foretold to mankind in 'Noahs Segen für Sem, verheißen dem Abraham, durch dessen Samen alle Geschlechter auf Erden sollten gesegnet sein' (1131) ['Noah's blessing of Shem, promised to Abraham, through whose seed all families of the earth should be blessed' (1270)]. His prophecy, in other words, crystallizes from the corpus of narratives inherited from the previous generations and is the result of a laborious and lengthy exegetical process. His 'Hang zur Gedankenverbindungen' (67) ['gift for connecting ideas' (70)] enables him to syncretize disparate narratives into one and to extract from them a prophecy and a legacy for himself, just as the Abraham of the tradition organizes all natural forces into the idea of the highest and only God.

Jacob's complaint that God is unclear is contradicted by his vivid dream of the heavenly ladder, the single vision where Yahweh appears to him as a powerful anthropomorphic deity with a blue beard who draws 'die Luft in seine Brust' (104) ['air deep into His chest' (111)] before he speaks.[7] Jacob's dream is psychologically motivated: his humiliated subconsciousness conjures up an extravagant vision to compensate for his recent encounter with Eliphaz. Might and power, embodied by Yahweh in the dream, are the two qualities which Jacob clearly does not possess when he begs Eliphaz to spare his life. Yahweh renews Abraham's covenant with Jacob, promising him fabulous posterity, reaffirming Jacob's compromised virility ('ich will deinen Samen zahlreich machen wie das Staubkorn der Erde' (104) ['I will make your seed as the dust of the earth' (111)]), and emphasizing his place in a line of spiritual heads of Israel: 'Ich bin Abirams Herr und Jizchaks und der Deine' (104) ['I am the Lord of Abiram and of Yitzchak and I am your Lord' (111)].[8] Yahweh's dramatic physicality in this vision is particularly striking. He is portrayed as a bearded God, a King enthroned in heaven, clad in a 'Mützenkrone der Macht [...] angetan mit einem Gewande aus Mondlicht, das Fransen hatte aus Feuersflammen' (104) ['caplike crown of the Almighty [...] whose raiment was of moonlight and fringed with little flames' (111)]. This image of Yahweh, his outstretched arms 'nervig von Kraft' (104) ['sinewy with great power' (111)], holding a sign of Life and a drinking vessel, is inspired by a depiction of the sun god Hammurabi. However, it recalls any number of other generic patriarchal deities, imagined as bearded men enthroned in heaven, such as the Olympian Zeus.[9] Jacob's dream heaven is full of fantastic and grotesque beings, 'Gefiederte Menschentiere, Cheruben, gekrönte Kühe mit den Gesichtern von Jungfrauen [...] Stiergötter' (103) ['Winged creatures, part man part beast, cherubim, crowned cows with the faces of maidens [...] Bull-gods' (110)]. This hyperbolic vision jars with the rest of the chapter stylistically. As in the other instances in *Joseph* where God is depicted as a King, namely in Eliezer's narratives, Jacob's ladder dream also seems to have been influenced by the narrative style of Jewish folklore. Indeed, his dream in bin Gorion's compilation is equally hyperbolic: the ladder is eight thousand miles- and the angels ascending it are two thousand miles wide.[10] There is a contradiction in the juxtaposition of an abstract disembodied God, God as an idea, in the tetralogy and the depictions that rely on a visualization of Him as an embodied figure or a natural phenomenon. The novel's intertextuality, and in this context, for want of a better word, the authenticity of Mann's portrayals of God, is revealing about his narrative strategy. Almost every time God is visualized in *Joseph*, His image turns out to be a form of a citation. Mann, a virtuoso writer — who brings the biblical patriarchs to life in the tetralogy through rich and subtle psychological characterization, more often than not chooses to closely follow external sources for his depiction of the Jewish God.

At different points in the narrative Jacob's God is represented as a voice, a peal of thunder, a face of mildness and an annihilating flame of fire, a clichéd patriarchal bearded deity and Elohim, a threefold unity (an allusion to the Christian Holy Trinity). For Jacob, Abraham's search for the universal prime cause evolves into a struggle with man's mortality.[11] In this context, if Abraham's conceptualization of the divine is empowering in its elevation of mankind, Jacob's understanding of God hinges on relinquishing control. Control or being in charge of one's own destiny is the distinguishing trait of Joseph's character and the subject of the next section.

Joseph: God's Favourite

Like Abraham in Eliezer's stories, Joseph defines God as 'das Ganze' (1054) [what is all] from the start.[12] His primary concern, therefore, is God's intentions rather than his identity. Mann's protagonist is often seen as a character who gradually adopts the role of a self-conscious 'Regisseur des Spiels' [director of the play] of his life, taking charge of his story.[13] However, there is also a strong case to be made for Joseph consciously shaping his story, which is intertwined with God's narrative in the novel, from his youth. His understanding of Yahweh is best illustrated in the dreams conjured up by his subconsciousness, both in waking reality and in his sleep.

At the end of fine discourse with Jacob in 'Zwiegesang', teenage Joseph exclaims that he wants to sing to the Lord 'mit flinker Zunge, flink wie der Griffel des Schreibers!' (86) ['with a nimble tongue, nimble as the stylus of the scribe' (91)] and then tells him about a recurrent dream. This dream does not appear in the Bible and is, in fact, Mann's montage of fragments from several psalms:[14]

> Denn sie sandten mir nach ihrer Haß und haben Fangstricke gelegt meinen Schritten, sie gruben ein Grab vor meinen Füßen und stießen mein Leben in die Grube, daß mir zur Wohnung wurde die Finsternis. Aber ich rief seinen Namen aus der Finsternis der Grube, da heilte er mich und hat mich entrissen der Unterwelt. Er machte mich groß unter den Fremden, und ein Volk, das ich nicht kannte, dient mir auf der Stirne. Die Söhne der Fremden sagen mir Schmeicheleien, denn sie würden dahinschmachten ohne mich. (86)

> [For in their hatred they sent for me and laid snares for my steps, they dug a pit before my feet, and thrust my life into the pit, where darkness became my dwelling place. But I called upon His name out of the darkness of the pit, and He healed me and He rescued me out of the underworld. He made me great among strangers, and a people I did not know serves me, touching their brows to the ground. The sons of strangers flatter me, for without me they would perish. (91)]

On the one hand, the dream describes a generic mythical schema of death and resurrection, fall and elevation. On the other, it reads as a programmatic paraphrase of Joseph's story in the tetralogy compressed into one paragraph, alluding as it does, in general terms, to his fall at the hands of his brothers, his incarceration in the well at Dothan, and his future rise to power in Egypt, where he is made the minister of agriculture and earns the love of the Egyptians for saving them from starvation. Indeed, Joseph himself retrospectively interprets his elevation in Egypt as a divine fulfilment of this particular vision, citing it in a message to Jacob: 'Gott gab mir den Vorrang unter den Fremden, und mir ist untertänig Volks, das ich nicht kannte' (1228) ['God has given me preeminence among these foreigners, and a people I did not know are subject to me' (1381)]. The roots of Joseph's dream appear to lie in the predictions about his future made by the oracle Rimut and his tutor Eliezer. Rimut prophesies to Rachel in general mythical terms that her child will fall into a pit and yet live, and foretells the raising up of his head from the death. The dream also echoes Eliezer's horoscope, which Joseph recounts to his father in minute detail, for it promises great journeys and a role in 'den Geschehnissen in den Reichen der Erde und an der Handhabung der Herrschaft' (79) ['the events of the empires of this earth and in the administration of authority' (83)].[15] Joseph's dream is an articulation of an aspiration, envisioned by him many times and based on Eliezer and Rimut's predictions, which he creatively merges into a single narrative and endows with a divine significance.[16] In fact, he admits to Jacob that the dream is his own invention: 'Das war nur schöne Rede [...] die ich machte, um dem Herrn ein Großes zu sagen. Und es ist der Mond, der mich etwas berückt' (87) ['These were merely pretty words [...] that I spoke to say something grand for my Lord. And it is the moon, too, which beguiles me somewhat' (91–92)]. If his life seems predestined in the tetralogy, it is because he deliberately stages it to make it appear so from the outset.

In his vision, a 'dream' only in the sense of it representing his aspiration, Joseph symbolically posits his life as a devotional narrative, an homage to his God. When he reframes the predictions about his future into a narrative that imaginatively mythologizes his life, he is simply imitating the examples available to him in his immediate environment. His heritage is instructive in demonstrating that anything can become a subject of fine discourse and, indeed, this is how he posits his own narrative when he casts it as 'schöne Rede' ['pretty words']. From Eliezer's stories, told with a double tongue and governed by the rolling sphere, Joseph learns about the poetic possibilities afforded by a mythical consciousness, understanding that any experience can simultaneously have an earthly and a heavenly aspect (literal and metaphorical to the readers but one as true as the other to Mann's characters).[17] Indeed, Joseph uses the words 'tongue' and 'moon' — associated in the tetralogy with fictional narration which is epitomized by Eliezer — when he speaks about his dream, suggesting that he too is engaged in an act of creative mythologization but on a completely different scale: his entire life becomes a canvas for a divine fantasy.[18]

The positioning of Joseph's first 'vision' before his other three prophetic dream sequences, which initially appear to be divinely inspired, is a narrative manoeuvre with important implications.[19] Central to all of Joseph's subsequent visions is the narcissistic motif of his elevation and adoration by the others.[20] These visions

include the dream of the sheaves, the sun and the moon, and the extravagant
Enoch–Metatron ascension vision. In essence, they merely repeat and translate the
vision that Joseph sets out to his father in 'Zwiegesang' into a more figurative visual
dream language. Joseph's ambition to be adored by a foreign people, for example,
is mirrored in all his other dreams, where the sheaves, the stars and the angels bow
down to him. His dreaming consciousness repeatedly reproduces and elaborates a
prophecy of his own making. The positioning of Joseph's vision in the narrative
means that Mann demythologizes his biblical dreams, which include the visions of
the sheaves and the stars, as vivid projections of his protagonist's subconsciousness.

There is, nevertheless, a certain amount of ambiguity linked to the attribution
of authorial responsibility for Joseph's story in the novel. Joseph's first 'dream' is
clearly his own invention. His brothers, with whom he presumptuously shares
the dreams of the bowing sheaves and the stars, see their origin in his arrogance.
In spite of that, both Joseph and the narrator insist that his prophetic dreams are
divinely inspired. The narrator states: 'Gott hatte ihm Träume gesandt' (594) ['God
had sent him dreams' (663)]. This contradiction is resolved through the framing of
divine intervention in the novel. Joseph is Abraham's true heir in his understanding
of God and self, or, more precisely, of the centrality of human agency in one's
intercourse with the divine, as essentially linked. One sublimates the other. The
notion of a symbiotic relationship between the divine and the human is absorbed
by Joseph from his role models: Eliezer and his father. Jacob's ingenious sheep-
breeding stratagem, masterminded to fulfil God's prophecies of wealth, is an
inspiring example. Eliezer also teaches Joseph to cast man as God's co-creator,
whose intellect enables him to structure and organize reality into a meaningful
narrative. According to Eliezer, reason is given to man by God to improve 'das
Heilige, aber nicht ganz Stimmende' (294) ['something holy, if not quite consistent'
(326)], a notion that takes root and evolves in Joseph's imagination. In the climactic
moment when Joseph is thrown into the well by his brothers the notion of agency,
inherent to his first playful and presumptuous vision, crystallizes into a firm belief
that the confrontation was necessary for the sake of God's future plans.[21] For the
first time in his life Joseph explicitly and literally interprets the circumstances that
have led to his fall as intended by God. Joseph's belief in the importance of human
agency translates into a conviction, which becomes more articulated with time, that
God means him to play an active and decisive role in the fulfilment of his plan:

> Man muß nur auf den Gedanken kommen, daß Gott es besonders mit einem
> vorhat und daß man ihm helfen muß: dann spannt sich die Seele, und der
> Verstand ermannt sich, die Dinge unter sich zu bringen und sich zum Herrn
> aufzuwerfen über sie. (673)

> [A man must happen upon the notion that God has something special in mind
> for him and that, in turn, he must help Him — then his soul spreads its wings
> and his reason plucks up its courage to bring things under its control and to step
> forward as their master. (751)]

Faith in God is cast in the novel as Joseph's belief in himself, his inflated self-
confidence. Joseph is God's favourite because he believes in the pliability of

circumstances and the world as a whole to his will. What begins as a symbolic and playful mythologization of Joseph's life in God's honour, ultimately translates into its literal narrativization in Egypt, guided by dream motifs. Keenly aware that 'das Entrückungsmotiv' (528) ['the motif of his being carried away' (589)] has to be complemented by the motif of his being raised up, Joseph enacts the aspiration of his youth and mythologizes his life as God's story, engineering his ascent as a symbolical panegyric.

Joseph's ambition to say something grand to the Lord is realized in the text in the symbol of a mouth ('Mund'). In the novel, the word 'mouth' is associated with Eliezer's creative narration but it also refers to a position of power as a representative of the highest authority, a role of a 'mouthpiece' or second in command. In Joseph's Enoch-Metatron dream vision, which he likewise has in his youth, God makes him his mouthpiece and overseer over the angels, commanding them to obey every word that he speaks in his name. This dream provides a model that is replicated and realized in each of Joseph's subsequent positions of power in Egypt as he takes on the roles of Potiphar's representative, Mont-kaw's deputy and 'oberster Mund' (710) ['the overseer's [...] mouth' (793)], Mai-Sachme's 'Mund' (972) ['mouth' (1089)] and adjutant in prison and, finally, the Pharaoh's mediator and 'Oberster Mund, [...] durch den des Königs Worte gingen, der Stellvertreter des Gottes' (1074) ['a Supreme Mouth [...] through which the king's words must pass, the god's deputy' (1205)].

Insofar as Joseph interprets the events of his life as a fulfilment of a divine plan, he assumes the role of God's symbolical mouthpiece and a mediator of his will, identifying himself with the moon, the star of Thoth, the speaker and scribe of the gods. Joseph models his relationships with figures of authority, such as Echnâton, on his relationship with God, conveniently and opportunistically seeing an earthly reflection of his divine authority in them. An insight into his relationship with the Pharaoh may therefore tell us more about his relationship with Yahweh. Joseph is referred to in the novel as the King's symbolical double and mouthpiece, for each of his words is regarded as the Pharaoh's own word. He assumes the role of a Hermes figure, an interpreter, an intermediary between what is above and what is below, who is 'wie der Mond zwischen Pharao, unserer schönen Sonne, und der unteren Erde' (1071) [[as 'the moon between Pharaoh, our beautiful sun, and the earth below' (1201)]. However, the will he conveys is always his own, only disguised as the Pharaoh's. This much is made obvious in his dialogue with Echnâton in the Cretan Loggia where he passes his words for the Pharaoh's as he ingeniously pretends to repeat to himself what the latter may say: ' "Genau so", sagte Joseph mit Erstaunen, "gedachte ich in der Höhle zu mir zu sprechen, wenn ich in Gedanken das Gespräch der Großen fortsetzen würde" ' (1049) ["That is exactly," Joseph said in amazement, "what I had planned to tell myself in my cave, in the continuation of my thoughts about the conversation of the greats." ' (1175)].

Each new step in Joseph's ascent is a realization of his wish to glorify God through the song of his life: a symbolical utterance of his creative mouth.[22] He is promoted thanks to his quick intelligence and eloquence, prompting the members of Potiphar's house to call him 'Mund' or 'mouth':

> denn der Jüngling sprach wie ein Gott [...] und sie wußten wohl, daß er durch
> schöne und kluge Rede [...] seinen Weg gemacht oder ihn sich doch bereitet
> hatte beim Herrn und beim Mont-kaw. (710)

> [for the young man spoke like a god [...] and they were well aware that it was
> with beautiful and clever words [...] that he had made his way or at least had
> prepared it both with the master himself and with his steward Mont-kaw.
> (793–94)]

Joseph's eloquence, his ability to exploit the creative potential of language, is
instrumental to his ascent to power. The novel, like the Gospel of John (John 1.
1), sets up Logos, the Word of God, as a creative principle. In the stories familiar
to Joseph, the world is created by God, described as the Word moving above the
primal waters. He regards language as divinely creative for it constructs what
it describes and enables man to emulate God. This is important to Joseph, who
believes that worship should always entail 'Anklang[] ans Höchste' (946) ['harmony
with what is Most High' (1060)]. The narrator, who frequently demystifies biblical
miracles elsewhere in the novel, presents Joseph's eloquence as truly extraordinary,
for his words have the power to either accelerate Mont-kaw's demise when he
wishes him good night or to hold death at bay with his stories. Joseph's creative
fluency is contrasted in the novel with Naphtali's eloquence: 'eine ziemlich
untergeordnete Zungenfertigkeit' (301) ['a rather trifling glibness' (333)] that has no
higher significance.

When Joseph tells Jacob that he wishes to glorify God in a song, he sets up
narrative creativity as a mode of worship. He recites his first dream in the framework of fine discourse, adding it at the very end as its logical continuation. Jacob
concludes by saying formulaically: 'So wird es dir gehen, wie du gesagt hast' (87) ['it
will come to pass as you have said' (92)]. Joseph's life story is ultimately translated
by Serach into a new panegyric song about God's jest:[23]

> Gott kann striemen und lindern.
> Ach, wie wunderlich ist er mit seinem Tun
> unter den Menschenkindern!
> Unbegreiflich ist es, wie er regiert,
> groß seiner Hände Geschäfte. (1243)

> [after His lash God gives healing.
> Ah, how wonderful are the works that He
> to His children is revealing!
> Far beyond our ken the reach of His rule,
> great each deed His breath enkindles. (1398)]

In the end, the words of Joseph's first dream perfectly construct what they describe.
Joseph worships Yahweh through a song of his life by creating a new myth of
the planning God who rescues Israel from starvation and by inspiring Serach's
song.[24] There is a promise at the end of the tetralogy that Joseph's aspiration
will be perpetually creative, the novel itself, of course, being one example of its
realization: 'Breite Lieder sollen strömen, die deines Lebens Spiel besingen, immer

aufs neue' (1311) ['Broad be the river of song that celebrates the playful story of your life, singing it ever new' (1477)]. Joseph's desire to sing 'something grand' to God appears to him to be realized in the preservation of Israel from starvation. On a different textual level, however, his fall into the well in Dothan is presented to the readers by the ambiguous man in the field (discussed in the next chapter) as a rehearsal of Christ's resurrection narrative, a story where Joseph unwittingly plays the symbolical role of his precursor. His story, like Tamar's, whilst important in itself, can also be read as a part of a wider salvific narrative that links the Old and the New Testaments, a significant literary statement at a time when attempts were being made to dejudaize the Bible.

Joseph's Enoch-Metatron dream, a variation of the elevation or ascension fantasy common to all of his visions, is the only instance in the novel when Yahweh is manifested to him. On other occasions, Joseph imagines God as a father figure doting on his favourite, a striking likeness of Jacob, idealized and sublimated, as he reveals to his brother Benjamin:[25]

> es schimmerte ihm der Bart mit dem Schläfenhaar seitlich dahin, und liefen Furchen hinein, gut und tief. Unter seinen Augen war's zart und müde drunter her, und waren nicht allzu groß, aber braun und glänzelnd, und spähten besorgt nach mir, da ich näher kam. (339–40)

> [For the beard and the hair at His temples glistened as they flowed to each side, and there were furrows there, deep and good. Lines of tenderness and weariness lay beneath His eyes, which were not all too large, but brown and bright, and they peered at me with concern as I approached. (377)]

Tellingly, in Egypt Joseph is saved from a transgression with Mut when his spirit produces a vision of the father, a collage of the figures of authority he had served, where Jacob's, Potiphar's and Mont-kaw's traits merge ambiguously with 'viel gewaltigere[n] Züge' (914) ['far more powerful features' (1025)].[26] The Metatron dream which he sees in his youth, however, offers an altogether different portrait of God. In this dream Joseph is carried to heaven by the angel Amphiel in the shape of an enormous horned eagle before being made Metatron by God, to the consternation of the angels. This dream, too, is a palimpsestic collage of a series of narratives familiar to Joseph, amalgamated and syncretized by his dreaming subconsciousness. Joseph fuses the myth about Etana's flight to Anu's heaven on an eagle, taught him by Eliezer, with the fine discourse narrative of the boy Hanok who is made Metatron. The hostile angels Aza and Azaël in Joseph's dream recall the protagonists of Eliezer's narratives. God's seat in this dream sequence is located in the highest heaven, Araboth on a mountain 'funkelnd von feuerigen Steinen' (339) ['flashing with fiery stones' (376)], a verbatim quotation of Eliezer's story, where God's residence is made out of a substance 'wie von feuerigen Steinen' (293) ['like fiery gemstones' (324)]. The dream is a testament to the unique creativity of Joseph's subconsciousness, which uses the material available to him to narrativize everything single-mindedly as the realization of Eliezer's horoscope and Rimut's predictions. Like Serach, he is an artist figure, able to aestheticize reality and endow it with a transcendental meaning. In this instance the prophecies about his future are realized as his rise to power as Metatron in heaven, which symbolizes a foreign land. Another indication that Joseph's subconsciousness simply inhabits familiar narratives in his dream is the fact that God does not interact with him and speaks about Joseph-Enoch in the past tense: 'den Knaben machte ich größer denn alle Wesen, in meiner Unbegreiflichkeit' (341) ['And by My incomprehensible will [...] I [...] made [this boy] [...] greater than all creatures' (379)]. It is clear that Joseph is merely projecting himself onto the mythical persona of Enoch whose narrative is reproduced by his dreaming subconsciousness.[27]

The fantastic and hyperbolic Enoch-Metatron dream includes elements which are stylistically unthinkable elsewhere in Mann's text, such as long catalogues: 'die Engel des Feuers, des Hagels, des Blitzes, des Windes, des Zornes und der Wut, des Sturmes, des Schnees und Regens, des Tages, der Nacht, des Mondes und der Planeten' (341) ['the angels of fire, of hail, of lightning, of wind, of anger, and of rage, of storm, of snow and rain, of day, of night, of the moon and the planets' (378)].[28] Heaven in Joseph's dream is populated by fabulous creatures, an army of singing angels armed with golden weapons and animals resting on pillows. In the dream Joseph-Enoch is given three hundred and sixty-five thousand blessings by God and sees enormous wheels covered with eyes, seven halls of Zebul built of fire, and seven fiery altars where a prince called 'Wer ist wie Gott?' (338) ['Who Is Like God' (376)] is making a sacrifice. The God of his dream is an autocratic King of midrashic folklore in a strained relationship with his entourage over his preference for mankind. He is one-dimensional — a cardboard figure whose speech is rigid and formulaic and who exists on a narrative plane different from the one occupied by Joseph. The depiction of a personified God enthroned in heaven jars conspicuously with the sophisticated and ironic style of Mann's narrative, which also portrays Yahweh as an ingenious human projection, a transcendent spiritual deity. Needless to say, this dream too is based on Mann's borrowing from *Die Sagen der Juden*.[29]

God in *Joseph* is constituted hermeneutically, through a critical contemplation of the world (Abraham) and interpretation of patriarchal narratives preserved in either fine discourse or in Eliezer's stories (Jacob and Joseph). The divine in the novel cannot be separated from the narrative and, more specifically, from the fictional. In a letter to Mann, written in 1934, Karl Kerényi referred to the *Buddenbrooks-Magic Mountain-Joseph* sequence as a '*Rückkehr* zum Urquell der Romanerzählung' ['*return* to the primal source of fictional narrative'], 'eine Art Beweis für meine Auffassung der Entwickelung des griechischen Romans' ['a kind of proof of my conception of the development of the Greek novel'] which he described as 'Mythos-Wundererzählung-bürgerliche Geschichte' ['myth-fabulous tale-bourgeois narrative'].[30] Although Eliezer's Abraham defines God in abstract terms as the highest he also represents a type of pre-modern consciousness which endows deities with an anthropomorphic form and has them interact with man on the same plane of reality. Eliezer, however, does not just embody mythical consciousness but also fictional narration. Joseph's imagination, so successful at inventing fiction and embodying it as lived reality of theological significance, is a product of that same mythical consciousness, which, in the novel, is associated with the symbol of the rolling sphere, that allows the earthly, human and literal to become the celestial, divine and metaphoric and vice versa. With time Joseph's understanding of the divine becomes more refined and abstract, aligned more closely to Eliezer's narrative of Abraham's conceptualization of Yahweh as the highest, until he comes to see God as an enlightening and structuring narrative principle, an empowering means for living a conscious future-oriented life.

The God of Israel

In the novel Yahweh manifests himself only to the patriarchs Abraham, Jacob and Joseph, or in other words, to those who are actively engaged in his contemplation. Indeed, there is a marked difference in the way that God is understood, experienced and represented by Abraham's descendants in faith, Jacob and Joseph, and their wider community, also known as Israel, many of whose members do not subscribe to the monotheism of the patriarchs. The ways in which they approach the divine are considered below.

Belief in Yahweh and 'geistliche Werbung und Verständigung' (95) ['spiritual wooing and accommodation' (101)] are the foundation of Abraham's faith community. This faith, however, is far from steadfast or exclusive. The community recognizes the highest God, 'den wahren Baal und Addu des Kreislaufs' (11) ['the true Baal and Adad of the grand cycle' (8)], in the God who had led the man of Ur out of Chaldea, one of many in the polytheist culture of the Near East in the novel. Jacob's brother Esau converts to Kuzach, the god of his Canaan wives. When Jacob and Rebecca part, she acknowledges in her heart that she may not see him again if her God or 'ein anderer es so wollte' (158) ['some other god willed it' (173)]. Rachel and Leah accept Yahweh out of love and loyalty to their husband, rather than out of religious conviction, and worship him as only one of many deities. Leah believes her fertility to be a gift from Jacob's God and the gods of her father. Rachel remains 'götzendienerisch' (264) ['idolatrous' (292)] in her heart, stealing Laban's teraphim to prevent them from aiding her father in his pursuit of Jacob and calling both on the gods of Babel and on her husband's God when she gives birth to Benjamin.

Jacob's sons, the heirs of Abraham's legacy, internalize their mothers' beliefs. The brothers' sincere attempts to understand whether Joseph's dreams are inspired by Yahweh testify to their faith. However, they also offer sacrifices to idols and when they swear to keep the circumstances of Joseph's disappearance secret, they call on both Abraham's God and the local Baals. The brothers' faith becomes more pronounced towards the conclusion of the novel, when they begin to see their misadventures in Egypt as God's punishment for their treatment of Joseph and Yahweh as 'ein Gott der Rache' (1176) ['a God of vengeance' (1322)]. The brothers' guilt prompts them to see God's involvement in everything that befalls them. They even interpret the events orchestrated by Joseph and Mai-Sachme, such as the appearance of money in their bags, as divine acts. Judah, in particular, has a strong sense of Yahweh as a source of punitive justice, seeing his sensuality as a punishment for his involvement in Joseph's disappearance. Of course, it is he, and not Joseph, who inherits the blessing and the spiritual leadership of the community, but, in contrast to the other patriarchs, his conceptualization of God lacks intellectual sophistication. He visualizes Yahweh as an entity 'von dessen Nase, wenn er zornig war, Dampf ging und verzehrend Feuer von seinem Munde, daß es davon blitzte' (1124) ['from whose nose steam came when He was angry, and destroying fire that came forth from His mouth as lightning' (1262)].

Even Jacob himself occasionally succumbs to superstition and idolatry. Showing remarkable flexibility when it suits him, he follows the practices that had not come from Yahweh but 'allenfalls doch von ihm kommen konnten' (250) ['could, after all, have come from Him' (277)], destroying and burying an image of the goddess Labartu in order to protect the pregnant Rachel and surreptitiously murmuring a prayer to the deity Ea with the same aim. He also believes that his wedding night belongs to Ishtar rather than Yahweh, a reflection of the polytheist culture of the world he is part of.

Isaak's single insight about God is informed by his identification with the original Isaak, his namesake and the rejected sacrifice, and is, in fact, also a prophetic allusion to the future sacrifice of Christ: 'es wird geschlachtet werden der Mensch und der Sohn statt des Tieres und an Gottes statt, und aber werdet ihr essen' (136) ['the man and the son will be slaughtered instead of the animal and in the place of God, and you will eat of it' (148)]. Misunderstanding his words as a reference to man's primal nature and to the time before Yahweh, his mourners are horrified by the prophecy because it is framed by references to animal worship.

If the members of the core family display such volatility and flexibility in their beliefs, even less can be said about monotheism taking firm root in the rest of the community. When Jacob leaves Shechem he collects and buries the idols that had appeared in his camp and that serve as a testament to his people's persisting idolatry, '[die] Neigung zum Rückfall und Abfall' ['a tendency [...] to relapse and fall away'] and interest in 'die fremden Götter' (1124) ['strange gods' (1262)]. With the exception of Joseph, who maintains and adapts his faith in Egypt, belief in Yahweh seems to cease after the link to the community had been broken. The children of the concubines, originally from outside of the faith community, lose their faith in 'El eljon, wenn sie sich je auf ihn verstanden hatten' (94) ['El-Elyon — if they ever had clung to Him' (100)] when they leave.

Tamar, a Canaan woman, is Jacob's single true convert and an interesting counterpoint to the polytheistic beliefs of the other wives. Her faith is commensurable with the faith of the patriarchs for she sees Yahweh as the future of the world.[31] Like Abraham, Tamar is a 'Sucherin' ['seeker'] led by her 'Bemühtheit um Wahrheit und Heil' (1127) ['effort to find truth and salvation' (1265)], who rejects belief in fertility deities because her soul senses that there is something else that is superior to them. Like Joseph, she imagines God to look like her teacher and mentor Jacob.[32] Unlike the patriarchs, however, Tamar shows no sign of wishing to ponder on His nature, desiring only to participate in his story.

In spite of the fact that faith in Yahweh often seems to be flexible, contingent and accommodating of polytheist beliefs, the end of the novel sees Abraham's community brought together and consolidated by its zest for the contemplation of the divine. Jacob's sermon about God, as Israel travels to Egypt, delights even the young members of the community who are all said to be more or less 'begabt in dieser Richtung' (1259) ['gifted in this way' (1416)]. God's apparent similarity to the other deities is treated by the community as an intellectual problem to overcome with wit, intelligence and their 'Begabung fürs Göttliche' (1261) ['talent for the divine' (1418)]. God, for them, is an exciting intellectual construct, constituted through an interpretative effort. Although monotheism is by no means shown to be unequivocally victorious in Jacob's community, 'Göttliches', 'die forterbende Arbeit an einem Gottesgedanken' (94–95) ['divine matters, the inherited task of thinking about God' (100)] forms the bond that holds it together.

Conclusion

In many ways, the patriarchs in *Joseph* see the Jewish God as a silence which demands to be interpreted.[33] Their interpretative effort takes different forms and has different outcomes. Like Abraham in Eliezer's stories, who understands silence as a form of a reply from God, Jacob similarly imbues the absence of an answer in response to his appeal to Yahweh with significance as an expression of His inscrutability and the unaccountability. Joseph's treatment of God is best described in Serach's words: 'wenn dem höheren Schweigen / menschlich deutend sich das Wort gesellt' (1240) ['when high silence is aided / by the telling word that man should know' (1395)]. Joseph sees his endeavour to fulfil what he believes to be a divine plan as an attempt to move 'Gott selbst, den gewaltigen Antwortlosen' ['God Himself, the great unanswering God'] to laughter 'über das Antwortlose' (1161) ['over what is unanswerable' (1304)]. God in Mann's ironic narrative is primarily constituted hermeneutically. There are, however, three ambiguous moments in *Joseph*, addressed in the next chapter, which contradict this reading and introduce a measure of ambiguity about the depiction of the divine and the supernatural in the tetralogy.

Notes to Chapter 5

1. Cunningham, *Myth and Politics*, p. 139. See also Gerth, *"Das Problem des Menschen"*, pp. 175–76.
2. Compare with Murdaugh: 'Just as human enlightenment progressed in splintered fashion, often broken by lapses [...] so the presence of God in his creatures took the form of multiplicity, and Jacob spoke for the human condition when he lamented' (Murdaugh, *Salvation in the Secular*, pp. 58–59).
3. Compare with Hatfield who asserts that Mann's God is 'genial and tolerant' (p. 83). See Henry C. Hatfield, 'Myth versus Secularism: Religion in Thomas Mann's *Joseph*', in *Crisis and Continuity in Modern German Fiction: Ten Essays*, ed. by Henry Hatfield (Ithaca, NY: Cornell University Press, 1969), pp. 78–89.
4. Tumanov postulates that Jacob fails as Abraham and 'assumes the persona of another father whose offspring is claimed by God: Job' (Tumanov, 'Jacob as Job', p. 289).
5. Marquardt believes that Jacob begins to narrate his stories as 'eine *Vorgeschichte des kommenden*

Christentums' [as *prehistory of the coming Christianity*] (Marquardt, *Erzählte Juden*, pp. 185–86). Jäger argues that Jacob's anachronistic reference to the Trinity and his theology are associative rather than logical in this instance (Jäger, *Humanisierung des Mythos*, p. 175). Beck asserts that the Christological subtext of the novel should only be understood as ironic play (Beck, 'Thomas Manns Josephstetralogie', p. 22).

6. Jacob's final words about Shiloh are that he will be 'so weiß wie Schnee, so rot wie Blut und so schwarz wie Ebenholz' (1308) ['white as snow, red as blood, black as ebony' (1473)]. Berger reads this as an allusion to the Snow White fairy tale (Berger, *Die mythologischen Motive*, p. 176). It can also be read as a reference to the episode from Wolfram von Eschenbach's *Parzival* which reinforces the messianic reference: 'Parzival, falsity's uprooter — his loyalty taught him to find three drops of snowy blood, which deprived him of his wits'. See Wolfram von Eschenbach, *Parzival and Titurel*, trans. by Cyril Edwards (Oxford: Oxford University Press, 2006), p. 125.

7. Berger points out Mann's combination of Egyptian motifs with Babylonian and Assyrian imagery in Jacob's dream (Berger, *Die mythologischen Motive*, p. 91).

8. It is interesting that when Jacob recalls this dream many years later he both describes God's voice as vague and remembers that it speaks to him urgently about the name Israel (p. 278 [p. 309]). Yahweh does not, in fact, say anything to that effect in the Luz dream.

9. Fischer suggests that Mann's description of God and of the Vizier standing before him largely follows the depiction of Hammurabi before the sun god (Fischer, *Handbuch*, p. 341). See Jeremias for the image of Hammurabi receiving laws from the sun god (Jeremias, *Das Alte Testament im Lichte des Alten Orients*, p. 261).

10. bin Gorion, 'Die Sagen der Juden', p. 311.

11. For Prickett the nature of Jacob's God is protean: 'one not merely of change but of dynamic evolution' (p. 252). See Stephen Prickett, *Origins of Narrative: the Romantic Appropriation of the Bible* (Cambridge: Cambridge University Press, 1996), pp. 247–63.

12. This is translated by Woods as 'the unified whole' (1182). However, in the German original Joseph uses the same words to define God as Abraham in Eliezer's story.

13. See Eckhard Heftrich, 'Der Homo oeconomicus im Werk Thomas Mann', in *Vom Märchenhelden zum Manager. Beiträge zum Ökonomieverständnis in der Literatur*, ed. by Werner Wunderlich, Facetten deutscher Literatur, St Galler Studien, 2 (Bern: Haupt, 1989), pp. 153–69 (p. 163). Swensen writes that Joseph and God stand in an ambiguous relationship to each other 'and it is unclear whose will it is, to which the narrative conforms and from which it takes shape' (Swensen, *Gods, Angels and Narrators*, p. 37). He argues that Joseph 'presents his story as if it were the work of a higher will' and since it 'lies outside the realms of human experience, no one can prove it his will and not that of a god' (p. 110). I argue that Joseph's first dream demonstrates that there is never really any ambiguity about the motivation of his story.

14. Berger, *Die mythologischen Motive*, p. 155. Fischer, *Handbuch*, p. 335.

15. Jäger points out that astrology in *Joseph* can have the same effect as dreams, which are fulfilled because the dreamers believe in them (Jäger, *Humanisierung des Mythos*, p. 274).

16. Nolte asserts that 'in crucial situations which will determine the further course of his life, he always acts in accordance with the prophecy' and, as a result, experiences 'a very powerful sense of destiny' (Nolte, *Being and Meaning*, p. 101). She argues that the Self present 'wholly and completely, from the beginning, contains also the whole, detailed blueprint of our life' (p. 99) and that at the end of the novel Joseph's understanding of individual life [...] corresponds closely to Schopenhauer's concept of *transcendent fatalism*' (p. 100). Noble states that Mann's depiction of Joseph as the chosen one recalls the Protestant predestination teaching (p. 35). See Cecil A. M. Noble, *Dichter und Religion. Thomas Mann, Kafka, T. S. Eliot*, Europäische Hochschulschriften. Reihe I, Deutsche Sprache und Literatur, 1014 (Frankfurt a.M.: Lang, 1987). Marx argues that 'Joseph himself shares what Thomas Mann ascribes to Jesus Christ himself — a mythical consciousness, the art of shaping life according to the scriptures' (p. 32). See Friedhelm Marx, 'Transfigurations of Christ in Thomas Mann', *Religion & Literature*, 33 (2001), 23–36.

17. Murdaugh writes that Eliezer is 'the myth bearer' who is 'excluded from the active "Gottessorge"' [care for God] but contributes to it 'by educating the young Joseph in the myths of his lineage' (Murdaugh, *Salvation in the Secular*, p. 39).

18. Bensch points out that there are parallels between dreams and fiction in the tetralogy but does not consider Joseph's first 'dream' (Bensch, *Träumerische Ungenauigkeiten*, p. 158).

19. Compare with Cunningham who reads Joseph's dreams of the sheaves, the sun and the stars as 'clear expressions of his perceived (and desired) identity as the bearer' of Abraham's 'blessing' and argues that Joseph 'uses them to bring about the destiny which he believes they prophesy' (Cunningham, *Myth and Politics*, p. 140).

20. Bensch argues that Joseph's dreams are motivated psychologically and that the elevation in his dreams is a reflection of his position in waking reality as Jacob's favourite (his only son to be educated) (Bensch, *Träumerische Ungenauigkeiten*, p. 151). She also points out that dreamers can be blind to the fact that their dreams express their subconscious wishes (p. 150). For another psychoanalytical reading of Joseph's dreams see Lothar Pikulik, 'Joseph vor Pharao. 'Die Traumdeutung in Thomas Manns biblischem Romanwerk *Joseph und seine Brüder*', *Thomas-Mann-Jahrbuch*, 1 (1988) 99–116 (p. 104).

21. Cunningham writes that 'this *Weltanschauung* — [is] a sort of halfway house between determinism and Free Will, in which one's destiny is chosen and indicated by God without being imposed' (Cunningham, *Myth and Politics*, p. 110).

22. Compare with Cunningham who stresses that Joseph's 'perceived duty to God is, in this respect, no more than self-glorification; not the service of any higher ideal, but of his own ego' (Cunningham, *Myth and Politics*, p. 113).

23. Jäger sees Serach's song as an example of Mann's attempt to unite truth and reality through art. He points out that the name of the chapter which features the song is 'Verkündigung' [Annunciation], a Christian term that, for him, refers to the reconciliation of truth and reality (Jäger, *Humanisierung des Mythos*, p. 204, p. 284).

24. Ehinger notes that Serach's song is 'sprachlich ... ungelenk' [linguistically ... awkward] (p. 194). See Franziska Ehinger, *Gesang und Stimme im Erzählwerk von Gottfried Keller, Eduard von Keyserling und Thomas Mann*, Epistemata Reihe Literaturwissenschaft, 516 (Würzburg: Königshausen und Neumann, 2004).

25. Seibt sees Christ's death as a fulfilment of Abraham's sacrifice of Isaac and of Jacob's 'sacrifice' of Joseph; he argues that Jacob is thus functionalized as a parallel to Yahweh here which explains why the God of Joseph's dream looks like Jacob (Seibt, 'Jaakobs Gott', p. 100).

26. Nolte reads this image as the father archetype (Nolte, *Being and Meaning*, p. 116).

27. Kenney argues that for Joseph the dream represents 'his potential and, on a mystical level, his actual relationship to God, and through the identity of Metatron with the primal man, we, at least, are able to recognize his model for that relationship and its potential as the perfect man, the heavenly man himself' (p. 56). See Joseph M. Kenney, 'Apotheosis and Incarnation Myths in Mann's *Joseph und seine Brüder*', *German Quarterly*, 56 (1983), 39–60.

28. Berger, in contrast, believes that the novel represents an epic whole whose stylistic unity is unmistakable even in those places where the text seems to consist only of montage (Berger, *Die mythologischen Motive*, p. 15).

29. Kenney notes that the passage at the end of the dream where Henoch (Enoch) is apotheosized into Metatron is taken almost verbatim from bin Gorion's compilation (Kenney, 'Apotheosis and Incarnation Myths', pp. 41–42).

30. Kerényi, *Gespräch in Briefen*, p. 46, *Mythology*, pp. 42–43 (1 March 1934). Borchmeyer writes that for Mann myth (according to its original meaning as 'Erzählung' [narrative]) has a specific narrative structure (Borchmeyer, 'Zurück zum Anfang', p. 18).

31. See Heumann on Mann's use of different fragments of the biblical text for Tamar's figure (Heumann, 'Some Major Biblical Sources', p. 101).

32. Josipovici calls Mann's Tamar a 'knower' in reference to her religious certitude (p. 289). Gabriel Josipovici, *The Book of God* (New Haven, CT: Yale University Press, 1988). Spininger sees Tamar's narrative as 'a thematic antithesis' to Joseph's story insofar as his sexual restraint is inversed by her exploitation of sexuality 'illustrating ... [its] efficacy' 'within the divine scheme of salvation' (p. 157). Dennis J. Spininger, 'The "Thamar" Section of Thomas Mann's *Joseph und seine Brüder*: A Formal Analysis', *Monatshefte*, 61 (1969), 157–72.

33. For a discussion of the impossibility of understanding God expressed as 'Gottesferne' [distance

from God] see Anna Hellersberg-Wendriner, *Mystik der Gottesferne. Eine Interpretation Thomas Manns* (Bern: Francke, 1960), p. 98. Compare with Swensen, *Gods, Angels and Narrators*, p. 117.

CHAPTER 6

❖

Angelic Narrators and Pagan Deities

There are three brief but significant interventions into the patriarchs' world in *Joseph* by supernatural agents whose presence in the narrative is otherwise rationalized by the narrator's sceptical voice. They include Jacob's vision of a deity Ea-Oannes, Joseph's encounter with the man in field, who may or may not be an angel, and the second prelude, which is narrated by the angels. The supernatural characters' participation in the narrative and its telling creates confusion about the ways in which the different levels of the novel, that otherwise consistently demythologizes the miraculous biblical stories, fit together. In what follows these interventions are considered chronologically, as they appear in the text.

Ea-Oannes: A Local Sprite

Jacob's many visions of Yahweh and his dream encounter with an angel at Jabbok are easily rationalized as psychologically motivated projections of his subconsciousness. This is true for all of his experiences of the supernatural in the tetralogy bar one: his vision of Ea-Oannes, a Babylonian deity of the watery depths. The implications of Jacob's encounter with this deity, for the way that Mann approaches the divine in his retelling of the Old Testament story, are considered below.

Jacob experiences a powerful sensation as he walks across a field, 'ein eigentümlich brennendes Zucken, als treffe ihn der Blitz' (188) ['a peculiar burning spasm, as if he had been struck by lightning' (206)] just before he sees Ea-Oannes, a creature with a bearded human head under that of a fish. The figure draws something from the ground into a bucket and pours it out before gliding into the earth. Unsurprised, Jacob immediately interprets the vision as a message from Yahweh, concluding that it could have taken place only 'auf Veranstaltung Ja's, des Einzigen, des Gottes Isaaks' (189) ['at the behest of Yah, the God of Isaak, the one and only God' (207)] and explains its fantastical form to himself as his God's concession to the local spirit. After digging in the place indicated by Ea for a day and a half, Jacob finds a water spring much needed by Laban's household, which consolidates the power of the paternal blessing he urgently wishes to demonstrate to Rachel's father.

Ea's apparition stands out from Jacob's other encounters with the supernatural by its lack of ambivalence, insofar as it takes place in his waking reality. It occurs in the twilight, 'da Mond- und Tagesschein sich stritten' (188) ['for moonlight and daylight still stood at odds' (206)], which in the novel symbolizes a border between

the irrational and the rational, lunar grammar and the clarity of the sun, truth and
reality, the upper celestial and the lower earthly aspects of the rolling sphere. In this
liminal zone Ea's apparition assumes the air of absolute reality. The narrator's claim
that Jacob's revelation could have stemmed from the 'innere Spannung' (188) ['inner
tension' (206)] of his urgent wish to demonstrate the power of the blessing to Laban,
does not explain how it translates so directly into the concrete result of finding water
in that specific location, given that the spring is hidden deep underground. This
minor episode jars with the psychologizing and secularizing narrative philosophy at
the core of Mann's ironic modern retelling of the biblical narrative.

Jacob's encounter with Ea is a marginal episode in the tetralogy, two short
paragraphs in over a thousand pages of text, and the few critics who address it fail
to provide a satisfactory explanation for the deity's incongruous appearance in the
narrative, where the supernatural is consistently demythologized and ironized.[1]
The failure to account for Ea's apparition is important. His manifestation to Jacob
is a deliberate but minor incongruity, since Ea appears only briefly and on the
periphery of the narrative. The significance of Jacob's vision lies in its power of
suggestion, for, just like Yeshua's single act of healing in *The Master and Margarita*,
it ushers in doubt and the possibility of existence of the supernatural in the novel
in more than just the patriarchs' stories and imagination. It is a persuasive but
easily missed indication that there is a layer of the narrative where God (and not
the one all-powerful God but one of the many) may exist not as a metaphor or a
human projection, but as a narrative reality in His own right. An equally suggestive
episode, where Joseph meets the mysterious man in the field, is discussed below.

The Man in the Field: A Guiding Angel

The character of the man in the field is primarily based on two verses in the Book of
Genesis, where he is portrayed as a chance traveller who meets Joseph on his way to
his brothers (Genesis 37. 15–17), and *Die Sagen der Juden*, where he is depicted as the
angel Gabriel.[2] A multivalent figure, he plays at least two other important roles in
Joseph's story in the novel, guiding him across the desert to Egypt, the symbolical
Underworld in the tetralogy, in the chapter 'Ein Wiedersehen' ['A Reencounter']
and introducing Christological discourse on the resurrection into the narrative in a
conversation with Ruben by the empty well in 'Ruben kommt zur Höhle' ['Ruben
Comes to the Grave']. In what follows, I consider the significance of his encounter
with Joseph.

If the tiny fish-headed Ea is clearly a deity, a grotesque supernatural apparition
that is immediately recognized as such by Jacob, the identity of the man in the field
is more ambiguous. Ostensibly, he is a messenger delivering a letter whose path
happens to coincide with Joseph's and who offers to guide him to Dothan, as the
narrator surmises, in exchange for a ride on his donkey. Neither Joseph nor Ruben
perceive the man as anything other than human in spite of his peculiar behaviour.[3]
The man is helpful one minute and unpleasant the next. Every time he grows
particularly rude, his eyes start moving in circles in their sockets and he reluctantly

apologizes, as if remembering his manners.[4] He seems to have the gift of foresight, alluding to the donkey's accident just before it happens and predicting that he will play the role of a watchman, which soon comes to pass when he offers to look after Hulda. All this, including the man's passing references to Eliezer and Jacob's experience at Jabbok, strangely fails to excite Joseph's curiosity.[5] He rationalizes the man's clairvoyant reference to Hulda by suggesting that his inattentiveness to the road is the reason for her injury. As a result, his wilful blindness once again allows him to follow the path that leads to the fulfilment of Rimut and Eliezer's prophecies about his future.

The man bears a strong resemblance to the misanthropic angels, the protagonists of Eliezer's stories, and conspicuously takes their side on several occasions. It becomes clear retrospectively, hundreds of pages later, that he speaks in the idiom of the angels in the second prelude.[6] He criticizes Joseph's world of duality and calls mankind superfluous, unclean and unrighteousness, a race that he and others like him are forced to tolerate for the sake of 'höherer Angelegentlichkeit' (397) ['the zeal shown from on high' (442)]. He also makes an irritable veiled reference to the midrashic story about Adam's naming of the animals, something that the linguistically unproductive angels are unable to do, when he criticizes Joseph for defending Hulda's build. In another hint to the readers, the man dismisses Eliezer's narrative about the angels' promiscuity before the Deluge as gossip, suggesting that they were seduced out of contempt for the daughters of men.

When Joseph quizzes the man about the source of his knowledge of that story, his interlocutor cryptically replies: 'Fragst du deinen Eliezer auch, woher er es weiß, was er dich lehrt?' (397) ['Do you likewise ask your Eliezer how he knows what he teaches you?' (442)]. It is clear that Joseph's guide has a privileged narrative perspective and that he moves freely in the novel between the levels of the characters and the narrator, earth and heaven, just like Eliezer when he is engaged in inspired storytelling. Both in the narrative and outside it, the man is able to comment on it and to quote from it at will, including the parts that the readers have not yet reached.[7] His description of Joseph as 'bekanntlich hübsch und schön' (395) ['as everyone knows [...] handsome and beautiful' (440)] recalls the narrator's discussion of his fabled beauty in the chapter 'Ruhm und Gegenwart' ['Fame and Reality']. By calling the boy a calf, without rhyme or reason, the man is actually referencing the narrator's future analogy between Joseph, the calf, and Jacob, the cow that follows it to the edge of the field, which stands for Egypt in the novel. His warning to Joseph against being too friendly with the others points to his future catastrophic encounter with Mut-Em-Enet. Indeed, he cites Joseph's monologue about beauty to Mut word for word (or, of course, it may also be the case that Joseph later subconsciously repeats the man's words).[8] The man's treatment of Joseph's life as a quotable story is a mischievous allusion to his divine privileged perspective.

Up until this point in the novel, the realm of the angels has been represented as a citable world of Eliezer's entertaining fictional narratives. However, the man in the field makes it clear that it is Joseph's world that is citable when he tells Ruben who has come to the empty well:

diese Geschichte hier [ist] bloß ein Spiel und Fest [...] ein Ansatz nur und
Versuch der Erfüllung und eine Gegenwart, die nicht ganz ernst zu nehmen,
sondern nur ein Scherz und eine Anspielung ist, so daß wir blinzelnd und
lachend einander anstoßen mögen dabei [...] diese Geschichte [ist] im Werden
[...] und nicht schon geworden. (454)

[this story is itself play and festival, [...] merely a beginning, an attempt at
fulfilment, and at present not to be taken all too seriously, but is instead a jest
and an allusion, so that in response we may nudge one another with a wink
and a laugh. [...] this entire story is still becoming and has not already become.
(506)][9]

The angel's commentary on the 'story' momentarily disrupts its telling and operates
on a number of levels. The brief shift of perspective from the characters' level to that
of the narrator, of the told to the telling, emphasizes the artifice of the narrative and
its literary nature. To Ruben these words must seem like mockery at his despair at
Joseph's disappearance, but they are addressed primarily to the reader who should
recognize in the angelic figure guarding an empty 'tomb' a reference to the New
Testament resurrection narrative.[10] Indeed, according to the man, the time will
come in the future when the stone will be truly rolled away from the hole. In this
current trial narrative Joseph's role, or at least one of his roles, is that of Christ's
precursor. The control over his life shifts implicitly to God, who is using his story
as a template for another future narrative. The delight the angel invites Ruben to
share is that of a narrator winking and nudging his readers to recognize the multiple
levels of meaning in the allusions embedded in the narrative.[11] The man's mention
of an incomplete and becoming story may also, of course, be read as a reference to
Joseph and His Brothers. It is the readers' turn to take Joseph's place before a roguish
narrator and to acquiesce in his narrative in delight unclouded by considerations
of logic. The rolling sphere turns and the earthly characters' mythologization and
sublimation of their experience in stories about God finds its reflection in the angel's
narrativization of Joseph's life as a divine jest, which anticipates Serach's song.

The appearance of what seems to be an angel on Joseph's path has been treated as
'a small flaw in the fabric, a wilful self-indulgence of the creative imagination', an
incongruity in the narrative.[12] This, however, is Mann's very intention, constituting
an integral part of his poetic design. It should not simply be interpreted away. Mann
had admitted that the man in the field is 'nicht recht am Platze' [out of place] in
the narrative, which is 'eine "natürliche" Geschichte' [a 'natural' story], writing:
'Zwar habe ich die Hintertür halbwegs offen gelassen, daß er allenfalls doch ein
etwas wunderliches Menschenkind sein kann; aber sie ist recht schmal, und man
kommt fast nicht hindurch' [Even though I have left the back door half open so
that he could still be considered a rather odd son of man, the crack is really small
and it is almost impossible to squeeze through it].[13] The suggestion of divine
intervention, introduced by the man in the field, is anything but inconsequential,
but it is deliberately made ambiguous as Mann creates a range of interpretations for
this character. The man is an unpleasant eccentric messenger, an angelic guardian
of the empty tomb or Hermes Psychopompos, a guide of souls to the Underworld.
His angelic identity is one of many, a possibility.[14] He is an ambivalent figure

who evokes doubt and uncertainty and whose presence in Mann's ironic narrative demands an interpretative effort. When the coincidence of the man and the angels' words in the second prelude becomes apparent, it causes disquiet and prompts a desire to revisit his encounter with Joseph. It also suggests the coexistence of a supernatural realm in the tetralogy alongside the patriarchs' world, albeit one defined only in narrative terms. This narrative situation, the existence of two parallel worlds of the jealous angels and of the patriarchs, is anticipated in Eliezer's narrative in 'Wie Abraham Gott entdeckte,' where Abraham is observed by God and the angels but remains unaware of them. As in *The Master and Margarita*, the divine and the supernatural is also the metafictional, manifested through an unexpected shift in narrative perspective. This relativizes the patriarchs' world, itself a vivid retelling of a biblical story, as only one plane of existence and posits it in relation to another, transcendental reality, which is, in turn, represented in Eliezer's fabulous stories. In Mann's humorous narrative this higher reality is populated by the resentful and jealous angels. God appears in this context as the man's 'Auftraggeber' [commissioner], whose identity he pretends not to know: 'Wer dich eigentlich schickt, das weißt du gar nicht' (395) ['You don't even know who it is that has actually sent you' (439)]. The man capriciously calls the reason for sending him (apparently to act as Joseph's guide) 'unbegreifliche Angelegentlichkeiten' (395) [an 'incomprehensible zeal' (439)]. This distant and elusive God, who confirms Joseph's path to Egypt by sending an angel to guide him, is the God of Eliezer's narratives and the midrashic tradition.

The Second Prelude: The World as a Citable Text

The second prelude returns to the romance of the soul, a Gnostic creation myth recounted in the first prelude, first by the narrator and then by Eliezer.[15] It expands and reinterprets Eliezer's version of this story as a narrative about God's desire for immanence as the Jewish tribal deity, told from the perspective of the angels. The angelic protagonists of Eliezer's narratives become the narrators of their own story, characters in their own right who exist in the novel on a par with the patriarchs.[16] This important shift in narrative perspective merits a closer look, especially in the light of Joseph's encounter with the man in the field discussed above.

   Thanks to their obvious hostility towards mankind, the narrators of the second prelude are instantly recognizable as the misanthropic angels, the protagonists of Eliezer's fabulous narratives. They are portrayed in unmistakably midrashic terms as God's entourage, unpleasant scheming intrigants, 'stille Höflinge' (929) ['serene courtiers' (1042)] in a heavenly court in a strained relationship with God over his preference for mankind. However, in contrast to Eliezer's angelic protagonists who are, in many ways, no more than Mann's quotations from Midrash, the narrators of the second prelude are fully-fledged characters with a distinctive, self-satisfied voice.

   The shift in the narrative perspective in the second prelude is consistent with the rotation of the rolling sphere. Its movement creates parallel heavenly and earthly realities which have equal validity in the novel. They coexist and complement each other in patriarchal imagination in *Joseph*, but the second prelude also literalizes the movement of the sphere for the reader, as the vantage point is dramatically reversed. Up until this point in the narrative (with the exception of Ruben's conversation with the man in the field), the divine has been consistently positioned as the patriarchs' projection, mankind's intellectual construct in its pursuit of self-knowledge and spiritual emancipation. The second prelude changes the narrative dynamic as the readers' gaze shifts above from below. The transcendental and the divine is here humorously embodied in the anthropomorphous jealous angels who are just as interested in God's intentions as their human counterparts.

The inversion of the narrative perspective from below to above sets up an expectation of narrative privilege, otherwise associated with the narrator of the tetralogy, who has a bird's eye view of the story. The angels' position outside the patriarchal narrative in the second prelude also enables them to comment on it. Their narrative perspective is, however, delimited by their self-definition as a group antagonistic to mankind: God is discussed by the angels only in the context of his transactions with man. His traits, such as imprudence and obstinacy, and emotions such as embarrassment, are ascribed to Him by the angels based on a belief, motivated by jealousy and spite, that man is 'eine unleugbare Fehlschöpfung' (930) ['an undeniably botched creation' (1042)]. They are deeply offended by the existence of mankind, made in their image but fruitful, and humorously see its creation as a result of an 'Allmacht und Unumschränktheit im Hervorrufen' ['omnipotence that knows no boundaries in [...] calling things into being'], and a 'Bedürfnis nach Ausübung, dem puren Drange des "Nach diesem auch das noch"' (930) ['pure need to act and a pure urge for "if one thing, why not another"' (1042)]. God's other features, such as mercy and compassion, are deduced by the angels from the fact that he often spares the undeserving mankind.

Indeed, the angels' narrative privilege, their 'Teilhaberschaft an der Allwissenheit' ['share in omniscience'], and thus also their understanding of God's intentions, turns out to be 'beschränkt[]' (933) ['limited' (1046)]. They see Joseph's fall as a punishment for his presumption, a concession to their sense of righteousness and propriety, carried out 'unter dem Druck des Reiches des Strenge' (929) [as 'the result of pressure from the Realm of Sternness' (1041)]. In contrast, the narrator, who has an 'Einblick in ein oberstes Seelenleben' ['ability to peer into that most exalted mind'], reveals that in punishing Joseph God only appears to appease the angels, 'indem er die Kunst übt, zu heilen, womit er schlägt' (900) ['by practicing the art of healing even as He chastises' (1008)]. The angels' understanding is clouded by prejudice and their knowledge, in spite of their superior vantage point, is limited and based on rumour and unsupported opinion.[17] The intonation of the second prelude is that of an intimate conversation behind closed doors. The angels implicate the readers in their gossipy conversation and take them into their confidence by using phrases such as 'Unter uns gesagt' (933) ['Just between us' (1045)]. Behind the angels' rumour-mongering is an interpretative effort, similar to that of the patriarchs, an attempt to understand the intentions of an inscrutable God and His fascination with mankind. The angels' faux reverence for God, who is much criticized and ridiculed by them as obstinate, eccentric and misguided, coupled with their hostility towards mankind, leads them to suspect the involvement of an exiled fallen angel called Sammael, who, they believe, is manipulating God's desires and curiosity in order to cause Him embarrassment. In this context, the angels speak of God's suspected but 'unbeweisbare' (930) ['unverifiable' (1042)] clandestine relationship with Sammael, an intrigue, which they believe, centres on the latter's temptation of God with 'blutvoll-fleischliche Existenz als göttlicher Volksleib' (936) ['full-blooded, fleshly existence as the divine body of a nation' (1049)], His desire for immanence and vitality.[18] They judge God's choice of Abraham's community, whom they regard as unimpressive, as an embarrassing loss in status in relation to the other deities in a humorous reminder that the patriarchal world in the tetralogy is polytheistic. In addition, they fear that God will be unable to regain his defining features, 'Außerweltlichkeit, Allheit und Geistigkeit' ['extraworldly nature, His totality and spirituality'] and to return 'ins Jenseitig-Allgütig-Geistige' (937) ['to a beyond of spiritual omni-efficacy' (1050)] without the help of Abraham's community, who will have to first learn to understand him in these terms to enable his restoration. There is a comical incongruity in the fact that God is understood as transcendent, spiritual and all-embracing by the personified anthropomorphic angels. The angels' reliance on rumour to fill in the gaps in the narrative echoes Bulgakov's exploration of the role of myth-making in Yeshua's representation and legacy. At the same time, by stressing the central importance of the Jewish people in God's evolution from the immanent to the transcendent, Mann highlights the progressive and civilizing trajectory of their intellectual engagement with the notion of the divine. In their conceptualization of God, the patriarchs embody Mann's notion of the religious as 'sorgend achtsame Empfindlichkeit gegenüber den Regungen des Weltgeistes' ['a concerned, attentive receptivity to the movements of the universal spirit'].[19] In *Joseph* Abraham represents the entirety of humanity in his bold aspiration to serve only the highest. The enlightened humanism inherent in the patriarchs' intellectual effort in the novel, therefore, has a significance for mankind as a whole.

The angels' portrait of Yahweh is unreliable since it emerges from their self-centred holier-than-thou perspective. They posit themselves as the realm of severity and upholders of morality, who reject darkness in favour of light and evil in favour of good. From their subjective perspective, creation of mankind that introduces evil into the world is an incomprehensible act, a mistake which could only have been committed at the instigation of a rogue angel. The angels' moralistic posturing and self-presentation as the opposite to sinful mankind, however, turns out to be profoundly hypocritical. The story of their promiscuity with the daughters of man before the Deluge, repeated five times in the novel (sometimes as the story of Semhazai's pursuit of Ishchara), is brought up once again in the second prelude, only to be rejected by them as gossip.[20] Its reiteration undermines the angels' self-stylization as the Realm of Sternness, revealing that their misanthropy is simply masquerading as righteousness.

The angels' representation of God is not to be trusted for one other reason. In

Joseph God encompasses light and darkness, good and evil, and, as a result, thanks to the narrative logic of Mann's novel, vitality and creativity. In this context, mankind is 'das Produkt von Gottes Neugier nach Sich selbst' (931) ['the product of God's curiosity about Himself' (1044)] made in His image, His most faithful reflection and both good and evil. Pure light, represented by the angels and characters like Echnâton, is associated in the novel with decadence and impotence.[21] Unfruitful angels, [das] 'leid- und erlebnislose, nur eben zart klatschhafte Geschlecht' ['delicate gossipmongers, knowing neither suffering nor experience'], are unable to exploit the creative capital of language and do not have man's 'ideenverknüpfende[] Energie' (939) ['associative energy' (1052)]. In contrast, they use language only for gossip. As a result, they cannot fully grasp God's relationship with man.[22] This relationship is predicated on reciprocal reflection, encapsulated in Eliezer's paradoxical narrative, where Abraham, created by God, thinks Him into being. Man's imitation of God's creativity is an act of worship, unlike any that the angels can offer. Joseph, God's favourite, argues that worship should spring from the 'Anklang[] ans Höchste' ['harmony with what is Most High'], a bold and imaginative emulation of God and not 'langweilige[] Halleluja' (946) ['tedious hallelujah' (1060)], an expression which brings to mind the angels' formulaic praise in his dreams. Joseph takes this notion to its logical conclusion when he performs an act of ultimate devotion by narrativizing his entire life as a panegyric to God.

The borders between fiction and reality, as posited in *Joseph* and *The Master and Margarita*, in other words, the world of the patriarchs and the Soviet Moscow haunted by the Devil, are porous. The playful reversal of narrative perspective in the second prelude recalls the revelation in Bulgakov's novel that the poetic world of the Master's imagination is more true and real than the one which he has left behind. In *Joseph*, of course, both the world of the angels and that of the patriarchs emerge from stories recounted in, primarily but not exclusively, Jewish folklore and the Old Testament. God and the angels in the novel exist in the imagination of the select few members of Abraham's household, in their fictional entertaining stories and mythologization of personal experience. However, the angels also treat the world of the human characters as the 'erzählbare Welt des Geschehens' (934) ['narratable world of events' (1047)] created by God. This sentiment is, in fact, shared by Joseph who believes that 'Durch das Wort [...] war die Welt entstanden' (301) ['The world had come to be by the Word' (332)]. The two realities, where man thinks God into being and God creates man, exist in parallel to one another, as they do in Eliezer's story in 'Wie Abraham Gott entdeckte.' Both are true and logically irreconcilable. This creates an irresolvable contradiction or an Aporia, that is consistent with the notion of God's transcendence in *Joseph*, if He is defined as *Makom*, greater than his creations and thus impossible to comprehend with a human mind.[23] However, in *Joseph* the contradiction which is logically irresolvable, is mediated poetically through the rolling sphere.

In a sense, in both *Joseph* and *The Master and Margarita* the notions of Aporia and the divine are linked to the question of the ultimate creating authority behind the text. Yeshua is both the protagonist and the reader of the Master's fictional text.

Yahweh is man's creator and projection, paradoxically an authoring subject and object of man's stories. The angels are both the protagonists of Eliezer's stories and the narrators of Joseph's narrative, able to quote from it at will. The divine, in other words, is associated with the search for the origin of stories told in *Joseph*, mediated through a series of *mise en abyme* or frames which frustrate this search and lead the reader around in circles or, more accurately, up and down, following the movement of the rolling sphere.[24] The narrative and the divine define each other in the novel in terms underwritten by its idiosyncratic internal logic.[25]

There is one more shift in the narrative perspective in the second prelude that is worth mentioning here. The narrator interrupts the angels and reminds the readers that what they have before them is a novel, a fictional narrative:

> Um recht zu verstehen, was hier unterwegs und im Gange war, muß man sich bestimmter Daten und Nachrichten aus den Voraussetzungen und Vorspielen der hier laufenden Geschichte erinnern. Gemeint ist nichts anderes, als der "Roman der Seele", der dort mit den dafür zur Verfügung stehenden Worten kurz referiert wurde. (934).

> [In order to understand what was in progress and at work here, it is necessary to recall certain information and facts found in the premise and prelude to our current story. The reference here is to none other than the "romance of the soul" briefly recounted now in the terms available here. (1047)]

The playful self-referentiality of the text draws attention to its artifice, resulting in a metalepsis. The narrator identifies the romance of the soul as a meta-narrative by enclosing its title in quotation marks. Using his prerogative, he briefly steps outside the story, shifts between narrative levels and depicts God and the angels as narrative constructs, but not the constructs of the patriarchs. The angels' gossiping voices in that moment become the 'terms', to use Mann's word, in which the narrative humorously reflects back on itself.

Conclusion

Yahweh primarily appears in the novel as the subject of a series of narratives told by its characters and is constituted hermeneutically through their interpretative effort. His representation, like Yeshua's in *The Master and Margarita*, is polyphonic. In Eliezer's stories God is the highest, the transcendental prime cause but also the subject of delightful pleasurable fiction, a comical anthropomorphic figure. To the Abraham of the tradition, God is, amongst other things, the source of promises about fabulous posterity and land. Jacob and Joseph believe that Yahweh directs and sublimates their lives, an enterprise which requires their full attention and ingenuity for its proper execution. Their wider community, when not worshipping strange gods, looks to ancestral stories for new insights about Yahweh but also defines Him flexibly in terms of his relationship to the other deities in their cultural milieu. Finally, the angels regard God as a fallible eccentric, easily manipulated and motivated by incomprehensible needs. God represents different things to different sets of characters in the tetralogy but, common to all stories about Him, is His relationship with mankind, embodied in *Joseph* by Abraham's spiritual descendants, at once His means and object for sublimation and spiritual emancipation.

Mann's narrative strategy for depicting the divine is contradictory at its core. Yahweh's representation as an ingenious human construct, the highest, a transcendent spiritual deity, stands side by side with his portrayal as an anthropomorphic figure in the novel. At the heart of this contradiction is Mann's syncretic play with sources, such as the Old Testament, Gnostic myths and Jewish folklore, where the divine is imagined and pictured in different ways.[26] Some of these sources are deliberately more poetically integrated into the novel than others. The naïve and often humorous intonation of folkloric narratives contrasts with the patriarchs' interpretative effort, which sees God defined in abstract terms as an idea whose progressive humanist potential is significant for the entire human race.

The second prelude, which posits the angels as independent supernatural agents, is located in the beginning of what is the most secular volume of the novel.[27] Together with the apparitions of Ea and Joseph's angelic guide, it disrupts the narrative that consistently demythologizes the figure of God as a human projection and produces doubt. Abraham's doubt is depicted in the novel as a stimulus for his discovery and invention of God. The textual instances mentioned above have a similar generative effect by suggesting God's existence in the novel as a narrative possibility.[28] The novel portrays the figure of God as the characters' projection and provides psychological explanations for the visions they believe to be divinely inspired, but it also offers an idea of the divine as an inscrutable figure that exists on the level of text inhabited by the deity Ea.

Notes to Chapter 6

1. Berger points out that Mann's depiction of the Babylonian deity Ea-Oannes is informed by his reading of Alfred Jeremias, Bruno Meißner und Edgar Dacqué (Berger, *Die mythologischen Motive*, pp. 95–96). Bridges interprets Jacob's discovery of the spring as 'the result of his phallicism, water being a traditional attribute of the masculine principle' and ignores Ea (p. 40). George Bridges, *Thomas Mann's 'Joseph und seine Brüder' and the Phallic Theology of the Old Testament*, Stanford German Studies, 25 (Bern: Lang, 1995). Murdaugh argues that Mann connected Jacob 'with what might be the etymological ancestor of John the Baptist,' the fish-god Ea Oannes, to 'ornament' his role of 'prophet and harbinger for Christ' (Murdaugh, *Salvation in the Secular*, p. 54).

2. Lehnert, 'Thomas Manns Vorstudien', p. 472, and Berger, *Die mythologischen Motive*, p. 253. A number of scholars interpret the man as an angel. Maser suggests that his appearance was inspired by Ignaz Günther's 1763 statue *Guardian Angel* in Munich (p. 501). Edward A. Maser, 'Young Joseph's Guardian Angel: Salvage from a Case of Parallel Research', in *Art, the Ape of Nature. Studies in Honor of H. W. Janson*, ed. by Mosche Barasch, Lucy Freeman Sandler and Patricia Egan (New York, NY: Abrams, 1981), pp. 495–504. See also Hilary Heltay, 'Virtuosity in Thomas Mann's Later Narrative Technique', in *Thomas Mann*, ed. by Harold Bloom (New York, NY: Chelsea House Publishers, 1986), pp. 203–17 (p. 213) and Swensen, *Gods, Angels and Narrators*, p. 121. Nolte understands the man as 'not human' and consequently in possession of 'an interpreting consciousness' (Nolte, *Being and Meaning*, p. 150). Gerth sees the man in the field as a combination of three mythical entities: an angel from the romance of the soul or the second prelude, a Hermes figure and a New Testament angel (Gerth, *"Das Problem des Menschen"*, p. 188).

3. Cunningham argues that since neither Joseph nor Ruben see the man as a divine figure his function is 'only to broaden the reader's perspective, to add to the causality of earthly events a

vague and largely inconsequential element of divine superintendence' (Cunningham, *Myth and Politics*, p. 187).

4. Swensen reads this as a reminder from a 'higher authority — of the obligation he has to limit his divulgences and to conceal his identity' (Swensen, *Gods, Angels and Narrators*, p. 32).

5. Heltay mentions the man's 'unnatural insight into Joseph's family circumstances' and the 'latter's equally unnatural failure to react to it' (Heltay, 'Virtuosity', p. 213).

6. Compare with Swensen, *Gods, Angels and Narrators*, p. 34.

7. Swensen argues that the man and 'the angel-narrator seem to be one and the same' whose 'superior as such is the author' (Swensen, *Gods, Angels and Narrators*, p. 121).

8. Heltay also points out that Joseph's guard Kha'ma't quotes the man's words about the guard and the guarded (Heltay, 'Virtuosity', p. 211).

9. In this context Schwöbel interestingly writes that in the three monotheistic religions reading of sacred texts provides a key to understanding the world which is postulated as 'readable' ('lesbare Welt') (Schwöbel, *Die Religion des Zauberers*, p. 5).

10. Heltay reads the man here as Hermes and argues that his task is 'to sink into the soil of Reuben's subconscious mind the seed of expectation, or, in hermetic or mercurial terms, the knowledge of life beyond death' (Heltay, 'Virtuosity', p. 209). On a study of the ways in which metafictional narratives shift the burden and the responsibility of interpretation onto the readers by laying bare the conventions of storytelling, see Linda Hutcheon, *Narcissistic Narrative: the Metafictional Paradox*, University Paperbacks, 857 (New York, NY: Methuen, 1984), pp. 28–39.

11. Beck writes that the episode with Ruben features, for the first time in the novel, explicit reflection of the characters on the narrative in which they find themselves, voiced by the figures who are endowed with higher insights thanks to their unearthly nature (Beck, 'Thomas Manns Josephstetralogie', p. 52).

12. Heltay, 'Virtuosity', p. 203.

13. Hans Wysling and Cornelia Bernini, eds, *Jahre des Unmuts: Thomas Manns Briefwechsel mit René Schickele 1930–1949*, Thomas-Mann-Studien, 10 (Frankfurt a.M.: Klostermann, 1992), pp. 71 (3 July 1934). Compare with Heltay who argues that the man was 'consciously created [...] [supernatural] out of what might have been left as a simple human original' (Heltay, 'Virtuosity', p. 216).

14. Most scholars interpret the man in the field as a composite figure. Josipovici sees the man as Hermes Psychopompos, Satan and a Gnostic or a Manichean figure (Josipovici, *The Book of God*, pp. 282–83). Gerth understands him as a New Testament angel, the angel from the first and the second prelude and a Hermes figure (Gerth, *"Das Problem des Menschen"*, p. 188). Heltay sees the man as Anup-Hermanus, Hermes and the angel from the second prelude (Heltay, 'Virtuosity', p. 207, p. 205, p. 213). Murdaugh interprets him as Anubis but also as an angel, 'the divine messenger' and 'a rather ambiguous and still slightly demonic figure' (Murdaugh, *Salvation in the Secular*, p. 80). She reads God's messengers as 'bits of communication, and "intrusions" by the narrative consciousness into the unconsciousness or less conscious world "below"' (p. 79). Seen from this perspective, the man in the field is a messenger from 'the world of the narrator, of the highest moment of consciousness and deliberation in the novel which is playfully equated with "heaven"' (p. 82). In contrast, Beck argues that *Joseph* ironizes naive beliefs in divine providence, a heaven with God the Father and floating angels (Beck, 'Thomas Manns Josephstetralogie', pp. 53–54). He suggests that the man in the field is only a symbolical figure, who makes it seem that Joseph's fate is guided by God even if he admits that his supernatural nature is not fully repealed (p. 53).

15. For Mann's sources for the 'Urmensch' myth and the romance of the soul see Berger, *Die mythologischen Motive*, p. 245 and p. 247.

16. Compare with Swensen: 'The content of the legendary and mythical story is no longer treated as an expression of human imagination and thus an object for a history of ideas, but as a reality that is an object for a history of persons and events' (Swensen, *Gods, Angels and Narrators*, p. 58).

17. Vogelmann highlights the problematic nature of the angels' claims, their tendency to treat their own conjectures as facts which then serve as the basis for the next conjecture (Vogelmann, *Konstellationen von Mythos und Erzählen*, pp. 40–41).

18. Hamburger notes that Mann drew on Gnostic thought to describe the relationship of God and man as that between 'de[m] freien Ich mit der gebundenen Weltmaterie im Menschen' [the free I with the trapped world matter in man] (Hamburger, *Thomas Manns biblisches Werk*, p. 101). In the novel Mann conceives of a people or a tribe as a body, 'eine körperlich-materielle Substanz' [a bodily-material substance] that stands in the same relationship to God's spiritual entity as body towards soul (Hamburger, *Thomas Manns biblisches Werk*, p. 106). Fischer points out that one of the inspirations for the narrative of Yahweh as a biological tribal deity is Oskar Goldberg's *Die Wirklichkeit der Hebräer*. However, Mann reinterprets its wording where Yahweh's victory over the other Elohim implies 'die schließliche Weltherrschaft des auserwählten Volkes' [the ultimate world domination by a chosen people] (Fischer, *Handbuch*, p. 692). God's expedition into matter becomes a means for the Jews to learn his true nature in the novel and Goldberg's 'völkische Terminologie' [völkisch terminology] is given to Sammael (Fischer, *Handbuch*, pp. 691–92). Wolters writes in this context that only through a secularization of God's biological existence and a secular 'Verantwortungsethik' [ethics of responsibility] is it possible to engage with the fascist phenomenon from a moral perspective (Wolters, *Zwischen Metaphysik und Politik*, p. 288).

19. Kerényi, *Gespräch in Briefen*, p. 75. *Mythology*, p. 74 (7 October 1936).

20. See bin Gorion, '*Die Sagen der Juden*', p. 130.

21. See Berger, *Die mythologischen Motive*, p. 254.

22. Compare with Vogelmann who argues that the unfruitful angels cannot experience the 'Prozesshaftigkeit' [the processuality] associated with life which is thus not comprehensible to them as the basis for decision making or as a measure of judgement (Vogelmann, *Konstellationen von Mythos und Erzählen*, p. 44). Swensen similarly posits that because of the angels' 'austere purity they are unable to comprehend complexities' (Swensen, *Gods, Angels and Narrators*, p. 37).

23. Koopmann links Mann's notion of 'Weltgeist' [world spirit] to Aporia but only in passing, p. 41. See Helmut Koopmann, 'Ist Gott eine Hilfskonstruktion? Thomas Mann zur Religion, in seinen Essays', in *Zwischen Himmel und Hölle: Thomas Mann und die Religion. Die Davoser Literaturtage 2010*, ed. by Thomas Sprecher, Thomas-Mann-Studien, 44 (Frankfurt a.M.: Klostermann, 2012), pp. 35–52.

24. Swensen writes that beneath 'each story-teller's veil is always just another veiled story-teller', (Swensen, *Gods, Angels and Narrators*, p. 96).

25. Kurzke writes that Mann's God is a literary figure and that a God whom we encounter in texts is literature (p. 10). See Hermann Kurzke, *Der gläubige Thomas. Glaube und Sprache bei Thomas Mann*, Schriften des Ortsvereins Bonn-Köln der Deutschen Thomas-Mann-Gesellschaft e.V., 1 (Bonn: Bernstein, 2009).

26. In this context Berger writes about the 'souveräne Freiheit' [sovereign freedom] in the treatment of heterogeneous literary narratives that distinguishes the novel (Berger, *Die mythologischen Motive*, p. 120)

27. Hamburger asserts that in the fourth volume, Joseph's story becomes an invention of God precisely because it is plainly and unequivocally a narrative about man and not an ambiguous narrative about gods (Hamburger, *Thomas Manns biblisches Werk*, p. 75).

28. I am indebted to Professor Martin Swales for the term 'narrative possibility' in relation to the argument here.

CONCLUSION

❖

Joseph and His Brothers and *The Master and Margarita* represent unique literary phenomena in their contemporary culture. Yet what is said about one is often also true for the other. Bulgakov and Mann's masterpieces fill in the gaps in the scripture, imaginatively and often humorously probing and teasing out its characters' desires and motivations. In the process they interrogate and expand the biblical text, psychologizing and humanizing it in the midrashic exegetic tradition. Their poetic versions of biblical narratives, which both de- and remythologize the source text in the process of the telling, are characterized by syncretism and rich intertextuality.

One of the most intriguing similarities between *Joseph* and *The Master and Margarita* is their metafictional complexity: both novels play with conventions of storytelling, self-reflexively laying bare its processes.[1] At the very heart of this literary play is a reflection on the figure of an artist–creator, an inventor of a God, an author of a novel about Pontius Pilate. Fascination with the nature of human creativity is central to both Bulgakov and Mann's writing and it is a subject powerfully explored in the ways in which their vivid literary versions of biblical stories claim for themselves the status of an absolute artistic truth.

Joseph and His Brothers and *The Master and Margarita* treat the Bible as a source of universal significance, a text that lends itself to a poetic exploration of the human question. The divine provides a framework for the elucidation of the human. However, the religious also acquires a different moral and ethical meaning when it becomes aligned with the ideological values of an authoritarian state, as was the case in Soviet Russia and Nazi Germany.[2] Bulgakov and Mann's novels transcend their cultural, historical and literary contexts. They are greater than their time. Their political dimension should not, therefore, be overemphasized, but neither can it be ignored.

Mann and Bulgakov employ a deliberately contradictory narrative strategy for representing Christ and Yahweh. They demystify and desacralize their divine protagonists but leave the possibility of the existence of the transcendent open in the text, defined in both novels in narrative terms. This strategy creates uncertainty and results in the coexistence of two mutually exclusive, irreconcilable readings of Yeshua and Yahweh, or an Aporia, a perplexing difficulty. The feeling of doubt created through the incongruities and ambiguities inherent to the depictions of Yahweh and Yeshua operates as a dramatization of faith, if the latter is defined as belief, rather than certain knowledge.[3] By virtue of evading straightforward categorization and representation, Bulgakov's Yeshua and Mann's Yahweh are symbolically placed beyond the reach of anti-Semitic and anti-religious ideologues. Ineffable and contradictory, they represent a uniquely artistic truth.

Bulgakov and Mann's very interest in the gospels and the Old Testament in the political and cultural climate of atheist Soviet Russia and increasingly anti-Semitic Germany is significant.[4] Indeed, there are many ways in which each of the two novels clearly reflects back on its time. The Stalinist context, displaced from the Moscow narrative strand, is actualized in Yershalaim in *The Master and Margarita*.[5] The Passion of Christ plays out in a city of informers and secret police, political trials and interrogations. The Egyptian Amun cult in *Joseph* espouses the militaristic ethos and rhetoric of the Nazis.[6] Joseph's words about the consequences of the misuse of power are a direct challenge to Hitler's politics.[7]

There are, however, other subtle ways in which the narrative complexities of these two novels reflect back on the political and cultural backgrounds from which they have emerged, in strikingly similar ways. Mann and Bulgakov's narrative strategies for engaging with biblical texts and their divine protagonists may also be read as a mode of literary interaction with the monologist culture of Soviet and German totalizing states. The politicization of debates surrounding biblical criticism in Germany and Soviet Russia reflected a broader movement towards ideological homogeneity and orthodoxy. Policing of cultural production in this context took many forms: censorship, the banning and burning of books, the dismantling of professional literary bodies and, in Soviet Russia, social command and an official endorsement of Socialist Realism as the dominant artistic method. Polyphony, central to the depiction of Yeshua and Yahweh as objects of multiple conflicting and, crucially, subjective points of view, is symbolically antithetical to the hegemony of a single narrative voice associated with an authoritarian state.[8] In this context, the productive power of language, its ability to create multiple truths, acquires symbolical capital.

Monologism is also powerfully indicted in *The Master and Margarita*, when Korovyev persuades a group of Entertainment Commission employees to join in a song.[9] He vanishes, but his victims continue to sing in unison, some in tears but unable to stop, intoning a prisoners' song against their will: 'хористы рассеянные в разных местах, пели очень складно, как будто весь хор стоял, не спуская глаз с невидимого дирижера' (672) ['although the choristers were scattered throughout different rooms, they sang very harmoniously, as if the whole chorus were standing in one place with its eyes glued to an invisible conductor' (161)]. The polyphony and subjectivity of *The Master and Margarita* is symbolically juxtaposed to such harmonious singing orchestrated by the invisible demonic conductor.

It would be a disservice to *Joseph* and *The Master and Margarita* to narrowly interpret them as commentaries on any particular contemporary debate. They are read here in the light of the shift in biblical hermeneutics and its politicization, as outlined in the introduction, only in order to illuminate their poetic complexities and their engagement with the scripture. In this context, the use of biblical exegesis, as a legitimating basis for state-sponsored anti-religious and anti-Semitic projects in Soviet Russia and Germany, is humorously neutralized in Bulgakov and Mann's novels through the persistent ironicization of the Bible as an authoritative text. The novels playfully suggest different ways in which events depicted in the gospels and the Pentateuch may be subject to misunderstanding, misrepresentation and distortion, both inadvertent and deliberate, often because of institutional pressure to legitimate a specific political agenda. Through narrative irony and depicting the canonical Bible as contingent, the novels implicitly discredit its use in service of ideas, such as, for example, the quest for the 'authentic' historical Christ.[10] In *Joseph*, Nineveh cuneiform texts which suggest that Babylonian myths had a formative influence on Judaism are represented as copies of copies of texts 'aus Gott weiß welcher Vorzeit' (15) ['from God knows what ancient time' (12)], relativizing their authority. Attempts to reconstruct such a distant past, Mann's narrator implies, will always involve a degree of fictionalization. Indeed, Mann called his narrator's approach to the biblical narrative in the tetralogy a 'Wahrheitsspaß' [an amusing game with the truth].[11]

Political implications of tendentious biblical exegesis are diffused in *The Master and Margarita* and *Joseph* in many ways. *Joseph* treats the Jewish God Yahweh as the patriarchs' ingenious invention, shaped by the creative appropriation of Near Eastern myths. In the process, it poetically reclaims myth from the Nazis and retells Old Testament stories from a humanist perspective, bringing the Hebrew Bible to life in German at a time when there were attempts to 'dejudaize' Christianity. In Mann's novel, borrowing from Babylonian mythology by the Jewish characters, interpreted as a sign of Judaism's inauthenticity and irrelevance in anti-Semitic circles in Germany, is cast as a positive syncretic act. Eliezer resignifies and 'judaizes' the Babylonian creation myth and appropriates its imagery when he claims that it was Abraham's God who had defeated the dragon of chaos and that 'der Jubelruf, mit dem bei der Schöpfung die Götter den Mardug gegrüßt hatten [...] gebührte Ihm' (313) ['the cries of jubilation with which the gods had greeted Mardug at creation [...] belonged by rights to Him' (347)].[12] Joseph's use of Etana's narrative in his Metatron dream is depicted as a similarly creative act. The process of borrowing from other systems of religious belief by Jewish characters is celebrated in *Joseph* as an expression of ingenuity and creativity.

The Master and Margarita engages with both historicist and mythological schools of biblical criticism, subverting their arguments by reproducing them and instilling them with ambiguity. Berlioz's claim that Christ is a myth, modelled on dying and resurrecting fertility deities of antiquity, is effectively contradicted in the novel by the Yershalaim narrative that vividly represents the Christian messiah as a historical figure, a mortal named Yeshua Ha-Notsri.[13] However, the Yershalaim chapters, which secularize and demystify the biblical text, are framed as the Master's work, itself, of course, part of Bulgakov's novel, its status as a fictional narrative playfully emphasized through a series of *mise en abyme*.[14] *Joseph* and *The Master and Margarita* parody the endeavour to reconstruct 'authentic' biblical events by explicitly setting up their versions of Old and New Testament stories, ostensibly framed as eyewitness accounts, as fictions, and thus humorously debunking truth claims which emerge from biblical criticism.

Notes to the Conclusion

1. See Hutcheon for the concept of a metafictional 'narcissistic' narrative defined as 'process made visible' (Hutcheon, *Narcissistic Narrative*, p. 6).

2. For Cunningham, *Joseph*'s engagement with myth, 'a politically loaded concept', gives it 'an inherent political dimension from start to finish' (Cunningham, *Myth and Politics*, p. 303). Beck similarly argues that *Joseph*'s engagement with its time hinges on its consideration of the problem of myth in the modern world (Beck 'Thomas Manns Josephstetralogie', p. 75). Schwöbel writes that Mann's novel draws attention to the fact that the religious sign system has a cultural significance and thus also concrete social and political implications (Schwöbel, *Die Religion des Zauberers*, pp. 274–75). Also see Wolters, *Zwischen Metaphysik und Politik*, p. 58 and p. 121.

3. Pope: 'the answer lies *somewhere* in the tension among the various possibilities, which, in a sense, is the same situation we often find in myth or in the Four Gospels' (pp. 17–18). Richard W. F. Pope, 'Ambiguity and Meaning in *The Master and Margarita*: The Role of Afranius', *Slavic Review*, 36 (1977), 1–24.

4. Borchmeyer identifies *Joseph*'s very 'Heiterkeit' [cheerfulness] and epic humour as a means of aesthetic resistance to the horror of the Nazi time (pp. 208–09). Dieter Borchmeyer, 'Heiterkeit contra Faschismus. Eine Betrachtung über Thomas Manns Josephsromane', in *Heiterkeit. Konzepte in Literatur und Geistesgeschichte*, ed. by Petra Kiedaisch and Jochen A. Bär (Munich: Fink, 1977), pp. 203–18. Wright asserts that Mann 'discovered in religion [...] the values necessary to withstand the threat of fascism' (Wright, *The Genesis of Fiction*, p. xi).

5. Proffer points out that one of the key similarities between Yershalaim and Moscow lies in 'the ways in which a tyranny is maintained through spies, denunciations and simple fear' (Proffer, *Bulgakov*, p. 532). Haber reads Yeshua as embodying 'spiritual power, which resides within individuals and prevents even the most tyrannical of states from totally obliterating personal creativity and independence of thought' (Haber, 'The Mythic Bulgakov', p. 357). Elbaum, too, makes a case for Yeshua as 'a symbolical character, typifying, in a most general form, the courage and stamina of those who defy the established order' (Elbaum, 'The Evolution of *The Master and Margarita*', p. 86).

6. Cunningham, *Myth and Politics*, p. 213.

7. Cunningham sees Joseph as a Roosevelt figure, 'a fictional portrayal of anti-Hitler' (Cunningham, *Myth and Politics*, pp. 203–04). Hartwich writes that Mann's depiction of 'Hebrew antiquity' in *Joseph*, which combines tradition with '"left-wing" humanism', represents an 'alternative to the anti-bourgeois, reactionary mass ideology of National Socialism' (Hartwich, 'Religion and Culture', p. 153).

8. Gudkova writes that '[i]n years when there was one official point of view on everything, Bulgakov retained an individual, personal, defiantly subjective vision' (p. 26). She remarks that an 'official point of view' is a 'fiction, something for which no one person is responsible', a situation 'impossible' in literature and 'in Bulgakov's novel events of world history are polemically refracted through one person's individual perception' (p. 26). Violetta Gudkova, 'From Salon to Samizdat', trans. by Lesley Milne, in *Bulgakov. The Novelist-Playwright*, ed. by Lesley Milne, Russian Theatre Archive, 5 (Luxembourg: Harwood, 1995), pp. 15–28.

9. Also see Liakhova, 'Dramatizm lichnogo slova', pp. 170–71.

10. In 1940 the *Institute for the Study and Eradication of Jewish Influence on German Church Life* published a dejudaized version of the New Testament *Die Botschaft Gottes* (*The Message of God*), a 'Volkstestament' [a people's testament] free from the 'many layers of later accretions within the text' (Heschel, *The Aryan Jesus*, pp. 106–08, (p. 108)). See also Clayton Koelb, *Legendary Figures: Ancient History in Modern Novels* (Lincoln: University of Nebraska Press, 1998). Koelb writes that *Joseph* 'presents us with a concept of history based firmly in rhetoric' (p. 58), whereas Lawson posits that 'the dogma of fascist ideology is parodied by the ironic narrator' through 'Mann's narrative method' which 'undermines excessive claims to authority' (pp. 174–75).

11. Kerényi, *Gespräch in Briefen*, p. 74. Mann described his narrator's erudition as a mask or a device and characterized *Joseph* as 'Pseudo-Essayistik', [ein] 'Spiel, dessen Regel das Festhalten an den Daten der Bibel ist, als wären sie "wissenschaftlich"' [a pseudo-essay, a game whose rules

involve the adherence to the dates of the Bible as if they were scientific] (Robert Faesi, ed, *Thomas Mann. Robert Faesi. Briefwechsel* (Zurich: Atlantis, 1962), p. 30). See also Hendrik Birus, ' "Nun weiß man doch, wie sich das alles in Wirklichkeit zugetragen hat!" Thomas Manns *Joseph und seine Brüder* als simulierte Mimesis', in *Mimesis und Simulation*, ed. by Andreas Kablitz and Gerhard Neumann, Rombach Wissenschaften. Reihe Litterae, 52 (Freiburg: Rombach, 1998), pp. 89–118. Niklaus also writes about Mann's attempt to approach the divine spirit using narrative means, thus preventing any 'Missbrauch' [abuse] of the absolute (p. 32). Peter Niklaus, 'Religion und Ironie', in *Zwischen Himmel und Hölle: Thomas Mann und die Religion. Die Davoser Literaturtage 2010*, ed. by Thomas Sprecher, Thomas-Mann-Studien, 44 (Frankfurt a.M.: Klostermann, 2012), pp. 17–33.

12. Hamburger notes that Eliezer connects the Jewish patriarchal world with the Babylonian cultural and mythical tradition (Hamburger, *Thomas Manns biblisches Werk*, p. 135). Fischer points out that Yahweh appears as a slayer of either the dragon or a serpent (depending on the translation of the Bible) in the Book of Job 26. 13 and Isaiah 51. 9 (Fischer, *Handbuch*, p. 328).

13. Pittman writes that '[b]y endowing the story with the guise of historicity' Bulgakov 'succeeded in ridiculing the Soviet atheists' unwitting rejection of the Christian myth, as well as in exposing the inadequacies of the rationalistic criteria, by which they had sought to prove that Jesus Christ did not exist' (Pittman, *The Writer's Divided Self*, p. 163).

14. In this context it might be interesting to consider *Joseph* and the Yershalaim chapters of Bulgakov's novel as 'historiographic meta-fictions,' in other words, as works which situate themselves 'within historical discourse without surrendering [their] autonomy as fiction' (Hutcheon, *Narcissistic Narrative*, p. 4); that is, of course, if the Bible is taken to be a historical document.

BIBLIOGRAPHY

❖

ACKRILL, JOHN LLOYD, ed, *A New Aristotle Reader* (Oxford: Clarendon, 1987)

AMERT, SUSAN, 'The Dialectics of Closure in Bulgakov's *Master and Margarita*', *Russian Review*, 61 (2002), 599–617

AMUSIN, MARK, '"Your Novel has Some More Surprises in Store for You" (The Specificity of the Fantastic in *The Master and Margarita*)', *Russian Studies in Literature*, 42 (2005–06), 80–91

APPELFELD, AHARON, 'The Bible and Thomas Mann', in *Vom Weitläufigen Erzählen*, ed. by Manfred Papst and Thomas Sprecher, Thomas-Mann-Studien, 38 (Frankfurt a.M.: Klostermann, 2008), pp. 63–71

ASSMANN, JAN, *Thomas Mann und Ägypten. Mythos und Monotheismus in den Josephsromanen* (Munich: Beck, 2006)

—— 'Zitathaftes Leben. Thomas Mann und die Phänomenologie der kulturellen Erinnerung', *Thomas-Mann-Jahrbuch*, 6 (1994), 133–58

AVINS, CAROL, 'Reaching a Reader: The Master's Audience in *The Master and Margarita*', *Slavic Review*, 45 (1986), 272–85

BAKER, HAROLD D., 'Socratic, Hermetic, and Internally Convincing Dialogue: Types of Interlocution in Bulgakov's *The Master and Margarita*', *Russian Review*, 57 (1998), 53–71

—— 'Voland's Seventh Proof: The Event in Bulgakov's *Master i Margarita*', *Russian, Croatian and Serbian, Czech and Slovak, Polish Literature*, 49 (2001), 1–23

BARRATT, ANDREW, *Between Two Worlds: A Critical Introduction to 'The Master and Margarita'* (Oxford: Clarendon, 1987)

BEATIE, BRUCE A. and PHYLLIS W. POWELL, 'Bulgakov, Dante, and Relativity', *Canadian-American Slavic Studies*, 15 (1981), 250–70

—— 'Story and Symbol: Notes Toward a Structural Analysis of Bulgakov's *The Master and Margarita*', *Russian Literature Triquarterly*, 15 (1978), 219–38

BECK, HELMUT, 'Thomas Manns Josephstetralogie und das Gestaltungsprinzip der epischen Ironie', in *Betrachtungen und Überblicke zum Werk Thomas Manns*, ed. by Georg Wenzel (Berlin: Aufbau, 1966), pp. 11–106

BELZA, IGOR F., 'Genealogiia *Mastera i Margarity*', *Kontekst*, 78 (1978), 156–248

BENSCH, GISELA, *Träumerische Ungenauigkeiten: Traum und Traumbewusstsein im Romanwerk Thomas Manns: 'Buddenbrooks' — 'Der Zauberberg' — 'Joseph und seine Brüder'* (Göttingen: V & R Unipress, 2004)

BERGER, WILLY R., *Die mythologischen Motive in Thomas Manns Roman 'Joseph und seine Brüder'*, Literatur und Leben. Neue Folge, 14 (Cologne: Böhlau, 1971)

BETHEA, DAVID M., 'History as Hippodrome: The Apocalyptic Horse and Rider in *The Master and Margarita*', *Russian Review*, 41 (1982), 373–99

BIRUS, HENDRIK, '"Nun weiß man doch, wie sich das alles in Wirklichkeit zugetragen hat!" Thomas Manns *Joseph und seine Brüder* als simulierte Mimesis', in *Mimesis und Simulation*, ed. by Andreas Kablitz and Gerhard Neumann, Rombach Wissenschaften. Reihe Litterae, 52 (Freiburg: Rombach, 1998), pp. 89–118

BOND, GREG, '"Der Brunnen der Vergangenheit": Historical Narration in Uwe Johnson's

Heute neunzig Jahr and Thomas Mann's *Joseph und seine Brüder'*, *German Life and Letters*, 52 (1999), 68–84

BORCHMEYER, DIETER, 'Heiterkeit contra Faschismus. Eine Betrachtung über Thomas Manns Josephsromane', in *Heiterkeit. Konzepte in Literatur und Geistesgeschichte*, ed. by Petra Kiedaisch and Jochen A. Bär (Munich: Fink, 1977), pp. 203–18

—— '"Zurück zum Anfang aller Dinge." Mythos und Religion in Thomas Manns "Josephsromanen"', *Thomas-Mann-Jahrbuch*, 11 (1998), 9–29

BRANDES, GEORG, *Jesus: A Myth*, trans. by Edwin Björkman (London: Brentano, 1927)

BRAUN, JULIUS, *Naturgeschichte der Sage*, 2 vols (Munich: Bruckmann, 1864–65), I (1864)

BRIDGES, GEORGE, *Thomas Mann's 'Joseph und seine Brüder' and the Phallic Theology of the Old Testament*, Stanford German Studies, 25 (Bern: Lang, 1995)

BUKOWSKI, EVELYN, 'Jüdisches Erzählen und mythische Erinnerung in Thomas Manns *Joseph*-Romanen', in *Thomas Mann (1875–1955)*, ed. by Walter Delabar and Bodo Plachta, Memoria, 5 (Berlin: Weidler, 2005), pp. 169–80

BULGAKOV, MIKHAIL A., *Belaia gvardiia. Teatral'nyi roman. Master i Margarita*, ed. by V. Volina, Anna Saakiants and A. Vinogradov (Moscow: Khudozhestvennaia literatura, 1973)

—— '*Master i Margarita': Polnoe sobranie chernovikov romana. Osnovnoi tekst. V dvukh tomakh*, ed. by Elena Iu. Kolysheva, 2 vols (Moscow: Pashkov dom, 2014)

—— *"Moi bednyi, bednyi master..." Polnoe sobranie redaktsii i variantov romana 'Master i Margarita,'* ed. by Viktor I. Losev (Moscow: Vagrius, 2006)

—— *Sobranie sochinenii v piati tomakh*, ed by Gennadii S. Gots and others, 5 vols (Moscow: Khudozhestvennaia literatura, 1989–1990), V: *'Master i Margarita'. Pis'ma*, ed. by Lidiia Ianovskaia, Violetta Gudkova and Elena Zemskaia (1990)

—— *Sobraniie sochinenii v vos'mi tomakh*, ed. by Losev, Viktor I., 8 vols (St. Petersburg: Azbuka-klassika, 2002–04)

—— *The Master and Margarita*, trans. by Diana Burgin and Katherine Tiernan O'Connor (London: Picador, 1997)

CHEDROVA, A., 'Khristianskie aspekty romana Mikhaila Bulgakova *Master i Margarita*', *NovZ*, 160 (1985), 175–83

CHUDAKOVA, MARIETTA, 'Tvorcheskaia istoriia romana M. Bulgakova *Master i Margarita*', *Voprosy Literatury*, 20 (1976), 218–53

—— *Zhizneopisanie Mikhaila Bulgakova*, 2nd edn (Moscow: Kniga, 1988)

CUNNINGHAM, RAYMOND, *Myth and Politics in Thomas Mann's 'Joseph und seine Brüder'*, Stuttgarter Arbeiten zur Germanistik 161 (Stuttgart: Heinz, 1985)

CURTIS, JULIE A. E., *Bulgakov's Last Decade: The Writer as Hero* (Cambridge: Cambridge University Press, 1987)

—— *Manuscripts Don't Burn. Mikhail Bulgakov: A Life in Letters and Diaries*, trans. by Julie A. E. Curtis (London: Bloomsbury, 2012)

—— *Mikhail Bulgakov*, Critical Lives (London: Reaktion Books, 2017)

DAIAN, G., 'K istorii religii', *Bezbozhnik*, November 1926, pp. 11–14

DAVIES, J. M. Q., 'Bulgakov: Atheist or "Militant Old Believer"? *The Master and Margarita* Reconsidered', *ASEES*, 6 (1992), 125–33

DELITZSCH, FRIEDRICH, *Die grosse Täuschung. Kritische Betrachtungen zu den alttestamentlichen Berichten über Israels Eindringen in Kanaan, die Gottesoffenbarung vom Sinai und die Wirksamkeit der Propheten*, 2 vols (Stuttgart: Deutsche Verlags-Anstalt, 1920), I

—— *Zweiter Vortrag über Babel und Bibel. 26. bis 30. Tausend. Mit 20 Abbildungen und einem Wort 'Zur Klärung'* (Stuttgart: Deutsche Verlags-Anstalt, 1903)

DRAVE, ELISABETH, 'Strukturen jüdischer Bibelauslegung in Thomas Manns Roman *Joseph und seine Brüder*: das Beispiel Abraham', in *Bibel und Literatur*, ed. by Jürgen Ebach and Richard Faber (Munich: Fink, 1995), pp. 195–213

DREWS, ARTHUR, *The Christ Myth*, 3rd edn, trans. and rev. by Cecil Delisle Burns (London: Fisher Unwin, 1910)

EDWARDS, T. R. N., *Three Russian Writers and the Irrational. Zamyatin, Pil'nyak and Bulgakov* (Cambridge: Cambridge University Press, 1982)

EHINGER, FRANZISKA, *Gesang und Stimme im Erzählwerk von Gottfried Keller, Eduard von Keyserling und Thomas Mann*, Epistemata Reihe Literaturwissenschaft, 516 (Würzburg: Königshausen und Neumann, 2004)

EL'BAUM, GENRIKH, *Analiz Iudeiskikh Glav 'Mastera i Margarity' M. Bulgakova* (Ann Arbor, MI: Ardis, 1981)

ELBAUM, HENRY, 'The Evolution of *The Master and Margarita*: Text, Context, Intertext', *Canadian Slavonic Papers*, 37 (1995), 59–87

ERICSON, EDWARD E., 'The Satanic Incarnation: Parody in Bulgakov's *The Master and Margarita*', *Russian Review*, 33 (1974), 20–36

FAESI, ROBERT, ED, *Thomas Mann. Robert Faesi. Briefwechsel* (Zurich: Atlantis, 1962)

FARYNO, JERZY, 'Istoriia o Pontii Pilate', *Russian, Croatian and Serbian, Czech and Slovak, Polish Literature*, 18 (1985), 43–62

FEUERLICHT, IGNACE, 'Der Erzähler bei Thomas Mann', *German Quarterly*, 43 (1970), 418–34

FIENE, DONALD M., 'A Comparison of the Soviet and Possev Editions of *The Master and Margarita*, with a Note on Interpretation of the Novel', *Canadian-American Slavic Studies*, 15 (1981), 330–54

——'"Pilatism" in Mikhail Bulgakov's *Master i Margarita*', in *Bulgakov: The Novelist-Playwright*, ed. by Lesley Milne, Russian Theatre Archive, 5 (Luxembourg: Harwood, 1995), pp. 125–39

FISCHER, BERND-JÜRGEN, *Handbuch zu Thomas Manns "Josephsromanen"* (Tübingen: Francke, 2002)

FRANK, MARGOT K., 'The Mystery of the Master's Final Destination', *Canadian-American Slavic Studies*, 15 (1981), 287–94

FREI, HANS W., *The Eclipse of Biblical Narrative: A Study in Eighteenth and Nineteenth Century Hermeneutics* (New Haven, CT: Yale University Press, 1974)

GASPAROV, BORIS M., 'Iz nabliudenii nad motivnoi strukturoi romana M. A. Bulgakova *Master i Margarita*', *Daugava*, 10 (1988), 96–106; 11 (1988), 88–96; 12 (1988), 105–13; 1 (1989), 78–90

GERTH, KLAUS, *"Das Problem des Menschen". Zu Leben und Werk Thomas Manns* (Seelze: Friedrich, 2004)

GOLSTEIN, VLADIMIR, 'What Does a Saint Do amidst MASSOLIT Revelers? Mikhail Bulgakov, Father John of Kronstadt, and Julien Benda's *La Trahison des clercs*', *Russian Review*, 63 (2004), 673–87

GORION, MICHA JOSEF BIN, *'Die Sagen der Juden': Mythen, Legenden, Auslegungen gesammelt von Micha Josef bin Gorion*, 3rd edn (Berlin: Schocken, 1935)

GUDKOVA, VIOLETTA, 'From Salon to Samizdat', trans. by Lesley Milne, in *Bulgakov*, ed. by Lesley Milne, Russian Theatre Archive, 5 (Luxembourg: Harwood, 1995), pp. 15–28

HABER, EDYTHE C., 'The Lamp with the Green Shade: Mikhail Bulgakov and His Father', *Russian Review*, 44 (1985), 333–50

——'The Mythic Bulgakov: *The Master and Margarita* and Arthur Drews's *The Christ Myth*', *Slavic and East European Journal*, 43 (1999), 347–60

——'The Mythic Structure of Bulgakov's *The Master and Margarita*', *Russian Review*, 34 (1975), 382–409

HAMBURGER, KÄTE, *Thomas Manns biblisches Werk: Der Joseph-Roman, Die Moses-Erzählung, "Das Gesetz"*, Fischer Taschenbücher, 1280 (Frankfurt a.M.: Fischer, 1984)

HART, PIERRE R., 'The Master and Margarita as Creative Process', Modern Fiction Studies, 19 (1973), 169–78

HARTWICH, WOLF-DANIEL, 'Religion and Culture: Joseph and his Brothers', trans. by Ritchie Robertson, in The Cambridge Companion to Thomas Mann, ed. by Ritchie Robertson (Cambridge: Cambridge University Press, 2006), pp. 151–67

HATFIELD, HENRY C., 'Myth versus Secularism: Religion in Thomas Mann's Joseph', in Crisis and Continuity in Modern German Fiction: Ten Essays, ed. by Henry Hatfield (Ithaca, NY: Cornell University Press, 1969), pp. 78–89

HEFTRICH, ECKHARD, 'Der Homo oeconomicus im Werk Thomas Mann', in Vom Märchenhelden zum Manager. Beiträge zum Ökonomieverständnis in der Literatur, ed. by Werner Wunderlich, Facetten deutscher Literatur, St Galler Studien, 2 (Bern: Haupt, 1989), pp. 153–69

HELLERSBERG-WENDRINER, ANNA, Mystik der Gottesferne. Eine Interpretation Thomas Manns (Bern: Francke, 1960)

HELTAY, HILARY, 'Virtuosity in Thomas Mann's Later Narrative Technique', in Thomas Mann, ed. by Harold Bloom (New York, NY: Chelsea House Publishers, 1986), pp. 203–17

HESCHEL, SUSANNAH, The Aryan Jesus. Christian Theologians and the Bible in Nazi Germany (Princeton, NJ: Princeton University Press, 2008)

HEUMANN, FRED S., 'Some Major Biblical Sources in Thomas Mann's Joseph Tetralogy', Notre Dame English Journal, 14 (1982), 87–112

HOHMEYER, JÜRGEN, Thomas Manns Roman 'Joseph und seine Brüder'. Studien zu einer gemischten Erzählsituation, Marburger Beiträge zur Germanistik, 2 (Marburg: Elwert, 1965)

HUGHES, KENNETH, 'The Sources and Function of Serach's Song in Thomas Mann's Joseph, der Ernährer', Germanic Review, 45 (1970), 126–33

——— 'Theme and Structure in Thomas Mann's Die Geschichten Jaakobs', Monatshefte, 62 (1970), 24–36

HÜHN, PETER, JOHN PIER, WOLF SCHMID and JÖRG SCHÖNERT, eds, Handbook of Narratology (New York, NY: Walter de Gruyter, 2009)

HUTCHEON, LINDA, Narcissistic Narrative: the Metafictional Paradox, University Paperbacks, 857 (New York, NY: Methuen, 1984)

IANOVSKAIA, LIDIIA, 'Pontii Pilat i Yeshua Ga-Notsri. V zerkalakh bulgakovedeniia', Voprosy Literatury, 3 (2010), 5–72

——— Treugol'nik Volanda: K istorii romana 'Master i Margarita' (Kiev: Libid', 1992)

——— Tvorcheskii put' Mikhaila Bulgakova (Moscow: Sovetskii Pisatel', 1983)

——— Zapiski o Mikhaile Bulgakove (Moscow: Tekst, 2007)

IAROSLAVSKII, EMELIAN, Kak rodiatsia, zhivut i umiraiut bogi (Moscow: Gosudarstvennoe Antireligioznoe Izdatel'stvo, 1938)

IOVANOVICH, MILIVOE, 'Evangelie ot Matfeia kak literaturnyi istochnik Mastera i Margarity', Canadian-American Slavic Studies, 15 (1981), 295–311

JÄGER, CHRISTOPH, Humanisierung des Mythos — Vergegenwärtigung der Tradition. Theologisch-hermeneutische Aspekte in den Josephsromanen von Thomas Mann (Stuttgart: M&P, 1992)

JEREMIAS, ALFRED, Das Alte Testament im Lichte des Alten Orients. Handbuch zur biblisch-orientalischen Altertumskunde (Leipzig: Hinrichs, 1904)

JONES, MALCOLM, 'The Gospel According to Woland and the Tradition of the Wandering Jew', in Bulgakov, ed. by Lesley Milne, Russian Theatre Archive, 5 (Luxembourg: Harwood, 1995), pp. 115–24

JOSIPOVICI, GABRIEL, The Book of God (New Haven, CT: Yale University Press, 1988)

KAZARKIN, ALEKSANDR P., 'Tipy avtorstva v romane Master i Margarita', in Tvorchestvo Mikhaila Bulgakova, ed. by Iuliia A. Babicheva and Nikolai N. Kiselev (Tomsk: Izdatel'stvo Tomskogo Universiteta, 1991), pp. 11–27

——'"Vechnyi siuzhet" i avtorstvo v romane *Master i Margarita*', in *Problemy istoricheskoi poetiki v analize literaturnogo proizvedeniia*, ed. by Valerii I. Tiupa, Mikhail N. Darvin and others (Kemerovo: Kemerovskii Gosudarstvennii Universitet, 1987), pp. 125–35

KENNEY, JOSEPH M., 'Apotheosis and Incarnation Myths in Mann's *Joseph und seine Brüder*', *German Quarterly*, 56 (1983), 39–60

KEJNA-SHARRATT, BARBARA, 'Narrative Techniques in *The Master and Margarita*', *Canadian Slavonic Papers*, 16 (1974), 1–13

KERÉNYI, KARL, ed, *Thomas Mann — Karl Kerényi. Gespräch in Briefen* (Zurich: Rhein, 1960)

KISEL, MARIA, 'Feuilletons Don't Burn: Bulgakov's *The Master and Margarita* and the Imagined "Soviet Reader"', *Slavic Review*, 68 (2009), 582–600

KLEBERG, LARS, 'Roman Mastera i Roman Bulgakova', *Slavica Lundensia*, 5 (1977), 113–25

KOELB, CLAYTON, *Legendary Figures: Ancient History in Modern Novels* (Lincoln: University of Nebraska Press, 1998)

KOOPMANN, HELMUT, 'Ist Gott eine Hilfskonstruktion? Thomas Mann zur Religion, in seinen Essays', in *Zwischen Himmel und Hölle: Thomas Mann und die Religion. Die Davoser Literaturtage 2010*, ed. by Thomas Sprecher, Thomas-Mann-Studien, 44 (Frankfurt a M.: Klostermann, 2012), pp. 35–52

KORABLEV, ALEKSANDR, 'Khorosho predumannoe prorochestvo', *Lepta*, 5 (1991), 165–70

——'Tainodeistvie v *Mastere i Margarite*', *Voprosy Literatury*, 5 (1991), 35–54

KREPS, MIKHAIL, *Bulgakov i Pasternak kak romanisty. Analiz romanov 'Master i Margarita' i 'Doktor Zhivago'* (Ann Arbor, MI: Ermitazh, 1984)

KRISTIANSEN, BØRGE, 'Ägypten als symbolischer Raum der geistigen Problematik Thomas Manns. Überlegungen zur Dimension der Selbstkritik in *Joseph und seine Brüder*', *Thomas-Mann-Jahrbuch*, 6 (1993), 9–36

KRUGOVOY, GEORGE, *The Gnostic Novel of Mikhail Bulgakov: Sources and Exegesis* (Lanham, NY: University Press of America, 1991)

——'The Jesus of the Church and the Yeshua of Mikhail Bulgakov', *Transactions of the Association of Russian-American Scholars in the USA*, 18 (1985), pp. 201–22

KURZKE, HERMANN, *Der gläubige Thomas. Glaube und Sprache bei Thomas Mann*, Schriften des Ortsvereins Bonn-Köln der Deutschen Thomas-Mann-Gesellschaft e.V., 1 (Bonn: Bernstein, 2009)

KUSHLINA, OLGA and IURII SMIRNOV, 'Magiia slova (zametki na poliakh romana M. Bulgakova *Master i Margarita*', *Pamir*, 5 (1986), 152–67

——'Nekotorye voprosy poetiki romana *Master i Margarita*', in *M. A. Bulgakov — Dramaturg i khudozhestvennaia kul'tura ego vremeni*, ed. by Aleksandr A. Ninov and Violetta V. Gudkova (Moscow: Soiuz teatral'nykh deiatelei RSFSR, 1988), pp. 285–303

KUZIAKINA, NATALIA, 'Mikhail Bulgakov i Demian Bednyi', in *M. A. Bulgakov — dramaturg*, ed. by Aleksandr A. Ninov and Violetta V. Gudkova (Moscow: Soiuz teatral'nykh deiatelei RSFSR, 1988), pp. 392–410

LAWSON, ANN, '"Die schöne Geschichte": a corpus-based analysis of Thomas Mann's *Joseph und seine Brüder*', in *Working with German Corpora*, ed. by Bill Dodd (Birmingham: University of Birmingham Press, 2000), pp. 161–80

LEATHERBARROW, WILLIAM J., 'The Devil and the Creative Visionary in Bulgakov's *Master i Margarita*', *New Zealand Slavonic Journal*, 1 (1975), 29–45

LEHNERT, HERBERT, 'Thomas Manns Vorstudien zur Josephstetralogie', *Jahrbuch der Deutschen Schillergesellschaft*, 7 (1963), 458–520

LESSKIS, GEORGII A., '*Master i Margarita* Bulgakova (manera povestvovaniia, zhanr, makro-kompozitsiia)', *Izvestiia Akademii Nauk SSSR*, Seriia literatury i iazyka, 38 (1979), 52–59

LEVENSON, ALAN, 'Christian Author. Jewish Book? Methods and Sources in Thomas Mann's *Joseph*', *German Quarterly*, 71 (1998), 166–78

LIAKHOVA, E. I., 'Dramatizm lichnogo slova v romane M. A. Bulgakova *Master i Margarita*', in *Literaturnoe proizvedenie i literaturnyi protsess v aspekte istoricheskoi poetiki*, ed. by Valerii I. Tiupa, Mikhail Darvin and others (Kemerovo: Kemerovskii Gosudarstvennyi Universitet, 1988), pp. 169–76

LONGINOVIĆ, TOMISLAV, *Borderline Culture: The Politics of Identity in Four Twentieth-Century Slavic Novels* (Fayetteville, AK: University of Arkansas Press, 1993)

LÖRKE, TIM, 'Politische Religion und aufgeklärter Mythos: der Nationalsozialismus und das Gegenprogramm Hermann Brochs und Thomas Manns', in *Totalitarismus und Literatur. Deutsche Literatur im 20 Jahrhundert — Literarische Öffentlichkeit im Spannungsfeld totalitärer Meinungsbildung*, ed. by Hans Jörg Schmidt and Petra Tallafuss, Schriften des Hannah-Arendt-Instituts für Totalitarismusforschung, 33 (Göttingen: Vandenhoeck & Ruprecht, 2007), pp. 119–34

LOSEV, VIKTOR I., ed, *Mikhail i Elena Bulgakovy. Dnevnik Mastera i Margarity* (Moscow: Vagrius, 2004)

LOVELL, STEPHEN, 'Bulgakov as Soviet Culture', *Slavonic and East European Review*, 76 (1998), 28–48

LOWE, DAVID, 'Gounod's *Faust* and Bulgakov's *The Master and Margarita*', *Russian Review*, 55 (1996), 279–86

LUBKEMANN ALLEN, SHARON, 'From the Grotesque to the Sublime: Logos and Purgatorial Landscape of *Dead Souls* and *Master and Margarita*', *Slavic and East European Journal*, 47 (2003), 45–76

LUUKKANEN, ARTO, *The Religious Policy of the Stalinist State. A Case Study: The Central Standing Commission on Religious Questions, 1929–1938*, Studia Historica, 57 (Helsinki: SHS, 1997)

MCDONALD, WILLIAM E., 'Deep is the Well of the Past. Should we not call it Bottomless' in *Third Person: Authoring and Exploring Vast Narratives*, ed. by Pat Harrigan and Noah Wardrip-Fruin (Cambridge, MA: MIT Press, 2009), pp. 243–51

MAKSUDOV, SERGEI, '*Master i Margarita* — teatral'nyi roman v piati izmereniiakh (prostranstvo, vremia, etika)', *NovZ*, 196 (1995), 202–44

MANN, THOMAS, *Gesammelte Werke in dreizehn Bänden*, 13 vols (Frankfurt a.M.: Fischer: 1960)

——*Joseph and His Brothers. The stories of Jacob, Young Joseph, Joseph in Egypt, Joseph the Provider*, trans. by John E. Woods (New York, NY: Alfred A. Knopf, 2005)

——*Joseph und seine Brüder* (Frankfurt a.M.: Fischer, 2007)

MANN, THOMAS and KARL KERÉNYI, *Mythology and Humanism. The Correspondence of Thomas Mann and Karl Kerényi*. trans. by Alexander Gelley (Ithaca, NY: Cornell University Press, 1975)

MARQUARDT, FRANKA, *Erzählte Juden: Untersuchungen zu Thomas Manns 'Joseph und seine Brüder' und Robert Musils 'Mann ohne Eigenschaften'*, Literatur — Kultur — Medien, 4 (Münster: LIT, 2003)

MASER, EDWARD A., 'Young Joseph's Guardian Angel: Salvage from a Case of Parallel Research', in *Art, the Ape of Nature. Studies in Honor of H. W. Janson*, ed. by Mosche Barasch, Lucy Freeman Sandler and Patricia Egan (New York, NY: Abrams, 1981), pp. 495–504

MARX, FRIEDHELM, 'Transfigurations of Christ in Thomas Mann', *Religion & Literature*, 33 (2001), 23–36

MECHIK-BLANK, KSENIIA, 'Na rassvete *shestnadtsatogo* chisla vesennego mesiatsa Nisana... (Apofatizm romana *Master i Margarita*)', in *Mikhail Bulgakov na iskhode XX veka. Materialy VIII mezhdunarodnykh Bulgakovskikh chtenii v S.-Peterburge (mai 1997 g.)*, ed by Albert S. Burmistrov, Anatolii A. Grubin and Aleksandr A. Ninov, Biblioteka Sankt-Peterburgskogo Bulgakovskogo literaturno-teatral'nogo obshchestva, 2 (St. Petersburg: Rossiiskii Institut Istorii Iskusstv, 1999), pp. 134–44

MEREZHKOVSKII, DMITRII, *Taina trekh. Egipet i Vavilon*, ed. by Aleksandr N. Nikoliukin, Sobranie sochinenii D. S. Merezhkovskogo, 3 (Moscow: Respublika, 1999)

METZGER, BRUCE M. and JOHN BARTON, eds, *The Holy Bible Containing the Old and New Testaments. New Revised Standard Version. Anglicized Text. Cross-Reference Edition* (Oxford: Oxford University Press, 2003)

MILNE, LESLEY, *'The Master and Margarita'. A Comedy of Victory*, Birmingham Slavonic Monographs, 3 (Birmingham: Birmingham University Press, 1977)

MURDAUGH, ELAINE, *Salvation in the Secular: The Moral Law in Thomas Mann's 'Joseph und seine Brüder'*, Stanford German Studies, 10 (Bern: Lang, 1976)

NAIMAN, ERIC, 'The Morality of Punishment and Execution in *The Master and Margarita*', *Russian, Croatian and Serbian, Czech and Slovak, Polish Literature*, 18 (1985), 63–90

NATTERER, CLAUDIA, *Faust als Künstler. Michail Bulgakovs 'Master i Margarita' und Thomas Manns 'Doktor Faustus'*, Beiträge zur Slavischen Philologie, 9 (Heidelberg: Winter, 2002)

NEUSNER, JACOB and ALAN J. AVERY-PECK, eds, *Encyclopaedia of Midrash: Biblical Interpretation in formative Judaism*, 2 vols (Leiden: Brill, 2005), I

NIKLAUS, PETER, 'Religion und Ironie' in *Zwischen Himmel und Hölle*, ed. by Thomas Sprecher, Thomas-Mann-Studien, 44 (Frankfurt a.M.: Klostermann, 2012), pp. 17–33

NOBLE, CECIL A. M., *Dichter und Religion. Thomas Mann, Kafka, T. S. Eliot*, Europäische Hochschulschriften. Reihe I, Deutsche Sprache und Literatur, 1014 (Frankfurt a.M.: Lang, 1987)

NOLTE, CHARLOTTE, *Being and Meaning in Thomas Mann's 'Joseph' Novels*, MHRA texts and dissertations, 44, Bithell series of dissertations, 22 (Leeds: Maney for the Modern Humanities Research Association and the Institute of Germanic Studies, University of London, 1996)

OJA, MATT F., 'The Role and the Meaning of Madness in *The Master and Margarita*: The Novel as a Doppelgänger Tale', in *Bulgakov*, ed. by Lesley Milne, Russian Theatre Archive, 5 (Luxembourg: Harwood, 1995), pp. 142–54

ORT, CLAUS-MICHAEL, 'Körper, Stimme, Schrift: semiotischer Betrug und "heilige" Wahrheit in der literarischen Selbstreflexion Thomas Manns', in *Die Erfindung des Schriftstellers Thomas Mann*, ed. by Michael Ansel, Hans-Edwin Friedrich and Gerhard Lauer (Berlin: de Gruyter, 2009), pp. 237–71

PAGET, JAMES CARLETON, 'Quest for the historical Jesus', in *The Cambridge Companion to Jesus*, ed. by Markus Bockmuehl (Cambridge: Cambridge University Press, 2001), pp. 138–55

PEARCE, C. E., 'A Closer Look at Narrative Structure in Bulgakov's *The Master and Margarita*', *Canadian Slavonic Papers*, 22 (1980), 358–71

PERIS, DANIEL, *Storming the Heavens. The Soviet League of the Militant Godless* (Ithaca, NY: Cornell University Press, 1998)

PIKULIK, LOTHAR, 'Joseph vor Pharao. Die Traumdeutung in Thomas Manns biblischem Romanwerk *Joseph und seine Brüder*', *Thomas-Mann-Jahrbuch*, I (1988), 99–116

—— *Thomas Mann und der Faschismus: Wahrnehmung, Erkenntnisinteresse, Widerstand*, Germanistische Texte und Studien, 90 (Hildesheim: Olms, 2013)

PITTMAN, RIITTA H., 'Dreamers and Dreaming in M. A. Bulgakov's *The Master and Margarita*', in *Bulgakov*, ed. by Lesley Milne, Russian Theatre Archive, 5 (Luxembourg: Harwood, 1995), pp. 157–70

—— *The Writer's Divided Self in Bulgakov's 'The Master and Margarita'* (London: Macmillan in association with St. Antony's College, Oxford, 1991)

PODGAETS, O. A. 'Bezdomnyi, Latunskii, Riukhin i drugie', *Russkaia Rech'*, 3 (1991), 13–22

POKROVSKII, BORIS, 'O chem besedoval Voland s Berliozom: Filosofskie problemy romana Bulgakova *Master i Margarita*', *Transactions of the Association of Russian-American Scholars in the USA*, 24 (1991), 143–62

POPE, RICHARD W. F., 'Ambiguity and Meaning in *The Master and Margarita*: The Role of Afranius', *Slavic Review*, 36 (1977), 1–24

POSPIELOVSKY, DIMITRY V., *A History of Soviet Atheism in Theory and Practice, and the Believer. Soviet Antireligious Campaigns and Persecutions*, 3 vols (London: Macmillan, 1988), II

POWELL, DAVID. E., *Antireligious Propaganda in the Soviet Union: A Study of Mass Persuasion* (Cambridge, Massachusetts: the MIT Press, 1975)

PRICKETT, STEPHEN, *Origins of Narrative: the Romantic Appropriation of the Bible* (Cambridge: Cambridge University Press, 1996)

PROFFER, ELLENDEA, *Bulgakov. Life and Work* (Ann Arbor, MI: Ardis, 1984)

PRUITT, DONALD B., 'St. John and Bulgakov: The Model of a Parody of Christ', *Canadian-American Slavic Studies*, 15 (1981), 312–20

RAD, GERHARD VON, 'Biblische Josephserzählung und Josephsroman', in *Joseph: Bilder und Gedanken zu dem Roman 'Joseph und seine Brüder' von Thomas Mann*, ed. by Gisela Röhn (Hamburg: Witting, 1975), pp. 141–49

REISS, GUNTER, *'Allegorisierung' und moderne Erzählkunst. Eine Studie zum Werk Thomas Manns* (Munich: Fink, 1970)

RENAN, ERNEST, *The Life of Jesus*, [n. trans], Thinker's Library, 53 (London, Watts, 1935)

ROGACHEVSKAYA, EKATERINA, 'Thomas Mann's *Mario und der Zauberer* and Bulgakov's *The Master and Margarita* as Political Commentaries on the Events of the 1930s', *Australian Slavonic & East European Studies*, 9 (1995), 119–28

ROSENSHIELD, GARY, '*The Master and Margarita* and the Poetics of Aporia: A Polemical Article', *Slavic Review*, 56 (1997), 187–211

SANDOMIRSKAJA, IRINA, 'Aesopian Language: the Politics and Poetics of Naming the Unnamable', in *The Vernaculars of Communism. Language, Ideology and Power in the Soviet Union and Eastern Europe*, ed. by Petre Petrov and Lara Ryazanova-Clarke, Routledge Studies in the History of Russia and Eastern Europe, 21 (London: Routledge, 2015), pp. 63–88

SAVEL'EVA, OLGA, 'Russkii apokrificheskii Khristos: K postanovke problemy', *Slavia Orientalis*, 52 (2003), 159–78

SCHWÖBEL, CHRISTOPH, *Die Religion des Zauberers: Theologisches in den großen Romanen Thomas Manns* (Tübingen: Mohr Siebeck, 2008)

SEIBT, GUSTAV, 'Jaakobs Gott', in *Das Buch der Bücher — gelesen: Lesearten der Bibel in den Wissenschaften und Künsten*, ed. by Steffen Martus and Andrea Polaschegg, Publikationen zur Zeitschrift für Germanistik, 13 (Bern: Lang, 2006), pp. 85–100

SENICHKINA, ELENA P., 'Aktualizator vyskazivaniia "POCHEMU-TO" i ego rol' v khudozhestvennom tekste. (Na materiale romana M. Bulgakova *Master i Margarita*'), in *Khudozhestvennaia rech': obshchee i individual'noe*, ed. by Olga I. Aleksandrova and others (Kuibyshev: Kuibyshevskii gosudarstvennii pedagogicheskii institut imeni V. V. Kuibysheva, 1980), pp. 78–97

SHAVIT, YAACOV and MORDECHAI ERAN, *The Hebrew Bible Reborn: From Holy Scripture to the Book of Books. A History of Biblical Culture and the Battles over the Bible in Modern Judaism*, trans. by Chaya Naor, Studia Judaica 38 (Berlin: De Gruyter, 2007)

SKOLNIK, FRED and MICHAEL BERENBAUM, eds, *Encyclopaedia Judaica*, 2nd edn, 22 vols (Detroit, MI: Macmillan Reference USA in association with the Keter Publishing House, 2007), I

SOLOMON, HOWARD, 'The Sin of Cowardice: The Mystery behind Bulgakov's Ambiguity', *Russian, Croatian and Serbian, Czech and Slovak, Polish Literature*, 44 (1998), 241–52

SPARIOSU, MIHAI I., *Modernism and Exile. Play, Liminality, and the Exilic-Utopian Imagination* (Basingstoke: Palgrave Macmillan, 2015), pp. 161–79

SPININGER, DENNIS J., 'The "Thamar" Section of Thomas Mann's *Joseph und seine Brüder*: A Formal Analysis', *Monatshefte*, 61 (1969), 157–72

STAPANIAN-APKARIAN, JULIETTE R., 'Ironic "Vision" as an Aesthetics of Displaced Truth in M. Bulgakov's *Master and Margarita*', in *Russian Narrative & Visual Art: Varieties of Seeing*, ed. by Roger Anderson and Paul Debreczeny (Gainesville: University Press of Florida, 1994), pp. 173–200

STRAUSS, DAVID FRIEDRICH, *The Life of Jesus Critically Examined*, trans. by George Eliot (London: SCM, 1973)

SWALES, MARTIN, *Thomas Mann: A Study* (London: Heinemann, 1980)

SWENSEN, ALAN J., *Gods, Angels and Narrators. A Metaphysics of Narrative in Thomas Mann's 'Joseph und seine Brüder'*, Studies in Modern German literature, 57 (New York: Lang, 1994)

SZILÁRD, LÉNA, 'Der Mythos im Roman und der Wechsel der literarisch-stilistischen Formationen: Von Joyce und A. Belyj zum späten Th. Mann und zu M. Bulgakov,' in *Evolution of the Novel. L'Evolution du Roman. Die Entwicklung des Romans. Proceedings of the IXth congress of the International Comparative Literature Association*, ed. by Zoran Konstantinovič, Eva Kuschner and Béla Köpeczi, Innsbrucker Beiträge zur Kulturwissenschaft. Sonderhefte, 53 (Innsbruck: Institut für Sprachwissenschaft der Universität Innsbruck, 1982), pp. 347–52

TALBOT, NATHALIE MAHIEU, 'Giving the Devil His Due: The Register of Voices in *The Master and Margarita* and in York Höller's Operatic Adaptation of the Novel', trans. by Julie A. E. Curtis, in *Bulgakov*, ed. by Lesley Milne, Russian Theatre Archive, 5 (Luxembourg: Harwood, 1995), pp. 187–200

TARANOVSKI JOHNSON, VIDA, 'The Thematic Function of the Narrator in *The Master and Margarita*', *Canadian American Slavic Studies*, 15 (1981), 271–86

TUMANOV, VLADIMIR, 'Jacob as Job in Thomas Mann's *Joseph und seine Brüder*', *Neophilologus*, 86 (2002), 287–302

UTEKHIN, NIKOLAI, '*Master i Margarita* M. Bulgakova (ob istochnikakh deistvitel'nykh i mnimykh)', *Russkaiia Literatura*, 4 (1979), 39–109

VOGELMANN, KATHARINA, *Konstellationen von Mythos und Erzählen in Thomas Manns 'Josephs'-Romanen: unter besonderer Berücksichtigung der Figur des Jaakob*, Studien zur Germanistik, 15 (Hamburg: Kovač, 2005)

VON ESCHENBACH, WOLFRAM, *Parzival and Titurel*, trans. by Cyril Edwards (Oxford: Oxford University Press, 2006)

VULIS, ABRAM, 'Poetika "Mastera". Kniga o knige', *Zvezda Vostoka*, 10 (1990), 130–36; 11 (1990), 107–23

WEEKS, LAURA D., 'Hebraic Antecedents in *The Master and Margarita*: Woland and Company Revisited', *Slavic Review*, 42 (1984), 224–41

—— 'In Defense of the Homeless: On the Uses of History and the Role of Bezdomnyi in *The Master and Margarita*', *Russian Review*, 48 (1989), 45–65

WILLIAMS, GARETH, 'Some Difficulties in the Interpretation of Bulgakov's *Master and Margarita* and the advantages of a Manichean Approach, with Some Notes on Tolstoi's Influence on the Novel', *Slavonic and East European Review*, 68 (1990), 234–56

WOLTERS, DIERK, *Zwischen Metaphysik und Politik. Thomas Manns Roman 'Joseph und seine Brüder' in seiner Zeit*, Studien zur deutschen Literatur, 147 (Tübingen: Niemeyer, 1998)

WRIGHT, ANTHONY COLIN, *Mikhail Bulgakov. Life and Interpretations* (Toronto: University of Toronto Press, 1978)

WRIGHT, TERRY R., *The Genesis of Fiction: Modern Novelists as Biblical Interpreters* (Aldershot: Ashgate, 2007)

WYSLING, HANS and CORNELIA BERNINI, eds, *Jahre des Unmuts: Thomas Manns Briefwechsel mit René Schickele 1930–1949*, Thomas-Mann-Studien, 10 (Frankfurt a.M.: Klostermann, 1992)

ZERKALOV, ALEKSANDR, 'Iisus iz Nazareta i Yeshua Ga-Notsri', *Nauka i Religiia*, 9 (1986), 47–52

——'Voland, Mefistofel' i drugie. Zametki o "teologii" romana M. Bulgakova *Master i Margarita*', *Nauka i religiia*, 8 (1987), 49–51

ZIGELIS, ANDREW, 'Bulgakov's *Master i Margarita*: Three Types of Reductive Ambiguity', *Russian Language Journal*, 30 (1976), 119–30

ZLOCHEVSKAIA, ALLA, 'Paradoksy Zazerkalia v romanakh G. Gesse, V. Nabokova i M. Bulgakova', *Voprosy Literatury*, 3 (2008), 201–21

INDEX

❖

9 781781 885468